What does it mean to be working class in the twenty-first century, decades after industrial jobs and strong unions have given way to low-wage service jobs, contingent labour, and precarity? This book traces how deindustrialisation literature wrestles with this question, revealing how class itself is being reimagined and reshaped by economic restructuring and neoliberalism – while also introducing readers to a range of engaging and entertaining books worth reading.

—*Sherry Lee Linkon, Georgetown University, USA*

This book makes a compelling case for the intersections between class and contemporary literature. It brings the academic study of working-class writing bang up to date.

—*Nicola Wilson, University of Reading, UK*

The Working Class and Twenty-First-Century British Fiction

The Working Class and Twenty-First-Century British Fiction looks at how the twenty-first-century British novel has explored contemporary working-class life. Studying the works of David Peace, Gordon Burn, Anthony Cartwright, Ross Raisin, Jenni Fagan, and Sunjeev Sahota, the book shows how they have mapped the shift from deindustrialisation through to stigmatisation of individuals and communities who have experienced profound levels of destabilisation and unemployment. O'Brien argues that these novels offer ways of understanding fundamental aspects of contemporary capitalism for the working class in modern Britain, including, class struggle, inequality, trauma, social abjection, racism, and stigmatisation, exclusively looking at British working-class literature of the twenty-first century.

Phil O'Brien has written on working-class fiction and theatre for *Textual Practice* and *Literature & History* and in *Accelerated Times: British Literature in Transition* (Cambridge University Press) and *Working-Class Writing: Theory & Practice* (Palgrave). He is the secretary of the Raymond Williams Society, on the editorial board of *Key Words*, and editor of *Culture & Politics* (Verso) by Raymond Williams. He has taught at the University of Manchester and Liverpool John Moores University. This is his first book.

Routledge Studies in Contemporary Literature

33 Urban Captivity Narratives
Women's Writing After 9/11
Heather Hillsburg

34 The Humanist (Re)Turn
Reclaiming the Self in Literature
Michael Bryson

35 Approaches to Teaching the Work of Edwidge Danticat
*Edited by Celucien L. Joseph, Suchismita Banerjee, Marvin
Hobson, and Danny Hoey*

36 Contemporary Capitalism, Crisis, and the Politics of Fiction
Literature Beyond Fordism
Roberto del Valle Alcalá

37 Dissent and the Dynamics of Cultural Change
Lessons from the Underground Presses of the Late Sixties
Matthew T. Pifer

38 Collage in Twenty-First-Century Literature in English
Art of Crisis
Wojciech Drąg

39 Patrick McGrath and His Worlds
Madness and the Transnational Gothic
Edited by Matt Foley and Rebecca Duncan

40 The Working Class and Twenty-First-Century British Fiction
Deindustrialisation, Demonisation, Resistance
Phil O'Brien

For more information about this series, please visit: https://www.routledge.com

The Working Class and Twenty-First-Century British Fiction

Deindustrialisation, Demonisation, Resistance

Phil O'Brien

Routledge
Taylor & Francis Group

NEW YORK AND LONDON

First published 2020
by Routledge
52 Vanderbilt Avenue, New York, NY 10017

and by Routledge
2 Park Square, Milton Park, Abingdon, Oxon, OX14 4RN

Routledge is an imprint of the Taylor & Francis Group, an informa business

Library of Congress Cataloging-in-Publication Data
A catalog record for this title has been requested

ISBN: 978-0-367-44148-7 (hbk)
ISBN: 978-1-003-00791-3 (ebk)

Typeset in Sabon
by codeMantra

MIX
Paper from
responsible sources
FSC
www.fsc.org
FSC™ C013985

Printed in the United Kingdom
by Henry Ling Limited

For Our Chris
(1975–2012)

Contents

Acknowledgements   xi

Introduction: Class, Culture, Politics   1

PART 1
Mapping Deindustrialisation   25

1   David Peace and the Strike Novel: Conflict,
    History, Knowledge   27

2   Gordon Burn and Working-Class Nostalgia:
    Region, Form, Commodification   47

3   Anthony Cartwright and the Deindustrial Novel:
    Realism, Place, Class   67

PART 2
Resisting Demonisation   91

4   Ross Raisin and Class Mourning: Masculinity,
    Work, Precarity   93

5   Jenni Fagan and the Revolting Class: Gender,
    Stigma, Resistance   114

6   Sunjeev Sahota and the Racialised Worker:
    Class, Race, Violence   133

    Conclusion: Class Matters   151

Bibliography   157
Index   169

Acknowledgements

It is difficult to place when, where, and how this book came together. It feels like a lifetime of work, one which I needed to write and for which I could identify a number of possible starting points: my parents Jimmy and Glenys, Goose Green, the Open University, Hallgate Sorting Office and my Great Acre delivery, the early evening Masters at the University of Salford. It is a book about social class and everything listed signifies reasons why I have wanted to write about the working class in particular. Being awarded Arts and Humanities Research Council funding and then moving to the University of Manchester to complete my doctorate enabled what I had felt and thought for a long time to begin to take the form it now does. Much of it has been completed in Salford, writing, revising, and editing when possible between spells of precarious employment and uncertainty. The person who has lived with it the longest and in closest proximity is Ruth who I cannot thank enough for her love, support, and friendship. My brother Chris passed away before I thought that this could be a book but he has been with me throughout in many ways, none more so than through the love and support of my mum and dad, my brother Jim, and my sister Marie. This is for you Chris.

I owe an unpayable debt to Ben Harker who it would not have been possible to start let alone finish this research. Thank you to Ursula Hurley, Glyn White, Rebecca Pohl, David Alderson, and Liam Harte for reading early drafts of the chapters and to Kaye Mitchell and Nick Bentley for examining the original thesis. The input from the anonymous reviewers of my article for *Textual Practice* ("'Takes you back even if you were never there originally": class, history, and nostalgia in Gordon Burn's *The North of England Home Service*', vol. 32, issue 8, 2018, pp. 1405–1423) greatly improved that piece as well as the sections included, in revised form, as Chapter Two. Thanks to the journal's publishers who granted permission for its use here. Sherry Lee Linkon, Nicola Wilson, and Nick Hubble offered much-needed guidance on how to bring the final manuscript together. Thank you to John Roache, Jonny Rodgers, Chris Vardy, and Stephen Dippnall for your invaluable friendship. And, finally, without the Raymond Williams Society I do not think I would have continued long enough in academia to finish the book so many thanks to Kristin Ewins, Tony Crowley, Emily Cuming, Elinor Taylor, and everyone involved with the society and with *Key Words*. Culture is ordinary: that is the first fact.

Introduction
Class, Culture, Politics

What place do the working class have in the contemporary novel? What role does class take in twenty-first-century Britain? What is the relationship between class, capital, and neoliberalism? This book sets out to answer such pressings questions by analysing articulations of class by contemporary British writers David Peace, Gordon Burn, Anthony Cartwright, Ross Raisin, Jenni Fagan, and Sunjeev Sahota. It looks in detail at eight novels in the following order: *GB84* (2004), *The North of England Home Service* (2003), *The Afterglow* (2004), *Heartland* (2009), *How I Killed Margaret Thatcher* (2012), *Waterline* (2011), *The Panopticon* (2012), *Ours are the Streets* (2011), and *The Year of the Runaways* (2015). These texts are located not as a source for 'representations' of class but rather as a way of analysing and configuring it. They map out an understanding of how class is formed and how it works; they are not simple 'reflections' but powerful interventions into both class discourse and the drastic changes to class formation in Britain brought about by the ideologies of neoliberalism. This book identifies writers and writings which take as their subject matter contemporary class formations and offer a theorisation of how they imagine, depict, and represent capital. If the novel 'presumes to conjure up in perceptible form a society that has become abstract', as Theodor Adorno has noted,[1] how can novelistic representations in the twenty-first century map what Fredric Jameson has described as 'the great global multinational and de-centred communicational network in which we find ourselves caught as individual subjects?'[2] Can fiction play an effective epistemological role within the confusing and complex development of neoliberalism? What can it reveal about unemployment, deindustrialisation, oppression, social inequality, and trauma? Cultural representations are sites in which both ideology and the struggle against hegemony are powerfully worked through and communicated. In what follows, there is a specific emphasis on mediation and upon the set of relations which are mobilised around and by a given text; to talk of class is to talk of a social relation.

Selected are writers who present a way of figuring and mapping contemporary capitalism from a class perspective. It is this foregrounding of and engagement with class and class formation which makes these novels distinctive. They provide an analysis of the process and dynamics of class as an evolving and shifting framework through which to read neoliberalism and its discontents. And they figure class as a decisive experience, placing a critical emphasis on the way it shapes social, political, and historical change. A central concern throughout will be the contradictions upon and through which neoliberal capital operates; namely a declaration of the death of class at the same time as a hardening of inequality and an intensification of capital's power, developments which have been accompanied by the generation of consent through the mobilisation of class stigma. The six writers chosen allow for a mapping of what I figure as the symbolic crystallisation of the neoliberal attack on the working class – the Miners' Strike of 1984/1985 – through to the latest development in the process that the forces of neoliberalism have released: the stigmatisation of those individuals and communities who have experienced deindustrialisation. Crucially, they provide sites of resistance to this move from deindustrialisation to demonisation and suggest productive ways of understanding and challenging such destructive processes as well as gesturing towards modes of class liberation.

The inclusion or exclusion of given class perspectives within a cultural text 'is always more than a "literary" or "aesthetic" decision', according to Raymond Williams, who argues that it is a choice which reveals more about class hierarchy and the struggle over who gets to write 'reality'.[3] Because working-class life, people, and communities are 'rarely written about and, by extension, poorly understood', says Lynsey Hanley, they are presented as 'either hopelessly sentimental or offensively vilifying'.[4] This sense of sentimentality can also quickly turn into vilification, a toxic move registered in comments by Tim Lott:

> Fiction writing, after all, is a "high" literary form (probably the same reason there aren't many working-class classical musicians). It requires eloquence and education. Neither are particularly prioritised, and may even be stigmatic, in working-class culture.[5]

The forms of eloquence and education Lott is referring to here are the standards set by the dominant class. What the working class may understand as education and eloquence, in all forms, would be very different. Both have long traditions within working-class culture: the public library, the home, adult education, the expansion of comprehensive education, trade unionism, the labour movement, co-operative societies, and the rich history of storytelling, writing and writing clubs, poetry, song, music, workers theatre. For Williams, working-class culture is not 'proletarian art, or council houses, or a particular use of language; it is, rather, the basic collective idea, and the institutions, manners, habits of thought, and intentions which proceed from this'.[6] Reflecting on criticism of the Labour Party's leader Jeremy Corbyn for often quoting from

Percy Bysshe Shelley's radical poem 'The Masque of Anarchy', Rhian E. Jones describes the response as 'depressingly predictable'. She adds that poetry is 'dismissed' by Corbyn's critics

> as a hopelessly pretentious art form [...] scorned by ordinary people. This argument ignores the centuries of culture created and made use of by ordinary people themselves, [...] and regularly produced in the course of political struggle, to record, reflect or guide it.[7]

Importantly, Jones notes how significant the 'cultural intertwining of art and politics' remains to the working class in the twenty-first century: 'its forging into channels of communication, encouragement or simply comforting consolation, was and remains an intrinsic part of working-class consciousness'.[8] Lott offers a much more restrictive and narrow view of working-class culture, particularly to the expansive and progressive (and correct) conception of it offered by Williams and Jones. He suggests that part of the blame for exclusion lies with the working class as a social, cultural, and political formation. He deploys several clichés and caricatures: the assumption that the working class are inarticulate, uneducated, and numb to the allure of 'high' art. It is the fault of their culture, Lott says, if they do not have a place in contemporary literature; they are responsible for their own exclusion. Such logic is symbolic of a specific mental conception which is central to neoliberal discourse; it is one in which, rather than focusing on structural inequalities, the blame is placed onto an 'othered' working class. The problem, it seems, *is* class but the problem is *made by* the working class.

One of the failures here is taking an individual experience to explain a wider social formation, a whole way of life, a structural condition. Once more, Rhian E. Jones provides a corrective. Representations of the working class 'have become so thin, so shallow, repetitive and unimaginative, that they do us all a disservice'; therefore, she adds: 'An injection of new imagination, borne of diverse and unacknowledged experiences, is necessary if we are to slip the coils of political regression and artistic monotony'.[9] What is needed is a variety of approaches to writing about and engaging with class as a social and historical relation. Kit de Waal, echoing Jones and Hanley, describes how stories of working-class life are often 'filtered through middle-class sensibilities or explained for an imagined middle-class reader'. She adds: 'This squashes the multiplicity of working-class experience into a few standard tropes: the misery memoir, the escape, the clever boy or girl "done good"'.[10] As a contemporary author and a prominent supporter of working-class writing, de Waal has helped shift the focus onto the publishing industry which, as she says, is the 'least socially diverse of all the UK's creative industries'.[11] Such inequality is political in that it links to power and class. What needs to be addressed is the systematic denial of access to the modes of communication which hinder articulations of working-class experience in all its forms. The shutting down of access to modes of representation is far more significant than lazy assumptions about education and eloquence being stigmatic. What we need to be thinking about are the sites of cultural production, the means of cultural production, and what access working-class writers and artists have to these sites.

The 2017 essay collection *Know Your Place* is a wonderful intervention here. It is described by its editor Nathan Connolly as being 'part of a communal process'.[12] It offers a rich, complex, and contrasting sense of what being working class means, partly able to do so because of its flexibility and form: twenty-three essays on culture, education, housing, music, accent, writing, and the novel. Its significance is registered in the first essay by Abondance Matanda who writes about the black working-class home as a site of culture and cultural production. She locates family photos and videos as a cultural archive. Here is education and eloquence. Taken together, the collection calls for greater equality but also for fundamental structural change, not modest tinkering and mild reform. And, as Renni Eddo-Lodge has argued, equality should only be a transitional demand: 'It's clear that equality doesn't quite cut it. Asking for a sliver of disproportional power is too polite a request. I don't want to be included. Instead, I want to question who created the standard in the first place'.[13] Eddo-Lodge is talking specifically about race here, and structural racism, but it is also an important insight into how all forms of structural inequality work, based on race, gender, and class. My point is not to present equivalents but to find moments of common ground amongst the growing calls for social transformation. Throughout this book, I engage with the intersection of class with both gender and race in order to probe the dynamics of structural inequality. And what my relatively small selection of novels engages with is the working class as a multi-ethnic, multi-racial formation by looking at black support for the miners' strike in *GB84* (albeit briefly described by Peace), the Empire Windrush in *The North of England Home Service*, a global workforce of service labour in *Waterline*, the racialised figure of the white chav in *The Panopticon*, and, through a more extended and expansive engagement with race and ethnicity, British Asian experience in novels by Cartwright and Sahota. Crucially, and according to Paul Gilroy, '"race" is a political category that can accommodate various meanings which are in turn determined by struggle'.[14] Like class, it is the result of a social and historical process and in this way can be understood as a political formation.

Many of the novels selected, except for those by David Peace and Sunjeev Sahota, have been produced by writers who have attracted little if any critical attention. One aim, therefore, is to give the due attention which the work of these authors demands (and which I foresee them receiving in forthcoming studies of twenty-first-century fiction). For that, it addresses a significant gap in the knowledge about their texts as well as in the theorisation of class within studies of contemporary literature. There is an emphasis placed on the ways in which these novels have engaged with contemporary class formations and specifically working-class experience. I have chosen to focus specifically on this century in order to provide a necessary sense of political urgency which I insist is required during what has been a prolonged period of neoliberal hegemony.

My book is split into two distinct parts: Part One takes deindustrialisation as its focus; Part Two maps the shift to (or expansion and acceleration of) demonisation. Chapter One on David Peace's *GB84* focuses specifically on epistemological concerns and the possible ways of knowing available to the novel's working-class characters. I approach the novel as an attempt to trace and comprehend the strike's profound political, social, and historical shifts by directly engaging with its complexities and confusions. In doing so, the chapter engages with the problems of seeing, knowing, and witnessing which ultimately the text cannot resolve. Chapter Two on Gordon Burn's *The North of England Home Service* focuses on what happens to class memory when it becomes commodified and appropriated by consumer society. I explore such a process through an engagement with and critique of the nostalgia mode and its accompanying experiences of sentimentality, trauma, and uncertainty. Chapter Three examines how Anthony Cartwright's first three novels (*The Afterglow, Heartland,* and *How I Killed Margaret Thatcher*) engage with deindustrialisation as a physical manifestation of the neoliberal turn. I position his texts as interventions into debates concerning class, identity, race and racism, political agency, and neoliberal discourse. Chapter Four begins Part Two with Ross Raisin's *Waterline* as a novel which explores shame as a form of working-class masculinity and illuminates an understanding of how it connects to the neoliberal mantra that personal failure is a result of personal failings. The chapter examines the text's engagement with the destructive legacies of working-class patriarchy and industrial disease, and it illuminates an understanding of the racialisation of labour and neoliberal capitalism. Chapter Five gives a reading of Jenni Fagan's *The Panopticon* as a text which challenges conceptions of how working-class women should 'act' and 'perform'. Gender and sexuality form a central part of my reading; I examine how they intersect with class to produce numerous, interlocking inscriptions which are employed to label, define, and stigmatise. Chapter Six on Sunjeev Sahota examines the contemporary figuration of the abject, that of the racialised working-class 'other', following on from a critical exploration of the social abject in the previous two chapters. It explores the search for identity and belonging in Sahota's *Ours are the Streets* and *The Year of the Runaways* and analyses the ways in which the novels meditate upon history, empire, and the impact of deindustrialisation and unemployment on a working-class community.

As is apparent from my outlined approach to the work of these six writers, to talk of class is to talk of social hierarchy, inequality, conflict, class struggle, and ultimately conditions: economic, social, political, and historical. And this focus on development, on changing formations, is one which Imogen Tyler has described as 'practices and process of making'.[15] Informed by Jacques Rancière's conception of class as a homonym (a single word which can evoke different or multiple meanings), Tyler suggests two primary understandings of the term. While it is used to describe a group of people according to their place within society (based on their origin, employment status, and income), to give its true political meaning it must also be viewed as part of a struggle. This contestation, relating specifically to how the 'problem' of inequality is described, is, crucially, one in which those whom class attempts to define participate in. 'These struggles are always historically contingent and the names for class mutate and transform', argues Tyler.[16] Class naming, most commonly (but not always) deployed as a form of stigmatisation, is fundamental to the way in which class works in twenty-first-century Britain. Class has been declared dead under neoliberalism just as inequality has hardened and the power of capital intensified. Paradoxically, with an increase in poverty, precarious work, and the reinforcing of social immobility, class has also been mobilised to explain and justify inequality and to generate consent for neoliberal policy. Rhian E. Jones has characterised this as a cultural shift, one which has seen the 'vanishing factors of working-class, and especially female working-class, identity in public discourse' combined with the 'accelerated use' of class 'as an all-purpose whipping-post for a host of social ills and moral panics'.[17] 'Consciousness of class is resurgent', she argues, most notably with 'the increased visibility of "chav" as mocked and feared other in both politics and pop culture'.[18] So, how have these two phenomena operated in tandem while seeming to be so contradictory? E. P. Thompson, in *The Making of the English Working Class*, describes class as a 'relationship'.[19] He says: 'I am convinced that we cannot understand class unless we see it as a social and cultural formation, arising from processes which can only be studied as they work themselves out over a considerable historical period'.[20] Before moving onto the individual chapter readings of twenty-first-century British fiction and the working class, it will be instructive to map out in detail the historical, social, and political contexts appropriate to this study; it is a necessary and essential process if we are to understand class in the twenty-first century.

In Britain, New Labour's uncoupling of inequality from class goes some way to providing an explanation for the aforementioned contradictions. The party's dropping of a class analysis was, according to Tyler, 'part of a three-decades-long struggle on the part of the elites to jettison the language of class struggle as the perpetual framework through which to perceive social and economic (dis)advantage'.[21] Owen Jones has written of the determination of New Labour to 'scrub class from the country's vocabulary'.[22] When Tony Blair came to power in 1997 he was 'following in [Margaret] Thatcher's footsteps and pretending that class no longer existed'.[23] These movements against and away from class made it more difficult to talk both of class in the contemporary moment and of the working class as a social formation in and of the present; this is an effect which Cora Kaplan insists is ideologically and politically motivated. 'New Labour silently aligns the word and concept of class with the category of men, as if feminism hadn't thoroughly interrogated that assumption', says Kaplan. 'This backward intuition has been [...] part of a political strategy to make "class" itself, especially but not exclusively "working-class", obsolete or "history" as a term of social analysis', she adds. 'Consequently', Kaplan concludes, 'class becomes part of a version of the past where, if it were personified as a male, he would be one of the disappeared'.[24] So there are two things going on here: the male industrial worker is one of the disappeared, irrelevant, and a product of a distant past with no relevance in the present; and, by associating class exclusively with this figure, the concept of the working class is assigned the same fate. As Caplan reveals, this deliberately crafts an obstacle to overcome when seeking to explore the relevance and profundity of class formation in the twenty-first century. And crucially, this attempt by neoliberal logic to block off access to class analysis is part of the formation of class as, what Beverley Skeggs has called, a 'site of struggle'; it will always be such a location, insists Skeggs, because 'it encompasses interests, power and privilege'.[25]

I place my understanding of class as part of a historical development with a specific focus on neoliberalism's transformation from, what David Harvey has described as, 'relative obscurity' to become the dominant political doctrine of the late-twentieth and early-twenty-first century.[26] This particular history is analysed in more depth below, locating my account around Thatcherism as a political project built upon the leading principles of neoliberalism. Firstly, however, I wish briefly to discuss further the role of the mainstream political party most closely associated with the working class: Labour. The rebranding of the party as New Labour marks an important point in the history of this class formation in Britain. As Mike Wayne has described, New Labour, with its coupling of socially liberal policy and economic liberalism, 'accepted the Thatcherite settlement of a State ever more receptive to opening up markets for capital'.[27] In 1996, for instance, after seventeen years out of office, two of the leading architects of what become known as the 'Third Way', Peter Mandelson and Roger Liddle, wrote of the party's 'bold task'. They described such a move thus:

[T]o modernise Britain socially, economically and politically. In doing so [New Labour] aims to build on Britain's strengths. Its mission is to create not to destroy. Its strategy is to move forward from where Margaret Thatcher left off, rather than to dismantle every single thing she did.[28]

This acceptance involved submitting to the notion 'that entrepreneurship and aspiration would inevitably see what remained of the working class raised to the contented ranks of the middle class, ignoring or denying structural and systemic reasons [...] which might hinder this'.[29] Continuing the Thatcherite belief in individualism with 'almost religious zeal',[30] the 'Third Way' built upon the idea that everyone could get on in this new meritocracy. Owen Jones adds: 'In a new, supposedly upwardly mobile Britain, everyone would aspire to climb the ladder and all those who did not would be responsible for their own failure'.[31] This shift in who is responsible for the well-being of both the country and its people – a benevolent state or hard-working individuals – allows for the perpetuation of inequality: the message is that unemployment, poverty, poor housing, and poor living conditions can all be escaped by hard work. In *Chavs: The Demonization of the Working Class*, the central argument Owen Jones makes is that 'chav-hate' or the caricaturing and ridiculing of an undeserving poor is a way of justifying inequality. 'To admit that some people are poorer than others because of the social injustice inherent in our society would require government action', Jones argues. 'Claiming that people are largely responsible for their circumstances facilitates the opposite conclusion', he adds.[32] I will address this reading of how stigmatisation works and can be challenged in Chapter Five when I argue that Fagan's *The Panopticon* performs a double movement of resistance against such class naming and making.

The practice of 'manipulating language to control public perception', as Norman Fairclough describes it in *New Labour, New Language?*, was central not only to the 'Third Way' but remains so to the ongoing processes of class formation in twenty-first-century Britain.[33] This is one reason why, as Tyler argues, it is problematic to simply slot people into predetermined categories of class because such a move is 'actively engaged in the formation and establishment of the class hierarchies that it describes'.[34] Throughout this book, class formations are understood as dynamic processes, not as stable 'predetermined' categories. Close attention is paid to the way in which neoliberalism shapes ideas of class and class stigma. Again, language plays an important role here. For example, 'aspiration' has been used, by both New Labour and the Conservative Party, to describe a seemingly new class. 'It connotes endeavour', remarks Stefan Collini, 'making something of oneself, trying – as an older idiom had it – to improve one's station in life'.[35] As Collini points out, however, the notion of the 'aspirational class' performs an 'ideological function'. According to Tyler and Bruce Bennett, it works as 'a rhetorical device that seeks to whitewash a neoliberal economic and political project and the staggering inequalities it produces'.[36] Tyler and Bennett add: 'Aspiration is a political concept that seeks to replace not only the ideal of the compassionate and caring Welfare State, but along with it other political concepts such as class, democracy, exploitation, solidarity, justice, dignity, and rights'.[37] In many ways, it is a manipulation of language which has evolved out of New Labour's 'rhetoric of reconciliation' which was designed, according to Fairclough, to draw attention to 'assumed incompatibilities and [deny] them. It is a rhetoric of denial of expectations – things are not as they have been thought to be'.[38] So there can be 'social justice' alongside 'economic dynamism', 'ambition' with 'compassion', and 'fairness' as well as 'enterprise'.[39] And the labels which describe class inequality are rebranded: poverty is replaced by social exclusion, for example. According to Fairclough, the latter term became a lumping device into which '[p]roblems which might in different discourses be differentiated and separated are [...] made equivalent'.[40] As a result, 'social exclusion [...] is a condition people are in, not something that is done to them'.[41] Selina Todd has documented how the term working class became 'socially stigmatized [...] [and] increasingly interchangeable with "underclass"'.[42] And this is how class works, as a 'matter of inscription', according to Skeggs; it is predicated on 'concepts [which] are performative' and which 'have very real material, economic and political impacts'.[43] In what has become a key mental conception reshaped under neoliberalism, having a profound impact on ideas of class and social responsibility, 'personal failure is generally attributed to personal failings, and the victim is all too often blamed'.[44] Harvey argues: 'Ideological and political hegemony in any society depends on an ability to control the material context of personal and social experience'.[45] He identifies mental conceptions of the world, what he describes in *The Enigma of Capital* as one of the seven spheres of activity within the evolutionary trajectory of capitalism,[46] as playing a crucial role in such experience. It is through such conceptions that capital is, in one way, able to reproduce itself. And this relates back to a specific feature of neoliberalism; as Thatcher proclaimed, it was an ideologically driven project to 'change the soul' of the British people by the hand of a new form of contemporary capitalism.[47] So, as a result of the move to 'blame' individuals for what are structural problems (unemployment, for example), the poorest in society become a target during times of economic downturn; they are singled out as a drain on the economy in order to legitimise further reductions in, for example, the welfare state. So how did this shift to neoliberalism occur?

Harvey begins his account of the neoliberal turn (*A Brief History of Neoliberalism*) with a forecast: 'Future historians may well look upon the years 1978–80 as a revolutionary turning-point in the world's social and economic history'.[48] It was a period which saw the liberalisation of the Chinese economy led by Deng Xiaoping, the election of Margaret

Thatcher in Great Britain, and Ronald Reagan become President of the United States. While these three events offer symbolic moments in which to view the move towards neoliberalism becoming 'hegemonic as a mode of discourse', to get some perspective on its 'uneven geographical development' the immediate post-war period provides a useful starting point.[49] Like Harvey, Philip Mirowski traces the roots of neoliberalism back to the Mont Pelerin Society in 1947 which had amongst its founding members the free-market economists Friedrich Hayek and Milton Friedman. It is important to stress that Thatcherism, as Mirowski argues, was the culmination of a 'comprehensive long-term reform effort to [reshape] the entire fabric of society'.[50] Naomi Klein has described the 'Chicago School', of which Friedman was a leading figure in the 1950s, as a 'revolutionary bulwark against the dominant "statist" thinking of the day'.[51] The University of Chicago economists 'did not see Marxism as their true enemy', suggests Klein. 'The real source of the trouble was [...] the ideas of the Keynesians in the United States, the social democrats in Europe and the developmentalists in [...] the Third World'.[52] Neoliberalism's 'state-phobia', as Tyler describes it, was and is coupled, paradoxically, with the 'demands for continuous, repressive interventions by the state'.[53] It is a political doctrine which involves the state governing for the market, ensuring the market the optimum conditions in which to expand and grow which, in turn, means an increasing amount of intervention. 'So, it is a matter of a market economy without laissez-faire, that is to say, an active policy without state control', Michel Foucault has argued. 'Neo-liberalism should not therefore be identified with laissez-faire, but rather with permanent vigilance, activity, and intervention', Foucault concludes.[54] Mirowski stresses that this distinction between twentieth-century neoliberalism and nineteenth-century liberalism is key; 'most of the early neoliberals explicitly distanced themselves from what they considered the outmoded classical liberal doctrine of laissez-faire', he argues.[55] While it is problematic to reduce neoliberal ideology to the singular work of the Mont Pelerin Society, Mirowski stresses the distinctive nature of the international organisation's influence and highlights its relevance as a source-site of neoliberal thinking so as to challenge dangerous assumptions that neoliberalism is a 'hopelessly diffuse and ill-defined movement'.[56]

A number of key pre-1979 moments can therefore be highlighted in order to chart the development of neoliberalism. Following a crisis of global capital accumulation in the 1970s, both Chile (under the dictatorship of Augusto Pinochet from 1973) and New York City (during the fiscal crisis of 1975) are described by Harvey as testing grounds for a doctrine which sought to drive economic growth by deregulation, privatisation, financialisation, and the widespread withdrawal of state involvement in public and private life. Crucially, Britain has a pre-Thatcher history of implementing such a project of political and social management. In 1976, James Callaghan's Labour Government sought and received a multi-billion American dollar bail-out from the International Monetary Fund (IMF). In return for the loan, Callaghan had to approve large cuts in public spending. It was a form of nascent neoliberalism which Aaron Kelly has argued meant the Labour Party 'anticipated and facilitated Thatcherism rather than being overturned by it'.[57] Likewise, Todd has described it as a primitive form of Thatcherism. She says:

> The role of the international oil crisis was conveniently overlooked, while the IMF's stance was simply accepted as common sense, rather than as the calculated strategy of those bankers, financiers and right-wing politicians who controlled the IMF, and which promoted a global free market at the expense of workers' welfare.[58]

This brief history of nascent neoliberalism in Britain goes some way to understanding how Thatcherism was able to take hold. As Stuart Hall argued in one of the most important pieces of British political analysis in the twentieth century, 'far from simply conjuring demons out of the deep, [Thatcherism] operated directly on the real and manifestly contradictory experience of the popular classes under social-democratic corporatism'.[59] Thatcher won the General Election of May 1979 promising to tackle 'stagflation' – a period of rising inflation, declining economic growth, and rising unemployment – by curbing union power and deregulating the financial sector. According to Harvey, Thatcher's brand of neoliberalism, masterminded in part by her close ally Keith Joseph, was 'far more ideologically driven' than her counterparts across the Atlantic.[60] Thatcherism attacked entrenched forms of class power based upon aristocratic traditions and embraced the entrepreneurs and nouveaux riche who would form a new elite within British society. It also deployed measures to erode the gains, most notably the welfare state, of the post-war settlement (or post-war social contract). This compromise between capital and labour, as Harvey describes it, had been promoted as the 'key guarantor of domestic peace and tranquillity'.[61] Harvey says: 'The state in effect became a force field that internalized class relations. Working-class institutions such as labour unions and political parties of the left had a very real influence within the state apparatus'.[62] Todd has described this 'consensus' as follows: 'The government would guarantee the workers' welfare in return for their labour. To ensure that workers' needs were met at work as well as at home, the trade unions were assured a seat at the national negotiation table'.[63] It is this formation which I refer to when I use the term 'welfare capitalism', described by Alan Sinfield as promising 'all the people a stake in society and adequate share of its resources – a job, a pension or social security, a roof over your head, healthcare, education'.[64] Economic inequality eased during the post-1945 turn to such a form of political, economic, and social management. Lynsey Hanley observes: 'The gap between the incomes of the richest and those of the poorest in Britain reached its narrowest ever point in 1979'.[65] But neoliberalism directly challenged the forms of social solidarity which emerged in the period between 1945 and 1979. Harvey describes the distinctively right-wing project of neoliberalism as one of capitalist restructuring and stresses its impact on labour. He says:

> Capitalist class power was weakening relative to labour and other social movements and capital accumulation was lagging. The heads of leading corporations, along with media barons and wealthy individuals, many of whom [...] were scions of the capitalist class, went on the counter-attack.[66]

The state-finance nexus was reconstructed, overseeing the deregulation of financial operations, the opening up of both credit markets and international markets, and state withdrawal from social provision and welfare. The effect on labour was profound, picking apart the considerable gains of the previous three decades. After 1979 'the state's struggle for working-class assent to mainstream values and beliefs would shift decisively from the nurturing of consent to the politics of coercion', according to John Kirk.[67] This new approach would not only see the restoration of class power but also 'a profound remaking of the British working class'.[68]

The post-1979 period has seen the privatisation of almost all nationalised industries, widespread deregulation of the financial sector, the rise of the investment bank, the opening up of Britain to much-expanded foreign investment, the creation of both technological and global markets, increasing 'flexibility' in the labour market, a boom in credit-financed consumerism, and the commodification of services from health to higher education. Neoliberalism relies on the ability of capital to flow unhindered, so the concern is always with freeing up markets, transcending barriers, abolishing limits, and creating new markets to allow for consistent and perpetual (yet rarely achievable) growth. So, how was it possible to construct a 'common sense' neoliberalism, what Hall has described as the 'formation of a new hegemonic stage' in post-war British society?[69]

A central tenet of Thatcherism actively sought to change the way people thought and felt about class and society. Thatcherism was concerned with the winning and social construction of popular consent by grasping and reformulating the popular mentality and the common sense of the general populace. This was not predicated purely on an economic or political basis. Rather, it had the aim of reconstructing social life as a whole. Hall defines common sense as 'a structure of popular ideology, a spontaneous conception of the world, reflecting the traces of previous systems of thought that have sedimented into everyday reasoning'.[70]

One of the targets for such a struggle, and a section of society to whom Thatcherism, Hall argues, was in part able to appeal, was the British working class. 'What is particularly significant', Hall writes, 'is Thatcherism's capacity to become popular, especially among those sectors of the society whose interests it cannot possibly be said to represent in any conventional sense of the term'.[71] Despite its apparent tensions and contradictions as a 'populist political force' which operated by combining an 'imposition of social discipline from above' with a 'populist mobilization from below', Thatcherism was able to formulate a general and overarching world view which fed into local and personal concerns; it involved a 'plurality of discourses', as Hall describes it, which offered answers to political and social questions about 'the family, the economy, national identity, morality, crime, law, women, human nature'.[72] And its potency lay in being able to present a perception of unity despite the diversity of positions adopted within such areas of political debate and action. Crucially, Hall argues that such an ideology, 'a populist political force', was able to penetrate, fracture, and fragment 'the territory of the dominated classes [...] [and] their traditional discourses [...] laborism, reformism, welfarism, Keynesianism' and enlist 'popular consent among significant sections' of the working class.[73] As both Hall and Raymond Williams acknowledge, it would be misleading to assume that the working-class vote in the twentieth century went exclusively to the Labour Party and/ or for socialism.[74] However, Williams is more cautious, as I am, than Hall in his analysis of the level of working-class support for the initial emergence of neoliberalism. Whereas Hall proclaims that '[s]ubstantial sections of the skilled and semi-skilled industrial classes, [...] organised trade unionists, [...] the working-class urban vote, [...] the unemployed, [...] have gone over to Thatcherism, [...] abandoning their traditional loyalty to Labour',[75] Williams points to the significance of an expanded British political system, specifically during the 1983 General Election when the Social Democratic Party (SDP) formed out of a breakaway from the Labour Party.[76] 'The two-party system [Labour and Conservative] had always simplified, polarised and thus disguised the actual spread of political opinion', according to Williams. He adds: '[T]he "old working class" or "the classical proletariat" [...] did not vote "socialist" in the way that many interpretations presume or infer'.[77] Further, Eric Hobsbawm argued in 1978 in his essay 'The Forward March of Labour Halted?' that, following a peak of support for Labour in 1951, the working-class movement as a radical socialist movement 'seems to have got stuck'.[78] So, the crisis facing the left, during the rise of neoliberalism, was not as simple as stopping conversions to the right-wing ideology of Thatcherism but its inability to conceive of, to define, and win for itself an 'accepted concept of the general interest'.[79] This was also a concern of Hall's, who spoke of the urgent task, which the left must begin in earnest, of generating 'a whole alternative philosophy or conception of life' addressing the contemporary social and historical conditions.[80] 'It is the Labour Party which is committed to things as they are', noted Hall in January 1979.[81] 'Mounting a counteroffensive [to Thatcherism]', he argued a decade later, 'involves offering and setting in place alternative and equally powerful frames for life in the twenty-first century'.[82] As Andrew Milner has noted, such an analysis of Thatcher's popularity was 'claimed for Cultural Studies, rather than, say, Political Science, because [it] appeared to pertain to the social construction of consent'.[83] And regardless of the legitimate concerns raised by Williams over how to assess the level of working-class support for the Conservative Governments elected, specifically, in 1979 and 1983, Hall's assertion that neoliberalism was able to claim for itself the common sense of popular political and public debate and opinion was remarkably prescient. As Mirowski noted in 2013, five years after the global financial crisis of 2008, 'a kind of "folk" or "everyday" neoliberalism has sunk so deeply into the cultural unconscious that even a few rude shocks can't begin to bring it to the surface long enough to provoke discomfort'.[84] But, and increasingly so, class has been brought to the surface once more, troubling the dominant logic concerning its social and political (ir)relevance.

There have been repeated proclamations, particularly during the emergence of neoliberalism in Britain, announcing the death of class. However, as Selina Todd notes, 'in the early twenty-first century polls suggested that more than half of British people still considered themselves working class'.[85] One such poll, carried out on behalf of think-tank British Future, found that fifty-seven per cent of British people identify as working class while thirty-six per cent consider themselves to be middle class.[86] In contrast to this more traditional approach (asking people what class they are), the Great British Class Survey, conducted for the BBC by sociologists Mike Savage and Fiona Devine, created a new model of classification based on answers to an online questionnaire. It identified seven 'new' social classes: 'elite', 'established middle class', 'technical middle class', 'new affluent workers', 'emergent service workers', 'traditional working class', and 'precariat'.[87] Savage and Devine remark: 'We devised a new way of measuring class, which doesn't define class just by the job that you do, but by the different kinds of economic, cultural and social resources or "capitals" that people possess'.[88] There are a number of problems with such an approach. The three conceptions of capital used by the survey are presented as equivalents, with any dynamic between them seemingly absent. Due emphasis is not placed on the economic and, further, as Tyler points out, 'culture is understood as a diversity of "cultural products", and "cultural capital" is understood as expressed "likes" and "dislikes"'.[89] Therefore, culture is formulated by the survey as a matter of choice and depending on what you choose to like and dislike determines, partially at least, your class. To follow this logic through then, to move between classes simply involves changing your preference in 'cultural products'. Such logic does not take into account access to such forms of capital, often decided by economic factors, nor does it offer a theorisation of culture as a whole way of life, as an expression of lived experience. My book understands class formations as dynamic processes, not as predetermined categories, and in that way it approaches both class and culture in different ways to Savage and Devine.

Charles Umney argues in *Class Matters* that class should not be understood merely as a descriptive category but as defining 'the way in which society works'.[90] He adds that if we are to understand class in twenty-first-century Britain, then we must 'consider how the interactions between people with different economic roles affects the working of society as a whole'.[91] Such analysis has gained more substantial traction following the financial crisis of 2008 when, Umney argues, Britain 'had a brief glimpse of what we might call "class consciousness"'.[92] The global capitalist crisis – a crisis created by and of neoliberal ideology – saw the collapse of a number of high profile banks (exemplified by Lehman Brothers in September 2008), stock markets plummet, a sharp increase in home repossessions, and a dramatic expansion of national debt while unemployment peaked a few hundred thousand short of the symbolic three million mark in Britain. The crisis did not result in a sustained and successful class-based challenge to neoliberal hegemony, however; rather, it demonstrated the necessity of state intervention (in the form of bank bailouts) to protect capital and prop up neoliberalism.

Another 'rude shock' in Britain in the twenty-first century, in terms of its political and social impact, has been the result of the European Union (EU) Referendum in June 2016. Brexit immediately took on a class dimension and many political commentators explained the result as a working-class revolt.[93] Such analysis does not pay attention to the dynamics of capital nor to the fact that Brexit was mobilised and delivered by the ruling class. According to Umney, 'Brexit has been conducted as a conflict between different views on what is good for British capital'.[94] This is what often gets missed in the clammer to point the figure at an imagined working class. As research shows, the Leave campaign was not only orchestrated by those wedded to the ideology of neoliberalism but was also able to mobilise a 'broad-based coalition of voters which is much more wide-ranging than the "left behind"'.[95] An 'older working class' is amongst this coalition alongside 'affluent Eurosceptics'.[96] But any analysis of the working-class voters who opted to leave the EU must have at its centre a political, theoretical understanding of how capitalism works; such analysis should also include the relationship between the EU and the dynamics of global capital. Joe Kennedy in *Authentocrats* states: 'Brexit, of course, is the signal example in modern British history about what happens when liberal culture plays along with the idea that material inequalities are actually about culture'.[97] And, as

Wayne astutely observes, 'social liberalism aligned with economic liberalism built the conditions for a reactionary conservatism to win new recruits to illiberalism among the most disadvantaged'. He adds: 'New Labour effectively abandoned the working class whose communities, industries and cultural organs had been devastated by the "mark one" model of neoliberalism under Thatcherism and then Majorism'.[98] And the neoliberal consensus – as symbolised by the Conservative Party, the Liberal Democrats, and a considerable section of the Labour Party – has failed to produce adequate responses to the crash of 2008 or the chaos of the 2016 Brexit vote.

But out of the contradictions of neoliberalism – which partly explain both the crash and Brexit – has come a renewed acknowledgement of class. Both the Conservative Party and the Labour Party are talking about the working class again. As Richard Seymour has argued, 'class was as important as nation' during the 2017 General Election.[99] Despite predictions, Labour's shift to the left under Jeremy Corbyn did not result in a collapse of its working-class vote. The fact that there were not 'sweeping losses across the West Midlands, the North, and Wales is indicative', according to Seymour, 'that Labour succeeded in raising the turnout among "traditional Labour voters" as well as new voters'.[100] And what was clear from Labour's forty per cent vote, and specifically its 2017 manifesto, was that challenges to the neoliberal consensus were possible.

There are some major challenges accompanying this return to discussions about class following the EU referendum. There has been a subtle shift from explicit demonisation, although this persists amongst those who wish to 'blame' the working class for Brexit, to addressing 'legitimate concerns' apparently being voiced by the working class. But what exactly are these 'legitimate concerns' and who is really voicing them? As Kennedy points out, such concerns often tend to be about immigration, patriotism, and defence, but never about jobs, housing, and wage stagnation; they are never about material inequalities created by capitalism, foundational to neoliberalism. Umney shows how this, in part, links back to the post-crash political agendas of David Cameron, George Osborne, Nick Clegg, and the Conservative-Liberal Democrat Coalition Government of 2010–2015. 'The hardworking person became the model citizen of the austerity era: they accepted that we were "all in it together", and that you had to pull your weight by making sacrifices without complaining'.[101] The 'hardworking' were not to blame and those who were could be easily identified by deploying divisive logic: those on benefits, those who refused to work, immigrants both taking jobs and living off the state. Such toxic discourse was reconfigured by Theresa May when she became Prime Minister in 2016 – and here is the link to 'legitimate concerns'. Umney argues that Cameron's 'hardworking people' became May's 'working class'. In May's use of the term, from her deployment of it on the steps of 10 Downing Street as she gave her first speech as PM, working class describes 'people who worry about job security, who love the Queen, who want the death penalty and who want to leave the EU. And, of course, who dislike immigration'.[102] Umney adds that May's aim was to 'make sure that anti-immigration sentiment remained high-up on the list of working-class issues as she defined them'.[103] This question of definition – who decides who is working class and what working-class concerns are – has been a compelling feature of political commentary in the aftermath of the Brexit vote. Kennedy identifies a 'pseudo-ethnography central to political authentocracy that pretends to be getting away from "metropolitan elites" to tell it like it is but, in fact, has already decided what it wants to find when it gets there'.[104] He identifies how 'stories whose moral is the need to pay more attention to supposedly authentic people in actuality erase these people by turning them into metaphors for generic malaise'.[105] This is yet another projection and imposition, similar to the way in which class stigma works and is mobilised to justify inequality. This is an important development: from demonising the working class to deploying and constructing yet another stereotype while purporting to listen but in fact falsifying an image of a conservative, 'authentic', often white, working class. It is a construction which deflects from the political ideology which caused the problems in the first place. So, if it is demonisation or authenticity being mobilised, the outcome is the same: neoliberalism is off the hook. A necessary act of resistance is one which challenges such constructions of who the working class are and who they should be according to dominant class logic. Further, the political purposes of class naming need to be identified.

I draw attention to a small number of writers whose work, in offering illuminating engagements with contemporary class formations, offers sites of resistance to the dominance of neoliberal discourse. My chapters are case studies in a much wider debate that needs to be had about class and fiction. And I make important connections between all six to draw out some key facets of working-class experience and of twenty-first-century life under neoliberalism. A central concern is with deindustrial working-class communities and the first two chapters deal with industrial class experience predominantly from a male perspective. In the chapters on Cartwright and Raisin, the focus is on what is often misleadingly thought of as the 'traditional' British working class (a social formation predicated on heavy industry) and I engage directly with the intersections of gender and race with class in both. My chapter on Fagan's novel examines the female working-class experience of class stigma while the final chapter on Sahota pays specific attention to race, ethnicity, and particularly British Asian experience. That three of these six writers (Raisin, Fagan, and Sahota) were named amongst *Granta's* top twenty British writers under forty in 2013 demonstrates that fiction about class does not consign an author to obscurity.[106] Likewise, Peace was on the *Granta* list in 2003 and each of the six writers I discuss have enjoyed varying degrees of critical and commercial success: Burn's debut novel *Alma Cogan* (1991) won the Whitbread Award for Best First Novel; Peace's highest accolade has been the James Tait Black Memorial Prize for *GB84*; Cartwright earned a Betty Trask Award for *The Afterglow* and he was shortlisted for the inaugural Gordon Burn Prize in 2013; and Sahota was shortlisted for The Man Booker Prize in 2015 and also won the South Bank Sky Arts Award for Literature. So, here are six authors writing about the British working class in the twenty-first century, who have operated successfully within the mainstream publishing industry. The value of their texts, however, is not best judged by the accolades of what remains an unequal industry but in the way each maps, and therefore illuminates the workings of class in the twenty-first century.

What I hope to demonstrate, through a reading of these six writers, is that the formation of class continues to change but that class never goes away under the dynamics of a capitalist system. It is shaped, often dramatically, by alterations in economic and political practice, hence the continued disruptions to class formations. It is not a static structure, nor, according to Harvey, is it a 'stable social configuration'.[107] The complexities and contradictions of class in Britain must be understood in terms of its relationship to the complexities and contradictions of capitalism. That is why Jameson's proposal for an aesthetic of cognitive mapping which must hold true to the global nature of the third stage of capitalism is useful here.[108] This 'pedagogical political culture' will seek 'to endow the individual subject with some new heightened sense of its place in the global system'.[109] If experience is the link between being and consciousness, how is class experience under neoliberalism explored by cultural texts? An emerging critical discourse engaged in formulating contemporary conceptions of class provides a way of addressing such questions. And by mapping how it runs into discourses of fiction in the following chapters, I argue that the novels of Peace, Burn, Cartwright, Raisin, Fagan, and Sahota represent important interventions into evolving, contemporary discussions around class, capital, and neoliberalism.

Notes

1 Theodor W. Adorno, 'Reading Balzac', in *Notes to Literature: Volume One*, ed. by Rolf Tiedemann (New York, NY: Columbia University Press, 1991), pp. 121–136 (pp. 122–123).

2 Fredric Jameson, *Postmodernism, or, The Cultural Logic of Late Capitalism* (London: Verso, 1992), p. 44.

3 Raymond Williams, *Marxism and Literature* (Oxford: Oxford University Press, 1977), p. 175.

4 Lynsey Hanley, *Estates: An Intimate History* (London: Granta Books, 2008), p. 20.

5 Tim Lott, 'The Loneliness of the Working-Class Writer', *The Guardian*, 7 February 2015, www.theguardian.com/commentisfree/2015/feb/07/loneliness-working-class-writer-english-novelists. Lott has written two

novels concerned with issues of class in contemporary Britain: *White City Blue* (1999) and *Rumours of a Hurricane* (2002).

6 Raymond Williams, *Culture and Society 1780–1950* (Harmondsworth: Penguin, 1963), p. 313.

7 Rhian E. Jones, 'On Peterloo, Poetry, and the Politics of Protest History', *New Socialist*, 5th November 2018, https://newsocialist.org.uk/peterloo-poetry-and-politics-protest-history.

8 Ibid.

9 Rhian E. Jones, *Clampdown: Pop-Cultural Wars on Class and Gender* (Winchester: Zero Books, 2013).

10 Kit de Waal, 'Make Room for Working Class Writers', *The Guardian*, 10th February 2018, www.theguardian.com/books/2018/feb/10/kit-de-waal-where-are-all-the-working-class-writers-.

11 Ibid.

12 *Know Your Place: Essays on the Working Class by the Working Class*, ed. by Nathan Connolly (Liverpool: Dead Ink, 2017), p. 5.

13 Renni Eddo-Lodge, *Why I'm No Longer Talking to White People About Race* (London: Bloomsbury, 2018), p. 184.

14 Paul Gilroy, *There Ain't No Black in the Union Jack* (Abingdon: Routledge, 2002), p. 35.

15 Imogen Tyler, *Revolting Subjects: Social Abjection and Resistance in Neoliberal Britain* (London: Zero Books, 2013), p. 155.

16 Ibid., p. 155.

17 Rhian E. Jones, *Clampdown*, pp. 72–73.

18 Ibid., p. 95.

19 E. P. Thompson, *The Making of the English Working Class* (London: Penguin, 1991), p. 10. Thompson adds: 'I do not see class as a "structure", nor even as a "category", but as something which in fact happens (and can be shown to have happened) in human relationships', p. 8.

20 Thompson, p. 11.

21 Tyler, *Revolting Subjects*, p. 153.

22 Owen Jones, *Chavs: The Demonization of the Working Class* (London: Verso, 2011), p. 98.

23 Ibid., p. 98.

24 Cora Kaplan, 'The Death of the Working-Class Hero', *New Formations*, vol. 52, 2004, pp. 94–110 (p. 99).

25 Beverley Skeggs, *Class, Self, Culture* (London: Routledge, 2004), p. 44.

26 David Harvey, *A Brief History of Neoliberalism* (Oxford: Oxford University Press, 2007), p. 2.

27 Mike Wayne, *England's Discontents: Political Cultures and National Identities* (London: Pluto, 2018), p. 174. Wayne explains this opening up of the market under New Labour thus:

> Hence making the Bank of England "independent" (i.e. outside democratic political influence), the refusal to renationalise the railways, the use of private finance initiatives (PFIs) in health and transport, refusing to deflate the private housing bubble by building publicly owned housing on the scale necessary to meet demand, extensive outsourcing of State services to private corporations, creeping privatisation of health and education and as the logical extension of this economic liberalism, a cataclysmic alliance with US imperialism abroad at its most dangerous and destructive (the Bush-Cheney "axis of evil") p. 174.

28 As quoted in Keith Laybourn, *A Century of Labour: A History of the Labour Party* (Stroud: Sutton Publishing, 2001), p. 153.

29 Rhian E. Jones, *Clampdown*, p. 9.
30 Owen Jones, p. 250.
31 Ibid., p. 48.
32 Ibid., p. 37.
33 Norman Fairclough, *New Labour, New Language?* (London: Routledge, 2000), p. vii.
34 Imogen Tyler, 'Classificatory Struggles: Class, Culture and Inequality in Neoliberal Times', *The Sociological Review*, vol. 63, 2015, pp. 493–511 (p. 499).
35 Stefan Collini, 'Blahspeak', *London Review of Books*, vol. 32, no. 7, 8 April 2010, pp. 29–34, www.lrb.co.uk/v32/n07/stefan-collini/blahspeak.
36 Imogen Tyler and Bruce Bennett, 'Against Aspiration', *What Is Aspiration? How Progressives Should Respond by CLASS*: Centre for Labour and Social Studies, August 2015, pp. 6–8 (p. 6), http://classonline.org.uk/pubs/item/what-is-aspiration.
37 Tyler and Bennett, p. 6.
38 Fairclough, p. vii, p. 10.
39 Ibid., p. 10.
40 Ibid., p. 53.
41 Ibid., p. 54.
42 Selina Todd, *The People: The Rise and Fall of the Working Class* (London: John Murray, 2015), p. 358.
43 Skeggs, *Class, Self, Culture*, p. 44.
44 Harvey, *A Brief History of Neoliberalism*, p. 76.
45 David Harvey, *The Condition of Postmodernity: An Enquiry into the Origins of Cultural Change* (Oxford: Blackwell, 1990), pp. 226–227.
46 The other six: technological and organisational forms; social relations; institutional and administrative arrangements; production and labour processes; relations to nature; reproduction of daily life. David Harvey, *The Enigma of Capital and the Crises of Capitalism* (London: Profile Books, 2011), p. 123.
47 Margaret Thatcher quoted in Harvey, *A Brief History of Neoliberalism*, p. 23.
48 Harvey, *A Brief History of Neoliberalism*, p. 1.
49 Ibid., p. 3, p. 9.
50 Philip Mirowski, *Never Let a Serious Crisis Go to Waste: How Neoliberalism Survived the Financial Meltdown* (London: Verso, 2014), p. 48.
51 Naomi Klein, *The Shock Doctrine: The Rise of Disaster Capitalism* (London: Penguin, 2007), p. 49.
52 Ibid., p. 53.
53 Tyler, *Revolting Subjects*, p. 6.
54 Michel Foucault, *The Birth of Biopolitics: Lectures at the Collège de France* (Basingstoke: Palgrave Macmillan, 2010), p. 132.
55 Mirowski, p. 41.
56 Mirowski argues that the Mont Pelerin Society does not play the central role it once did. Neoliberalism is now a 'living, mutating entity' with universities, think-tanks, and media organisations more influential; Mirowski characterises this as the 'Russian doll structure of the Neoliberal Thought Collective'. See Mirowski, pp. 49–51.
57 Aaron Kelly, *Irvine Welsh* (Manchester: Manchester University Press, 2005), p. 8.
58 Todd, p. 311.
59 Stuart Hall, 'The Great Moving Right Show', in *The Hard Road to Renewal: Thatcherism and the Crisis of the Left*, ed. by Stuart Hall (London: Verso, p. 1990), pp. 39–56 (p. 50).

60 Harvey, *A Brief History of Neoliberalism*, p. 62.

61 Ibid., p. 10.

62 Ibid., p. 12.

63 Todd, p. 158.

64 Alan Sinfield, *Literature, Politics and Culture in Postwar Britain* (London: Continuum, 2004), p. xxxi. Sinfield convincingly argues that it has been the failure of welfare capitalism rather than the fall of Soviet communism which has wrong-footed the British liberal-left who continue to have faith in the post-war settlement. He says:

> [W]elfare-capitalism raises expectations, with a view to governing through popular consent rather than through threats of deprivation and coercion. But only for a while can the system produce enough wealth to keep pace with those expectations [...].*That is the failure that has perplexed us*, not the failure of Soviet-style, centralized direction.

Sinfield also makes the important observation that it has been the 'welfare' aspect of 'welfare capitalism' which has been accepted as failing, a key concept of Thatcherism and neoliberal logic, rather than this oxymoronic formation collapsing due to 'capitalism' itself. See Sinfield, p. xxxiii, and, for an extended discussion of welfare capitalism, pp. 315–352.

65 Hanley, p. 132.

66 Harvey, *The Enigma of Capital*, pp. 130–131.

67 John Kirk, *The British Working Class in the Twentieth Century: Film, Literature and Television* (Cardiff: University of Wales Press, 2009), p. 77.

68 Ibid., p. 108.

69 Stuart Hall, 'The Toad in the Garden: Thatcherism amongst the Theorists', in *Marxism and the Interpretation of Culture*, ed. by Cary Nelson and Lawrence Grossberg (London: Macmillan Education, 1988), pp. 35–73 (p. 37).

70 Ibid., p. 55.

71 Ibid., p. 41.

72 Ibid., p. 40, p. 53.

73 Ibid., p. 40, p. 42, p. 40.

74 Hall notes that '[b]etween a quarter and a third of the British working class, however defined, has traditionally voted conservative in [the twentieth] century'. Hall, 'The Toad in the Garden', p. 42.

75 Hall, 'The Toad in the Garden', p. 40.

76 The centrist SDP was created by two Labour MPs (David Owen and Bill Rodgers) and two former Labour MPs (Roy Jenkins and Shirley Williams) who formed an alliance with the Liberal Party during the 1983 and 1987 elections. Owen Jones believes this was an important factor in the success of the Conservative Party at the ballot box: 'Thatcher had lost half a million votes since 1979, but her fragmenting opposition allowed the Tories to come through the middle in constituencies across the country, giving her a landslide', p. 70.

77 Raymond Williams, *Towards 2000* (Harmondsworth: Penguin, 1985), p. 155.

78 Eric Hobsbawm, 'The Forward March of Labour Halted?', in *Politics for a Rational Left: Political Writing 1977–1988*, ed. by Eric Hobsbawm (London: Verso, 1989), pp. 9–22 (p. 21). In the 1951 General Election, Labour, led by Clement Attlee, lost to Winston Churchill's Conservative Party despite receiving a record number of votes (just under fourteen million); this surpassed the Tories by some 230,000 but gave Labour twenty-six fewer seats in the House of Commons.

79 Williams, *Towards 2000*, p. 165.

80 Hall, 'The Toad in the Garden', p. 64.

81 Hall, 'The Great Moving Right Show', p. 52.
82 Hall, 'The Toad in the Garden', p. 64.
83 Andrew Milner, *Class* (London: SAGE Publications, 1999), p. 118.
84 Mirowski, p. 89.
85 See Todd, p. 338 and p. 456 (notes).
86 Ipsos MORI, 'State of the Nation 2013 – Ipsos MORI poll for British Future', Ipsos MORI, 14 January 2013, www.ipsos-mori.com/researchpublications/ researcharchive/3111/State-of-the-Nation-2013.aspx.
87 Mike Savage and Fiona Devine, 'The Great British Class Survey – Results', *BBC*, 3 April 2013, www.bbc.co.uk/science/0/21970879.
88 Ibid.
89 Tyler, 'Classificatory Struggles', p. 503. Tyler is commenting specifically on the Economic and Social Research Council funded 'Cultural Capital and Social Exclusion' project which, as she says, 'formed the conceptual basis for the BBC's *Great British Class Survey*', p. 502.
90 Charles Umney, *Class Matters: Inequality and Exploitation in 21st Century Britain* (London: Pluto Press, 2018), p. 16.
91 Ibid., p. 21.
92 Ibid., p. 8.
93 John Harris, 'Britain is in the Midst of a Working Class Revolt', *The Guardian*, 17 June 2016, www.theguardian.com/commentisfree/2016/ jun/17/britain-working-class-revolt-eu-referendum.
94 Umney, p. 178.
95 Kirby Swales, 'Understanding the Leave Vote', *NatCen Social Research*, 7 December 2016, https://whatukthinks.org/eu/wp-content/uploads/2016/ 12/NatCen_Brexplanations-report-FINAL-WEB2.pdf.
96 Ibid. For more on the 'myth of Brexit as a working-class vote' see Lorenza Antonucci, Laszlo Horvath, and André Krouwel, 'Brexit Was Not the Voice of the Working Class nor of the Uneducated – It Was the Squeezed Middle', The London School of Economics and Political Science, 13 October 2017, http://blogs.lse.ac.uk/politicsandpolicy/ brexit-and-the-squeezed-middle/.
97 Joe Kennedy, *Authentocrats: Culture, Politics and the New Seriousness* (London: Repeater Books, 2018), p. 160.
98 Wayne adds:

> This abandonment led to the electoral decline of New Labour over time (five million votes were lost between the New Labour victory in 1997 and the General Election defeat of 2010). Centre-right Labourism tried belatedly and dismally to offer the working class cheap cultural and State solutions to material insecurity (on immigration, on national identity, on strong "law and order", etc.) in response to their weakening electoral prospects. This makes sense for the centre-right, as cultural compensation (and pumping up State coercion) is less threatening to neoliberalism and class inequalities than a real distribution of wealth. p. 180.

99 Richard Seymour, *Corbyn: The Strange Rebirth of Radical Politics*, 2nd edition (London: Verso, 2017), p. xxiv.
100 Ibid., p. 273.
101 Umney, pp. 10–11.
102 Ibid., pp. 13–14.
103 Ibid., p. 14.
104 Kennedy, pp. 78–79.
105 Ibid., p. 86.

106 *Granta 123: Best of Young British Novelists 4*, ed. by John Freeman (London: Granta Publications, Spring 2013).

107 Harvey, *A Brief History of Neoliberalism*, p. 31. In *The New Imperialism* (Oxford: Oxford University Press, 2003), Harvey notes: 'No matter how universal the process of proletarianisation, the result is not the creation of a homogeneous proletariat', p. 147.

108 Elsewhere, Jameson has described cognitive mapping as 'a code word' for class consciousness. Crucially, however, it is related to the 'need for class consciousness of a new and hitherto undreamed of kind'. See 'Marxism and Postmodernism' in *The Cultural Turn: Selected Writings on the Postmodern, 1983–1998* by Fredric Jameson (London: Verso, 1998), pp. 33–49.

109 Jameson, *Postmodernism*, p. 54.

Part 1

Mapping Deindustrialisation

1 David Peace and the Strike Novel

Conflict, History, Knowledge

The Miners' Strike of 1984/1985 remains a highly contested historical event; the doubts and suspicions which surround it have not been resolved by time. The forces which propelled the industrial dispute, what Raymond Williams described back in 1985 as 'new nomad capitalism', continue to evolve and shape in different ways the realities of twenty-first-century British life.[1] How that portentous year is understood is also unfinished. This chapter approaches GB84 as an attempt to open up the events of 1984/1985 for re-assessment and re-evaluation. Although part of Britain's wider neoliberal turn, an economic and political process which began (as discussed in the Introduction) before 1984, the strike has become crystallised in the historical imagination as the moment when the logic of Thatcherism became dominant. According to Mark Fisher, 'the fault lines of class antagonism were fully exposed' during the dispute and, as a moment which is imbued with such transformative power (socially, economically, and politically), it is 'at least as significant in its symbolic dimension as in its practical effects'.[2] So, 1984/1985 offers a site of active historical knowledge, one which is contested but one which continues to resonate as a source of understanding about both the past and the present. Katy Shaw has argued that GB84 directs 'its narratives to an end point: a marked fictionalisation of events'. She adds: 'In doing so, this counter-factual construction provides a neat closure to an inherently open-ended dispute'.[3] In contrast, however, I argue that there is no tidy resolution offered by Peace's text. Rather, it seeks to unlock the historical record in order to release the contradictory and incoherent mix of discourses present. It is a novel which Peace himself has described as devoid of 'any neat tie ups'. 'I wanted to leave the story in the mess it was in at the end of the strike', he says.[4] Using 'new' information about 1984/1985, the findings of retrospective investigations, for example, as well as revisiting overlooked narratives and neglected contemporaneous writings, the novel is an attempt to navigate within the enormity of one of the defining moments of the 1980s and demonstrate its wide personal and public reach. There are two specific reasons why there is no 'neat closure' presented by the book; these concern questions of literary form and of epistemology. The working class in the novel experience a profound and specific move away from knowing and understanding the strike as active historical actors to losing control both of its dynamics and of a collective knowledge of its increasingly convoluted developments.

So, *GB84* is an attempt to trace the political, social, and historical forces operating within and released by the strike, what are figured as manifestations of the neoliberal turn, by directly engaging with the complexity and confusion of the year-long struggle. In doing so, there arises a problem of seeing, knowing, and witnessing, which ultimately the text does not resolve. This is one way in which the novel is unfinished. The aim of presenting what Peace has called the 'whole "occult history" of the Miners' Strike' by examining the machinations and potentiality of the neoliberal state is both ambitious and necessary.[5] To describe the text's attempt to figure such forces as unresolved is not to argue that it is impossible to understand neoliberalism. Rather, the text's failure emphasises the immense task, in the Adornian sense, of 'representing' capital. Further, what *GB84* does is reveal the 'occult' nature of neoliberalism while plotting new ways in which to understand its dynamics as a project of right-wing intention. And it is with this Chapter One is primarily concerned. Therefore, it will be instructive to explore the term occult: a word frequently used by the writer himself and by seemingly every reviewer and critic of his work.

According to the *Oxford English Dictionary* (OED), the origins of the word, the use of which in English can be traced back to before the sixteenth century, are from the Latin terms 'occultāre', meaning 'to hide, conceal', and 'occultus', as in 'secret, hidden from the understanding, [...] to cover up'.[6] As a verb it implies 'to cut off from view' both 'by interposing something' and 'as part of [a] cycle of light and dark'. And while occult can also be used as a noun to connote a 'hidden or secret thing', it is as an adjective that it has been most commonly deployed. 'Not disclosed or divulged [...]; kept secret; communicated only to the initiated' is one set of meanings while another suggests something which is 'not manifest to direct observation; discoverable only by experiment; unexplained; latent'. It also carries an implication of the 'magical' or 'the supernatural' but Peace has stated that for him its value is in the signification of something which is 'hidden or occulted'.[7] As noted, it is a description which is repeatedly attached to Peace's fiction and yet the term itself has received minimal critical attention or pressure from critics.[8] Matthew Hart provides one exemplary exception. He calls *GB84* an 'occult history' of Thatcherism and argues that the occult is both a 'language' and a 'style' which works as an intensifying device in the novel.[9] It operates on two levels: uncovering the 'secret acts of violence and betrayal' carried out by the government, according to Hart, and linking these events with an 'under-mythology' or 'subterranean' history of Albion, the English Civil War, and the struggles of the labour movement; what he describes as 'a matter of bodies that will not stay buried'.[10] In my reading of *GB84*, however, a different emphasis is placed on occult in order to stress its relevance to the problem of knowing and representing capital. At one level, it aptly describes the actions of those who are aligned against the miners as well as the experiences of the National Union of Mineworkers (NUM) and its attempts to resist such forces. The intentions of the government and the state are 'not disclosed or divulged'; they are 'kept secret'. Attempts to figure out who the NUM and its working-class members are engaged in struggle with is unclear: is it the National Coal Board (NCB), the government, the intelligence services, the army, rogue individuals, a police state? Crucially, such forces remain 'mysterious' and therefore difficult to confront and overcome. However, it is what is 'not manifest to direct observation', to return to one of the *OED's* definitions, with which *GB84* is primarily concerned. Not only is it engaged in disclosing an alternative history of the strike but what the novel seeks to reveal – the forces of an emergent neoliberalism – is deliberately concealed, 'hidden from sight; [...] not exposed to view', and 'beyond ordinary understanding or knowledge'. Even though neoliberalism is now hegemonic as a mode of discourse, 'the enigma of capital', writes Harvey, is 'what political power always want to keep opaque'.[11] We are not only confronted by new 'faceless masters', as Fredric Jameson suggests,[12] but with the difficulty of placing and gaining purchase on the structures and practices of a capitalist system which has become ever more abstract and impersonal. It is this notion of the occult which informs my reading of *GB84*. Finally, it must be stressed that a conception of the term as magical or supernatural is problematic. The emphasis here is on the forces operating within the Miners' Strike as hidden and secretive, acts of concealment which are deliberate. This does not mean that they are part of the 'realm of the unknown', 'not apprehensible', and 'inexplicable', as the *OED* describes the occult. Rather, the challenge facing a contemporary British writer like David Peace is that such a profound sense of the occult is 'discoverable only by experiment'.

To encompass the political and social complexity of the year-long conflict, Peace weaves his story through six main characters, their narratives intersecting with each other elliptically. The fifty-three weeks of the strike are represented structurally by fifty-three individual chapters which form the five parts of the novel. For the purposes of this study of working-class fiction, I analyse *GB84* predominantly through the first-person accounts of Martin Daly and Peter Cox: two fictional miners on strike in the real-life village of Thurcroft in South Yorkshire. Their first-person narratives are told in two densely-packed columns on a single page at the beginning of each week: Martin during parts one, three, and five of the text, Peter in parts two and four. They are friends and work colleagues; Martin is a rank and file collier, Peter a delegate on the Thurcroft Strike Committee.[13] The miners' narratives do not provide the 'authentic' experience of the strike;[14] rather, these sections allow the text to illuminate something specific about the class experience of neoliberalism – one of disorientation, of deliberate concealment, and of problems of knowing.

While Martin and Peter represent the everyday struggle of the striking miners on the picket line, Terry Winters and Stephen Sweet are symbols of the higher-level workings of the strike. Winters is the chief executive officer of the NUM, the highest unelected position in the union. Stephen Sweet is a Hayekian businessman and flamboyant freelance journalist, the self-proclaimed 'eyes and ears' of Margaret Thatcher.[15] Sweet's role is presented through the third-person narration of Neil Fontaine. He is Sweet's driver and both himself and the third-person narrator refer to his boss as 'The Jew', suggestive of the anti-Semitism to which David Hart, Thatcher's special advisor on whom Sweet is based, was subjected.[16] However, Fontaine, a former police officer, also works as a quasi-agent for special branch and his narrative links in with that of two other central characters: David Johnson and Malcolm Morris. Like Fontaine, who is based on Hart's chauffeur Peter Devereux,[17] these two men are the secret foot-soldiers of the state. Morris is an Ulster-trained surveillance officer, covertly recording meetings and tapping phones. Johnson, referred to as the 'mechanic', is an undercover agent, acting in turn as both a strike-breaking and a striking miner, as a member of a paramilitary hit squad with extreme right-wing leanings, and as a police officer.

It is through this structural complexity that *GB84* attempts to track the forces operating within the dynamics of the strike. It is, to use Catherine Belsey's term, an 'interrogative text'. Such a text 'refuses a single point of view, however complex and comprehensive, but brings points of view into unresolved collision or contradiction'.[18] In Peace's novel, the reader is presented with six different narratives, none of which provide the definitive account. These multiple discourses, to use Patricia Waugh's formulation, 'question and relativize each other's authority'.[19] This occurs in *GB84* through the counter-play between the first-person accounts of the two miners and the third-person 'objectivity' of the main body of the novel; a collision which throws into ironic relief the dominant public narrative of the dispute. The speech Margaret Thatcher delivered to the Tory Party Conference of 1984, for example, the morning after the Irish Republican Army's (IRA) attempt on her life,[20] is relayed over three pages in the text. During this rare occasion when Thatcher is directly quoted, she denounces terrorism, the miners, and the unions, praises the actions of the working miners and the police, and proclaims that her government is fighting for democracy against 'extremists' (281). Following this verbatim report is an account of miner Martin Daly's experiences as the violence and chaos of the strike come to his own village of Thurcroft. While Thatcher talks of the police as being the 'admiration of the world' and 'British justice' as 'renowned across the world' (280–281), Martin Daly, on the page which immediately follows, is subjected to the brutality meted out by a country increasingly controlled as a police state: '[P]igs just keep on coming. Boots up your arse. Truncheon to your hands. Back of their shields into back of your neck. Truncheons to your head' (282). The miners are being beaten down, an act symbolic of the hierarchical structure which Thatcher and the New Right are seeking to uphold and restore. In her speech she talks of democratic values, of the rule of law, and of 'the best of British'; the last of these is characterised by Thatcher as those individuals who refuse to strike and who continue to work. In contrast, what Martin's narrative draws attention to are the class dynamics of the strike, highlighting the violent authoritarian tactics of the police and of the class hatred shown towards mining communities. This is class war. Peace writes:

> Tears in police eyes and all. Tears of laughter – Laugh at fucking lot of us, they do. Met. MacGregor. Thatcher. The lot of them. The whole bloody fucking lot of them – Laughing at us in our little villages with our little pits. Our little accents and our little clothes. (282)

This insight into the experiential processes of the strike destabilises the political rhetoric espoused by Thatcher; it also acts as a Brechtian rupture, questioning the consequences and effects of the manoeuvring and plotting portrayed in the main body of the text. Bertolt Brecht's notion of epic theatre is characterised, according to Walter Benjamin, by an 'interruption of happenings' which is part of the attempt to 'discover the conditions of life' through a process of alienation.[21] This focus on disturbing the narrative in order to present dissonant fragments which deny a sense of resolution and coherence is central to Peace's novel.

One focus in *GB84*, then, is on those normally marginalised by or absent from the mainstream narratives of the strike, demonstrating how they are excluded from such histories and therefore questioning the validity of any approach which is complicit with such exclusion. By '[r]epeatedly suggesting divisions', Shaw has described how 'these competing narratives unite to evidence a profound lack of communication between the public and private worlds of the strike, a mosaic of perspectives confusing and challenging our understanding of characters and the dispute itself'.[22] However, conceptualising the miners' narratives as symbolic of 'a profound lack of communication' does not go far enough, it does not place due emphasis on neoliberal agency. Here there is a link with Hart's reading of *GB84* as a novel which registers 'the violent chasm between a conception of politics as civic struggle and a commitment to politics as civil war'.[23] Hart concludes that the defeat of democracy is the price paid, inadvertently, for Thatcherism's political victory. *GB84* does depict a destruction of democracy but the novel also seeks to explore the dissonance between what rhetoric the state uses in public and the oppressive acts it initiates in private. The text works away at the myth that the Miners' Strike was a fight for democratic freedom, as espoused by Thatcher in the quote above, and it shows democracy being actively abused and destroyed, under the auspices of the New Right. Democracy's destruction is not portrayed as merely a by-product of political victory as Hart suggests, but as a necessary component of neoliberalism's success. Similarly, the lack of communication of which Shaw speaks is, importantly, a deliberate act, not an oversight or an unavoidable breakdown in correspondence between those involved in the dispute.

Crucially, it is through its working-class characters that *GB84* explores how the actions of the right-wing state are felt on a personal and private level. As noted, Peace places working-class voices, written in a distinctive South Yorkshire idiom, directly into the narrative, fashioned from the transcripts of interviews and discussions with striking miners and their families which were published in *Thurcroft: A Village and the Miners' Strike, An Oral History by the people of Thurcroft*.[24] This text, as one of Peace's primary sources, illuminates the experiential realities of the strike from a specific class perspective.[25] *GB84* can be directly cross-referenced with this oral history: first-hand accounts of police harassment, community solidarity, and individual hardship, peppered with humour and friendship, all traceable on a map published in *Thurcroft* of the mining village.[26] Rather than being reduced to anonymous parts of a homogenous mass of workers, the two miners are presented as individuals within a wider social struggle. And there is a commitment to accuracy in *GB84* which finds its greatest expression in these sections. After being attacked by riot police, Martin Daly's colleague Keith Cooper returns to the picket lines: 'Least Keith's back. Back with his new teeth—Police State took them out, he laughs. Welfare State put them back in – Fucking country, says other lad in with us' (312). Compare this with an account written by the editors of *Thurcroft* which summarises what happened after a group of miners, who remain anonymous, were beaten up by police:

> T, whose top teeth were on a palate, had them shattered into his upper gum. Because of the swelling it was three weeks before he could have any dental surgery. It took five visits after that to do the repair work. 'The police state took them out, the welfare state put them back' observed his brother.[27]

This has been condensed and pared down by Peace, giving it a greater urgency and potency which are amplified by the shift to the present tense. He also personalises the story by naming the miner who suffers the attack. Keith is a significant presence on the picket lines throughout the strike and one of the most vocal in his support for staying out. Peace's re-writing of this episode enhances the humour, which fits with Keith's personality, in order to highlight the absurdity of the treatment of the mining community. And the crucial line 'police state took them out, welfare state put them back' needs little adjustment: it is a ready-made metaphor for the growing tension between the policies of an authoritarian government and the structures of the post-war settlement or, more pointedly, between neoliberalism and welfare capitalism.

Such re-telling and re-imagining of 1984/1985 is part of *GB84*'s attempt to evoke a lived experience of the strike, calling upon the indicative tendencies of realism. The striking miners meet every morning at the welfare club and are given an envelope which includes the location of that day's picket. Their lives revolve around the club, the television, the picket lines, the motorways, and the rural lanes. It is a sense of the quotidian interrupted by the key moments of the strike itself, with an emphasis on how these moments are felt and understood by the miners. Every fatality on the picket line is documented and the demoralising practice of coal picking is faithfully recorded. This activity, which leads to the death of six young boys and men in Yorkshire, evokes a landscape synonymous with literary representations of working-class poverty and unemployment. There are similar depictions of 'scrambling for the coal' in George Orwell's *The Road to Wigan Pier* (1937),[28] a text which used the coalfields (specifically those of Wigan) as 'the characteristic landscape on which to define a particular class experience and habitus'.[29] But whereas Orwell's perspective is that of a detached outsider, the first-person narration of Martin Daly gives the scene in *GB84* an interiority which imbues it with both pathos and anger. For example, Orwell comments that the scramble for coal is 'well worth seeing'. He adds: 'Indeed I rather wonder that it has never been filmed'.[30] There is an ironic echo of such a remark in Peace's text when Martin describes the deaths of Paul and Darren Holmes, teenage brothers (aged 15 and 14, respectively) killed while picking coal in Goldthorpe, South Yorkshire in 1984.[31] 'Spoil heap fell on them', writes Peace. 'Crushed them. Buried them. Suffocated them. Killed them. There were no television cameras there to see it happen. No reporters' (330). So rather than the voyeuristic wonder expressed in Orwell's writing, Peace, by demystifying the scramble for coal, draws attention to the deliberate detachment of the mainstream press from the horrific realities of the strike for working-class communities.

Because of its commitment to the quotidian details of the strike, some critics have described *GB84* as operating within a realist register. Terry Eagleton calls it 'classical social realist', an 'abrasively realistic novel', and 'a gripping thriller, with no detriment to documentary realism'. Noting Peace's experimental approach, Eagleton concludes that the writer 'has found a form that combines the maximum flexibility with the maximum realism'.[32] Throughout this book I engage with the three dominant literary modes of realism, modernism, and postmodernism as flexible terms; I do not place them within a Jamesonian 'periodizing hypothesis' or as part of a fixed 'historical periodization', approaches which David Cunningham convincingly challenges.[33] Describing *GB84* as a 'classical social realist' novel is underplaying the dynamics of its form. Because of the 'non-action' of a strike, Joseph Brooker suggests, it is an event which 'sits ill with novelistic narrative's characteristic interest in individual development and agency'.[34] And Stephen Lacey has argued that industrial action raises specific questions about the 'political potential of realist forms'. With particular reference to film, he notes that 'a strike cast in the conventions of mimetic realism can only show the strike itself, not the underlying causes or possible solutions'.[35] Realism is 'a highly variable and inherently complex term' according to Raymond Williams who insists that an emphasis must be placed on intention as well as method in order to avoid reducing any discussion of it to a 'purely formalist analysis'.[36] It is this notion of intention, linked to the possibility of revealing underlying causes, which Dougal McNeill evokes when he suggests that in *GB84* Peace 'radicalises' the Lukácsian model of realism 'by *democratising* and collectivising its focus'.[37] Georg Lukács argued that the 'great' historical novelist (in this instance Walter Scott) 'never explains the age from the position of its great representatives'. 'For the being of the age', Lukács adds, 'can only appear as a broad and many-sided picture if the everyday life of the people, the joys and sorrows, crises and confusions of average human beings are portrayed'.[38] Lukács is concerned with locating the model for a more effective form of realism which is able to penetrate the surface of bourgeois society, unearthing prevalent social types and under-currents. McNeill makes the important observation that *GB84* strips its central historical figures (Thatcher and NUM leader Arthur Scargill) of their identifiable facets, figuring them as 'agents of a process, mere individuals in a wider social struggle' which allows the dispute's 'historical drive from below [to be] restored'.[39] However, treating the work exclusively as a historical novel in the Lukácsian sense overlooks *GB84's* manipulation of the tropes of realist fiction and does not pay due attention to its tendency to refuse and undermine notions of historical consensus or closure.

So, it does not enact a movement towards a purer form of realism, one which Jameson argued Lukács believed would allow for history to 'appear more effectively than its earlier, more specialised vehicle'.[40] It does, however, owe a debt to the modernist impulses of a historical novelist such as John Dos Passos. Peace's intersection of historical figures and the state with the lives of ordinary people shares an affinity with the latter's *U.S.A.* trilogy.[41] The juxtaposition between the quotidian and with what Donald Pizer has identified in Dos Passos as the 'superficial and clichéd expression' of the mainstream media and of political public rhetoric is a narrative device which *GB84* utilises.[42] Philip Nel has argued that the contrasting narratives and forms in *U.S.A.* create a 'jarring effect, inviting the reader to consider the connections and disjunctions between these perspectives and the different media through which these perspectives arrive'.[43] The impulse of modernism to manipulate realist forms with radical experimentation is one of the compelling features of Peace's body of work. While it finds its greatest expression in his novel *Occupied City* (2009), *GB84's* use of montage and intertextuality is extensive: interspersed within the latter text are references to first-person diaries, song lyrics, novels, the music of Dmitri Shostakovich, photographs, political speeches, scrapbooks, tape recordings, news reports, poetry, and political pamphlets. As well as sharing an obsession with quotidian detail, carrying an almost encyclopaedic ambition, *GB84* also evokes modernism's concern with documenting and manipulating time and movement, a move most apparent in the narratives of Martin and Peter.

As detailed in both *Thurcroft* and *GB84*, the strike evolves from a national over-time ban implemented during an initial dispute concerning the NCB's pit closure programme and pay rise offer of 1983. This leads the management at Manvers Main to alter break times; a situation which is quickly overtaken by the announcement on 1st March 1984 that twenty pits (including Cortonwood and Bullcliffe Wood in Yorkshire) had been selected for closure. Manton is the first pit picketed out by the Thurcroft miners, after their own colliery, and the sequence of subsequent pickets and escalating violence as documented in *Thurcroft* is mirrored by *GB84* (the most significant action taking place at Orgreave then Kiveton, Wath, and back to Thurcroft). However, the form of Martin and Peters' narratives, as streams of consciousness, pushes against the tendencies of 'documentary realism'. It gives their sections a sense of interiority and provides an opportunity for the miners to describe the strike on their own terms through their own, sometimes confusing and sporadic, thoughts and reflections. Further, not only do these internal monologues disrupt the text's realist tendencies but they are also disrupted as modernist techniques. They are punctured by fevered nightmares and daydreams, importantly ones which are part of a wider collective memory: submerged visions of Albion, the English Civil War and the War of the Roses, lines of poetry, song lyrics, the use of Old English, and memories of haunting defeats suffered by the working class. All these culminate in a dystopian vision of Great Britain 'swollen with black corpses and vengeful carrion' (462). When Martin Daly reflects on the progress of the strike, and its physical and emotional effects, his thoughts are interrupted by dreams interspersed with Anglo Saxon language:

It's been three months. Three fucking months – Lifted. Threatened. Beaten. Hospitalized. Broke in every fucking sense – I lie here and I listen to rain on our windows. To her tears – I turn over. I look at her – Her hopes. Her fears – All our hopes. All our fears – I close my eyes. Tight – *Under the ground, we brood. We hwisprian. We onscillan.*

> *Under the ground, we scream* – I open my eyes. Wide – She's not
> finished with us. Not finished with any of us. (110)

Martin is attempting to grasp what is happening to his marriage (his
wife Cath eventually leaves him and Thurcroft) and to his community.
There is a telling shift in perspective from the personal to the collective,
from 'I' (Martin) and 'her' (Cath) to 'our' (the miners) and 'we' (the
working class). The last movement is made by a use of Old English:
'hwisprian' as in to whisper or murmur and 'onscillan' as in to echo or
resound.[44] And this final definition of the word 'onscillan' is significant
because of the way in which the miners' narratives link to, or offer a
resonance with, a longer history of oppression, violence, and struggle.
GB84 is offering an alternative account of a country in which the myth,
according to the film director Ken Loach, 'has always been [of] a peace-
ful and stable society where violence is a teenage aberration'. Rather,
Britain is a nation, in Peace's text, 'founded on a violent past which
involves the forceful suppression of dissent'.[45] Hence the extract's final
move back to the personal pronoun deployed by Martin and out towards
the contemporary reality: 'she's not finished with us'. This relates to a recurring theme expressed in the clipped and terse interior monologues of
the two miners: an obsession with seeing, reading, watching, listening,
and understanding. 'I open my eyes. Wide.' says Martin, as if straining
the visual element of his senses to comprehend the gravity and profundity of the strike's dynamics.

When the brutality of the picket lines comes to Thurcroft, Martin
Daly insists:

> Folk can see them for what they are now. Folk can see through me-
> dia lies. [...] Now they've seen what police and government are like
> with their own eyes. Now it's in front of their faces. Here on their
> own bloody doorstep (290).[46]

On one level, it is possible to understand the 'truth' of the strike through
'direct observation'. And it is this sense of direct access to the strike –
'their own eyes' and 'in front of their faces' – on which the miners'
narratives are predicated. Their sections are presented as two narrow,
densely-packed columns of text, suggestive of the traditional design and
layout of a newspaper.[47] Martin and Peter are given the opportunity to
describe their own strike within a format normally reserved for what is
taken as the objective truth or what Peter's wife Mary prefers to describe
as 'Tory bloody lies' (350). And by stylistically parodying the traditional
print media, the narratives of these working-class men are ironically
referring to, in order to undermine, the subjective construction of news
by the mainstream press.

This is not a stable working-class record of the strike, however. It becomes increasingly difficult, as the dispute develops, for many of the individuals involved to grasp what is happening through direct observation; this is one reason why there is a shared obsession with the keeping of a personal historical record. The most prominent of these is constructed by Mary Cox whose three-volume *'True History of Great Strike for Jobs'* contains newspaper clippings each accompanied by her hand-written version of events which, by contradicting the 'official' record, tell the 'truth of matter' (350). Crucially, however, it is not just the working class who compile such histories. Theresa Winters keeps cuttings taken 'from the papers, [...] videos [...] made from the news'. Her husband Terry crafts his own story by cutting up classic spy novels while Malcolm Morris gathers, edits, and regularly listens to intelligence tapes intended for his secret service colleagues. Even David Johnson, responsible for several assaults, murders, and armed robberies as an undercover agent, collects 'every different paper [...]. He cuts out the stories. Sticks them in a scrapbook'.[48] All of these acts are attempts by those involved to archive their own history of 1984/1985. What they draw attention to are the ways in which, in a metafictional sense, different narratives of the strike are framed using contrasting methods and approaches. This is central to the idea of analysing history as a construct: what is included in and excluded from historical narratives, how events are portrayed and arguments structured, these are decisions which are fundamentally ideological. Therefore, what is presented is always a mediated form of information and knowledge.

Such attempts to construct the 'reality' of the strike are further complicated by the unreliability of information and the pervasive presence of the mainstream media. 'Everyone with a different fucking story' complains Martin Daly when conflicting reports from the picket lines flood into the miners' welfare club (10). The sense of confusion is compounded by the reliance, from rank and file colliers up to leading union officials, on the television, radio, Teletext, and national print media for news about the dispute. The *'Nine o'Clock News, News at Ten, Newsnight'* are followed avidly by all (6). Even Ian McGregor, the NCB chairman, is lambasted by Stephen Sweet for acting upon information gleaned from what Sweet sees as the unreliability of television news.[49] The dependence on such outlets for information is indicative of the daily routine of mining communities like Thurcroft. The men and women of the village are living through and with the strike and yet they increasingly come to rely on the often contorted representations of it in the mass media. 'There was this portable television we had in Welfare', says Peter Cox at the start of 1985. 'Folk would just sit there all bloody day and watch it. Just waiting for some news' (392). Importantly, this is how Peter discovers that the strike is over: from a television news bulletin interrupting the BBC's regular schedule of programmes. Again, here is another incident taken directly from *Thurcroft*: 'We were watching telly, it was Dads' Army, Sunday, when it came on "Newsflash. Miners' Strike is over". I was surprised, well, it made me feel sick in a way'.[50] Compare this with Peter's experience in *GB84*: 'Bloody miserable day – I was sat there. Cup of tea with no milk again – Middle of *Dad's Army*. Newsflash – *Miners' Strike is over* – That was it. Just like that – I thought I was going to pass out' (442). Peace has re-written this extract to give it an enhanced lugubrious tone: it is a 'miserable day' and there is 'no milk again'. But a central metaphor, once again, comes ready-made and needs little alteration: Peter as passive viewer. He is no longer playing a determining part in the strike; he is a spectator and the mundane way in which he hears such important news, sat at home watching repeats of a 1970s sitcom on the TV, is indicative of the disorientation felt by both himself and his working-class community.

So, there is a profound move away from knowing the strike to losing control of it. While acts of narrative construction such as Mary Cox's scrapbook contest the media's depiction of the coal dispute, it is a challenge which is ultimately insurmountable. Following violent clashes at Orgreave, Peace writes:

> The nation was outraged – Not by the assault on the miner. Not by the assault on the President. No – The TV had lied again. They had cut the film. They had stitched it back together – Stitched up the Union with it – Miners threw stones. Miners hurt horses. Miners rioted – '– *the worst industrial violence since the war –*'. (138)

The national news performs a similar action to Mary, Theresa and Terry Winters, Malcolm Morris, and David Johnson: selecting, editing, and re-formulating a narrative of the strike. In doing so, it is in deliberate and direct contradiction of the experiences of the miners on the picket lines; it is a tampering with the construction of historical knowledge, making it look like the miners started a riot, for example, rather than their actions being a response to police brutality. Further, attempts by the NUM and the mining communities to relay information about the strike to fellow workers, through the traditional methods of picketing and discussion, are routinely suppressed. The novel's characters give voice to the frustrations surrounding these issues of communication, suppression, and the manipulation of truth. However, they are increasingly powerless against the economic forces sweeping Britain and the profound political shifts taking place. While these developments remain hidden or abstract to the individual characters of the novel, *GB84* is an attempt to depict and place them in a wider context: the novel documents the mobilisation of the state's forces (the police, the judiciary, and the intelligence services) against the miners.

David Harvey has described this as the neoliberal state apparatus using 'its powers of persuasion, co-optation, bribery, and threat to maintain the climate of consent necessary to perpetuate its power'.[51] There is a danger that all such state-sanctioned action is explained as being driven exclusively by neoliberal doctrine, however. And there is another, contrasting danger here, one skilfully elucidated by Christopher Vardy. 'In *GB84*, the neoliberal transition in Britain is historicised within a thousand-year *longue durée*',[52] notes Vardy, who traces the history of violence and oppression figured by the text as being part of a longer class struggle stretching back as far as the eleventh-century Norman Conquest. This risks presenting neoliberalism, according to Vardy, as the inevitable or natural outcome of a much longer period of history, a figuration which does not offer a significant critique or understanding of the neoliberal transition as a specific moment in late-twentieth-century British history. Vardy adds: '[I]ts historicisation of neoliberalism within the *longue durée* of history as a continuum of conflict is paradoxically transhistorical, a depoliticised historicisation that risks naturalizing the very object of its critique: the ongoing legacies of the End of History'.[53] So, there are two potential simplifications here enacted by the novel: (1) all action is understood as being 'neoliberal'; or (2) all action is part of a more general, non-specific history, of which neoliberalism is the 'natural' end. These contrasting ways of reading *GB84* help to illuminate a sense of the novel as unfinished, as unable (in different ways) to place due critical pressure on the dynamics of neoliberalism. But my reading, one which foregrounds working-class experience, alleviates some of these tensions. The oppression and violence faced by Martin and Peter is placed in a wider historical context of working-class struggle: the General Strike of 1926 and the coal strikes of 1972 and 1974.[54] And the motivations behind the determination to defeat what Stephen Sweet labels the 'Red Guard' and 'The Shock Troops of Socialism' is infused with overtly Cold War rhetoric (56).[55] Equally, something specific happens to the working class in the novel; the class experience is not transhistorical, it is shaped by the dynamics of Thatcherism and, more broadly, neoliberalism. Seumas Milne's *The Enemy Within: The Secret War Against the Miners* reveals how the 'Tory government and its footsoldiers used any and every means to break the miners' union'.[56] Milne writes of the 'use of informers, infiltrators and *provocateurs*; pre-meditated police violence; attempted frame-ups; bugging and surveillance on a heroic scale; the spending of billions of pounds on facing down the strike and then on forcing through large-scale pit closures'.[57] These forces orchestrated against the working class and woven into *GB84* carry an explicitly contemporary aspect. Malcolm Morris works with increasingly sophisticated surveillance techniques, for example, utilising the latest technological advances.[58] These are not simply transhistorical practices but, rather, they reveal how the state acts on behalf of neoliberalism; here are the 'repressive interventions by the state' as described by Imogen Tyler.[59] '[P]ermanent vigilance, activity, and intervention', Foucault argues, are central facets of neoliberalism and, although they do also have a longer history, they take a specific, accelerated form in *GB84*, as experienced by the novel's working class.[60] Further, such 'repressive interventions' are part of Thatcherism's authoritarian populism, something which the Miners' Strike starkly reveals.

The miners are one of several targets of a campaign (which revolves around surveillance, violence, and media manipulation) against alleged subversives. And the mobilisation of forces against this section of the working class as a constructed 'other' is part of a wider movement against those groups labelled Britain's enemies within. These include members of the Socialist Workers' Party, the National Front, the IRA, and the Campaign for Nuclear Disarmament. Such groups, working for very different aims, are lumped together as equivalents. This aligns the miners with what the Government labels as terrorist organisations; conflating the IRA and the NUM as 'extremists', for example (281). Therefore, individuals like Martin and Peter are depicted as outside the imagined community of Britain, a move which facilitates a situation in which their individual and collective rights can be repeatedly denied. Benedict Anderson defines a nation as 'an imagined political community [...] imagined as both inherently limited and sovereign'.[61] The striking miners are drawn as outside the 'limited' boundaries of the British nation, they do not represent the 'best of British' according to Thatcher (280). Out of this process, however, comes the potential for inclusive forms of working-class solidarity which, crucially, connect a range of intersectional sites of struggle. Satnam Virdee argues that the authoritarian populist agenda of Thatcherism relied on the construction of the 'enemy within' which was 'made up variously of racialized minorities, trade unions, socialists, feminists and other alleged "social deviants"'.[62] As Ron Ramdin notes in *The Making of the Black Working Class in Britain*, 'there were approximately 3,000 black members in the National Union of Mineworkers' at the time of the strike.[63] Support from the black community comes as a surprise to Peter, however, when he is in London collecting money for the relief fund. Using language indicative of the types of division upon which the racialising nationalism of Thatcherism worked, Peter Cox describes how a 'coloured lad' donates a week's wages, minus two pounds, to the collection. 'It made me think, that did', reflects Peter.

> There were no coloured people in Thurcroft and there were them that were right glad about that. I wished they'd been here to see that – But I was same; grew up thinking that blacks had a chip on their shoulder and that Irish were all bloody nutters. I didn't think that now (182).[64]

So, *GB84* attempts to unpick the lie of British patriotism, of working-class racism, and the labelling of alleged subversive tendencies. It is a process described by Martin Daly, noted above, as 'folk' seeing through the 'lies' of the media, police, and government.[65] Crucially, the infamous 'enemy within' label is part of a process of naming and defining that intersects with class. It is a form of inscription, what Beverley Skeggs describes as the symbolic attachment of 'negative value', which the narratives of Martin and Peter seek to contest.[66]

The naming and 'othering' of these working-class men links in with the sense of disorientation both Martin Daly and Peter Cox experience. In another incident taken from *Thurcroft*, a group of colliers, including Martin, are attacked by police in their own village and thrown into a riot van. This is inspired by a page-length testimony of a miner in *Thurcroft*; it is worth quoting an extract of his experiences at length:

> Then they started taking us down the road towards Dinnington. Half of them were saying 'We're going to do you, you scummy bastards, rioting, breaking windows in a police van' [...]. Half a mile out of the village we turned off and went down a lane. Halfway down it they stopped the van and dragged us out again. One of them stuck me up against a post, [...] then turned me round and shoved me down the banking. He said 'Come on the Queen's Highway again this morning and you're arrested'. I was coming round then. ___ was more or less out. They did the same with him, but he landed on a barbed wire fence at the bottom.[67]

In *GB84*, Peace substantially re-writes this extract:

> You're fucked, you three, they tell us. Having you for riot [...]. Think maybe they're taking us to Dinnington. But then van turns off. Down a lane onto Common – Fucking hell, I think. No police stations down here. No fucking hospitals, either – Nothing. No one – Begin to think this is it. End of the road. Van stops. Doors open – They say, Get out, you fucking scum. [...] It's like fucking Nicaragua, this. They'll rape us and shoot us and stick us in this fucking ditch [...]. Fucking bastards kick us down banking into ditch [...] I lie there in that ditch and I want to scream at sky, I do – Fuck me. I wish them dead. I wish her dead. Her and every fucking cunt that ever voted for her – I get up off ground. I look round – Keith face down in ditch. Chris caught on some barbed wire. (264)

There is a literal experience of feeling disorientated, emanating from an uncertainty around where they are being taken and what is going to happen to them. And the reference to the 'Queen's Highway' accentuates the sense of the men being excluded from the imagined community of Britain: this road does not belong to them. Tellingly, the first deviation from *Thurcroft* which Peace makes is in the reference to the location at which the police van stops: Common.[68] It is an ironic destination; the land is not a place to share, it is no longer a common or commons in the collective sense of the word. And *GB84* intensifies the scene by exaggerating the fear felt by Martin: a fear of rape and death.[69] This exaggeration does risk undermining the quotidian reality of the miners' experiences. However, it also speaks of the text's attempt to place some of the forces operating against them: namely Thatcher and the police state. And it enhances the sense of bewilderment they feel about what is happening.

Peace's novel both maps an increasing sense of disorientation as well as tracking the socio-historical forces which were operating within and through the dispute itself. The strike was an attempt to disrupt, challenge, and change the course of socio-political history; and while there is a distinctive right-wing agency in operation, the miners were also fighting for a distinct purpose. Peace uses the flexibility of the novel form in an attempt to comprehend, represent, and illuminate this particularly confusing and contested moment. In this regard, it plots new and as yet, to return to a word Peace used himself to refer to the text,[70] 'unfinished' ways of reading an emerging, nomadic form of capitalism through its class dynamics. As a strike novel, *GB84* deploys a certain degree of coherence and resolution. The narrative of the dispute in Peace's text is re-created, at one level, along historically accurate lines: its use of dates, identifiable locations, and key historical figures. It seemingly offers a sense of finality because the strike ends: one side wins and the other loses. What *GB84* does, however, is probe the inconsistencies and contradictions within that rigid timeframe. It presents multiple discourses which overlap and intersect, exploring the hidden relations, consequences, and struggles at play within the strike. What remains 'occult' is how the alliance of forces, orchestrated by and around a distinctly neoliberal government, operate within the wider range of global capitalism. The novel is foregrounding the specific manifestations of the neoliberal project but a comprehensive and knowable overview of such a project remains out of its reach; *GB84*, rather, explores the processes and in doing so opens up a whole range of disparate and yet illuminating discourses. That it cannot assimilate all of these into a coherent whole is partly the reason why the novel disintegrates into the brutality and confusion of a traditional crime thriller: David Johnson's violent killing spree and Neil Fontaine's gruesome suicide, for example.[71] This irresolution can also be explained by Vardy's argument about the novel's depoliticisation of history as discussed above. But what it does draw attention to are the acts of concealment, the deliberate attempts to dislodge and obfuscate both working-class subjectivity and knowledge about the strike and its processes; further, it places due emphasis on the presence of right-wing agency and intention as a central and defining component of the neoliberal turn and in doing so, it foregrounds the dynamics and specifics of class as a way of reading and understanding the dynamics and specifics of historical change.

Such processes, of concealment and obfuscation, will now be theorised in a different context as I turn to a novel by a writer who was a friend of Peace's and one which also seeks to critique the ways in which historical memory and change are understood by what becomes the deindustrialised working class; whereas Peace's *GB84* raises questions about working-class subjectivity and direct knowledge of the dynamics of 'nomad capitalism' and an emergent neoliberalism, Gordon Burn's *The North of England Home Service* raises important questions about what happens to working-class memory when it is commodified and appropriated by consumer capitalism.

Notes

1 Raymond Williams, 'Mining the Meaning: Key Words in the Miners' Strike', in *Resources of Hope: Culture, Democracy, Socialism*, by Raymond Williams (London: Verso, 1989), pp. 120–127 (p. 124).

2 Mark Fisher, *Capitalist Realism: Is There No Alternative?* (Winchester: Zero Books, 2009), p. 7.

3 Katy Shaw, *David Peace: Texts & Contexts* (Brighton: Sussex Academic Press, 2011), p. 88.

4 Mike Marqusee, 'No Redemption', *Red Pepper*, March 2009, www.red pepper.org.uk/No-redemption/.

5 Matthew Hart, 'An Interview with David Peace', *Contemporary Literature*, vol. 47, no. 4, Winter 2006, pp. 547–569 (p. 566).

6 See 'occult, v.', *OED Online*, Oxford University Press, www.oed.com/view/Entry/130167; 'occult, adj. and n.', *OED Online*, www.oed.com/view/Entry/130166.

7 Matthew Hart, 'The Third English Civil War: David Peace's "Occult History" of Thatcherism', *Contemporary Literature*, vol. 49, no.4, Winter 2008, pp. 573–596 (p. 577).

8 A Faber press release described *GB84* as an 'occult history' according to Andy Beckett who questioned if such an account can be effectively definitive and realistic; Joseph Brooker notes how real-life characters are 'occulted' with fictional names in *GB84*; and Katy Shaw argues Peace's novels 'offer "occult" accounts of twentieth-century history'. See Andy Beckett, 'Political Gothic', *London Review of Books*, 23 September 2004, www.lrb.co.uk/v26/n18/andy-beckett/political-gothic; Joseph Brooker, 'Orgreave Revisited: David Peace's *GB84* and the Return to the 1980s', *Radical Philosophy*, vol. 133, September/October 2005, pp. 39–51 (p. 42); Shaw, *David Peace*, p. 1.

9 Hart, 'The Third English Civil War', p. 587.

10 Ibid., pp. 577–578 (p. 582).

11 Harvey, *The Enigma of Capital*, p. 241.

12 Jameson, *Postmodernism*, p. 17.

13 While both men are actively engaged in the strike, taking part in the activities which emerge out of the miners' welfare club, one narrative which is missing from such local action is that of the women of the village. Although the wives and daughters of the miners make appearances in *GB84*, such an omission of an important narrative from 1984/1985 is disappointing in a novel which otherwise demonstrates a commitment to depict the immense size of the dispute in terms of its social and political scale. For accounts of the role played by Women Against Pit Closures see 'Women's support group at Maerdy' by Barbara Bloomfield in *The Enemy Within: Pit Villages and*

the Miners' Strike of 1984–5, ed. by Raphael Samuel, Barbara Bloomfield, and Guy Boanas (London: Routledge & Kegan Paul, 1986), pp. 154–165; Loretta Loach, 'We'll Be Here Right to the End... And After: Women in the Miners' Strike', in *Digging Deeper: Issues in the Miners' Strike*, ed. by Huw Beynon (London: Verso, 1985), pp. 169–179.

14 This contrasts with Brooker who argues that 'the documentary realism of [the miners'] voices generally signals an authenticity, an ontological priority over the rest of the book'. However, Brooker, in an otherwise persuasive account of *GB84*, makes the important observation that '"the reality of the strike" is also that of Sweet and Fontaine'. See Brooker, p. 47.

15 David Peace, *GB84* (London: Faber and Faber, 2010), p. 11 Where appropriate, references for quotations taken from *GB84* will be provided in parentheses.

16 Seumas Milne, *The Enemy Within: The Secret War Against the Miners* (London: Verso, 2004), p. 323.

17 Devereux is discussed in Milne, *The Enemy Within*, p. 324.

18 Catherine Belsey, *Critical Practice* (London: Routledge, 1991), p. 92.

19 Patricia Waugh, *Metafiction: The Theory and Practice of Self-Conscious Writing* (London: Routledge, 2001), p. 6.

20 The Provisional IRA planted a bomb in Brighton's Grand Hotel in an attempt to murder Thatcher. The Prime Minister was there for the annual Conservative Party conference. She escaped injury but five people (including Tory MP Anthony Berry) were killed and thirty-four injured.

21 Walter Benjamin, 'What Is Epic Theater?', in *Illuminations: Essays and Reflections* by Walter Benjamin (New York, NY: Schocken Books, 2007), pp. 147–154 (p. 150).

22 Shaw, p. 81.

23 Hart, 'The Third English Civil War', p. 593.

24 Although attributed to 'the people of Thurcroft', this book, published a year after the end of the strike, was edited by Peter Gibbon and David Steyne from Sheffield City Polytechnic (now Sheffield Hallam University). See *Thurcroft: A Village and the Miners' Strike, An Oral History by the People of Thurcroft*, ed. by Peter Gibbon and David Steyne (Nottingham: Spokesman, 1986).

25 Including *Thurcroft*, Peace lists thirty-two sources at the end of *GB84*. He also interviewed four people involved with the strike, as well as consulting newspaper cuttings and calling upon his own personal memories of 1984 as a seventeen-year-old in his hometown of Ossett, West Yorkshire. See Hart, 'An Interview with David Peace', p. 555; and see Peace, *GB84*, pp. 464–465.

26 See map of Thurcroft village in *Thurcroft*, p. 12.

27 *Thurcroft*, p. 116. Although some central figures in the village are identified, many of the people interviewed for the book are not named. 'T' is described thus: 'Male. Age: about 30. Married (to W). Native and resident of Thurcroft area. Mining family background (Brother of U). Faceworker, 15 years in coal. Regular picket'. See *Thurcroft*, p. 273.

28 George Orwell, *The Road to Wigan Pier* (London: Penguin, 2001), pp. 94–95.

29 Kirk, p. 52.

30 Orwell, p. 94.

31 Richard Benson, *The Valley: A Hundred Years in the Life of a Family* (London: Bloomsbury, 2014), p. 420.

32 Terry Eagleton, 'At the Coal Face', *The Guardian*, 6 March 2004, www. theguardian.com/books/2004/mar/06/featuresreviews.guardianreview20.

33 David Cunningham, 'The Contingency of Cheese: On Fredric Jameson's *The Antinomies of Realism*', *Radical Philosophy*, vol. 187, September/October 2014, pp. 25–35, (pp. 31, 29).

34 Brooker, p. 41.

35 Stephen Lacey, *Tony Garnett* (Manchester: Manchester University Press, 2007), p. 65, p. 66.

36 Raymond Williams, 'A Lecture on Realism', *Screen*, vol. 18, no. 1, Spring 1977, pp. 61–74 (p. 61, p. 73).

37 Dougal McNeill, *Forecasts of the Past: Globalisation, History, Realism, Utopia* (Oxford: Peter Lang, 2012), p. 68. Original emphasis. McNeill's wider arguments about realism are extremely useful and persuasive. He suggests that, far from being exhausted, realism can offer a radical approach, often along class lines, which challenges social reality and mainstream ideology. See McNeill, p. xiii.

38 Georg Lukács, *The Historical Novel* (Harmondsworth: Penguin, 1969), p. 40.

39 McNeill, p. 77, p. 69.

40 Fredric Jameson, *The Antinomies of Realism* (London: Verso, 2013), p. 264.

41 *The 42nd Parallel* (1930), *1919* (1932), and *The Big Money* (1936).

42 Donald Pizer, 'John Dos Passos in the 1920s: The Development of a Modernist Style', *Mosaic*, vol. 45, no. 4, December 2012, pp. 51–67 (p. 61).

43 Philip Nel, 'DeLillo and Modernism', in *The Cambridge Companion to Don DeLillo*, ed. by John N. Duvall (Cambridge: Cambridge University Press, 2008), pp. 13–26 (p. 16).

44 See 'whisper, v.', *OED Online*, Oxford University Press, www.oed.com/view/Entry/228529; Lynne Grundy, Christian Kay, and Jane Roberts, *A Thesaurus of Old English* (Glasgow: University of Glasgow, 2015) http://oldenglishthesaurus.arts.gla.ac.uk/.

45 Ken Loach quoted in Anthony Hayward, *Which Side Are You On? Ken Loach and His Films* (London: Bloomsbury, 2004), p. 133.

46 Such shifts in opinion are described by a miner in *Thurcroft*: 'People who'd said we ought to have been back at work started to see how the police acted. It did us a favour'. See *Thurcroft*, p. 122.

47 Christopher Vardy has noted how the columns are 'poised somewhere between a journalistic account and a biblical testament'. Christopher Vardy, 'Historicising Neoliberal Freedom: *GB84* and the Politics of Historical Fiction', *Open Library of Humanities*, vol. 4, no. 2, 24 October 2018, pp. 1–32 (p. 4).

48 See Peace, *GB84*, p. 159, p. 284, p. 220, and p. 35.

49 See Peace, *GB84*, p. 12.

50 *Thurcroft*, p. 152. This quote is attributed to 'N' who is described as 'Male. Age: early 20s. Native and resident of Thurcroft area. Mining family background. Haulage worker, 7 years in coal. Sacked during strike. Regular picket'. See *Thurcroft*, p. 272.

51 Harvey, *A Brief History of Neoliberalism*, p. 40.

52 Vardy, p. 24.

53 Ibid., p. 26.

54 See Peace, *GB84*, p. 392 and p. 56.

55 The title of Peace's novel also evokes this history: it was most probably inspired by GB75, according to Eoin McNamee. This was a private army created by SAS founder David Sterling to fight the 'red menace'. In *Smear!: Wilson and the Secret State* (another of Peace's listed sources for *GB84*), GB75 is described as 'part of a grandiose project whose aim was to regenerate

British democracy, defeat the forces of the totalitarian left within and with-out the Parliamentary Labour Party and reverse Britain's economic decline'. See Eoin McNamee, 'Hand-Held Narrative', *The Guardian*, 30 April 2004, www.theguardian.com/books/2004/apr/30/news.comment; Stephen Dorril and Robin Ramsay, *Smear! Wilson and the Secret State* (London: Grafton, 1992), p. 265.

56 Milne, *The Enemy Within*, p. 36.

57 Ibid., pp. 35–36. Original emphasis.

58 See Peace, *GB84*, p. 127.

59 Tyler, *Revolting Subjects*, p. 6.

60 Foucault, *The Birth of Biopolitics*, p. 132.

61 Benedict Anderson, *Imagined Communities* (London: Verso, 2006), p. 6.

62 Satnam Virdee, *Racism, Class and The Racialized Outsider* (London: Palgrave, 2014), p. 148.

63 Ron Ramdin, *The Making of the Black Working Class in Britain* (London: Verso, 2017), p. 474.

64 Again, this is taken directly from the *Thurcroft* book, see p. 177.

65 See Peace, *GB84*, p. 290.

66 Skeggs, *Class, Self, Culture*, p. 96. See Chapter Five for more on Skeggs and class inscription.

67 *Thurcroft*, p. 115. The underscore symbol refers to an unnamed miner.

68 Laughton Common, to give it its full name, is a small village between Thurcroft and Dinnington.

69 By mentioning Nicaragua, the text is also making an oblique reference to the CIA-backed counter-revolution against the socialist government of the Sandinista National Liberation Front (FSLN). The socialists had toppled the dictatorship of Tachito Somoza in 1979, leading the United States to orchestrate an offensive against the FSLN by financing a rebel army (the Contras).

70 See Dan Davies, 'David Peace: In The Light', *Esquire*, 30 August 2013, www.esquire.co.uk/culture/article/4717/in-the-light-by-david-peace/.

71 See Peace, *GB84*, pp. 458–461.

2 Gordon Burn and Working-Class Nostalgia
Region, Form, Commodification

Gordon Burn was born in Gallowgate, 'a close neighbourhood in the poor but respectable, rough-and-ready, raggy-arsed west end of Newcastle'.[1] Leaving his home city at the age of eighteen, he forged a career as a freelance journalist, feature writer, art critic, and author. Although the working-class north of his birth is a recurrent theme and location in his work, *The North of England Home Service* is his only novel set predominantly in the North East. It is through a return to the concerns of regional British realism, coupled by an engagement with the postmodern formations of late-twentieth-century North American fiction, that *The North of England Home Service* is able to engage with and critique conceptions of working-class history in the twenty-first century. In this chapter, comparisons are drawn to the obsessions and narrative techniques of those writers who have sought to figure postmodernism as a historical and cultural turn, alongside presenting an analysis of how Burn's text engages with the tropes of North East working-class fiction and the region's cultural traditions. In what way the novel echoes and, in turn, works through the poetics of contrasting literary forms in attempting to map the experiences of a distinctly (de)industrial working-class community is a primary concern. Further, how Burn utilises, adapts, and resists a singular identification with either of these modes in order to articulate a sense of the neoliberal present will be a central consideration.

Like many of the novel's characters, comedian and former television personality Ray Cruddas has lost his sense of identity and belonging. He is compelled to return to the North East not only due to a faltering career in variety entertainment but also because of a lack of faith in himself and the contemporary moment. It is through Cruddas and his friend and personal assistant Jackie Mabe that the novel offers a meditation on the vast social and economic changes brought upon the landscape and the people of the industrial north by the dynamics of neoliberalism and deindustrialisation.[2] By offering very different evocations of two distinct periods in British history (the 1950s and the early-twenty-first century), the text examines the shifting trends within working-class culture and how, when both the present and future appear uncertain, there is an urge to return to the old symbols of apparent stability and assurance. 'It is no surprise', argues historian Bill Lancaster in an essay on Newcastle, 'that [the] disintegration of the old landscape and of the economic and social order which it supported is accompanied by social trauma'.[3] A return to the past is one manifestation of such trauma. And Burn's novel figures historical memory as a way in which Ray Cruddas's old working-class community could, possibly, understand the present and seek to respond to it, creating if not a better future then a way of coping with it. The novel's working-class characters are seeking 'to be reminded', writes Burn:

> when the circumstances of their lives sometimes seemed to be conspiring to make them forget it – the ninety-five channels, the call-waiting, the multi-tasking, the compound interest accruing on the credit-card bill – that they came from a specific place with a long history and a unique identity and were not in fact unrooted particulate individuals free-floating in infinite space.[4]

Here is an exploration of how the disruptions and dislocations of neoliberalism, understood as a speeding up and collapsing of temporality, have been experienced by a deindustrial community. In the novel, such an experience manifests itself through an obsession with, and nostalgia for, a heavily romanticised past which, in turn, raises important questions about working-class identity and agency. Mark Fisher has asked: 'Could it be that neoliberal capitalism's destruction of solidarity and security brought about a compensatory hungering for the well-established and the familiar?'[5] This is the experience of the characters in Burn's novel and the notion of rootedness is addressed below. What is portrayed in the text is a profound dislocation, as an effect of contemporary capitalism, from both a class and a place. Further, the specific nostalgic obsessions with a working-class past as articulated in *The North of England Home Service* are symptomatic of a crisis in belonging and self. The past, its presence felt as a spectral form, is a way of trying to deal with or seek solace from the contemporary moment. However, this compulsion to repeat banal and inauthentic modes of historical experience creates a cultural impasse, a form of hyperreality which blocks any access to a positive subjectivity. Thus, history is understood through, what Guy Debord described as, the spectacle, transforming images of the past into a commodity and breeding a false consciousness of time and culture.[6] Through its humour and a detailed evocation of the worlds of light entertainment and popular culture, the novel figures such an impasse as an 'experience of a time that is out of joint';[7] it suggests a type of working-class historical memory formed out of the vulgar caricatures of the past. It is a novel which, with the present dominated by capital and drained of meaning and representation, imagines a contemporary culture unable to provide a progressive or enabling future.

Burn has Ray Cruddas manage Bobby's, a new type of social club which is named after the famous (real-life) local comedian Bobby Thompson.[8] Described as a nostalgia enterprise, the venue is located in Elswick, an old industrial area on the banks of the River Tyne, and is the kind of place 'that takes you back even if you were never there originally' (29). This distinctly postmodern promise offers the club's patrons the chance to experience a night out dressed as miners and Jarrow marchers in flat caps and workmen's scarves, or as mill girls and maids in heavy woollen shawls and white cotton pinafores. There are outside toilets at Bobby's rather than modern indoor conveniences, proletarian theme nights (Monday night is washday), and passionate renditions of old industrial folk songs fuelled by strong bitter. Each evening Ray Cruddas becomes Bobby Thompson, wearing his old stage garb (more flat caps and woodbines) to deliver the late comedian's routine with its geographically-specific jokes and anecdotes. Partly funded by local businessman Ronnie Cornish, the club is Cruddas's vision, evoking a timeless yet indistinct early-twentieth century, of a working-class city he left in the mid-1950s; it is a construction which denies the reality of the North East in 2001, the year of the novel's setting, and the traumatic horror of the foot-and-mouth crisis which provides a disturbing backdrop to the text.

Ray Cruddas's embracing of a working-class milieu he once dismissed, originally forging a way up and out of his class to become a successful light entertainment star, is matched to some extent by Burn's own return to the texts of regional realism.[9] The writer has spoken of how, as a reader, he revisited the forms and nuances of British social realism after a thirty-year absence, shortly before the publication of *The North of England Home Service*.[10] Tellingly, it is a form he once shunned. Burn describes seeing Sid Chaplin in Newcastle Central Library in the sixties and greeting him 'with a superior adolescent sneer'. He adds:

> I suppose [...] what I had against poor Sid Chaplin, a Coal Board officer as well as writer [...] [was] that he was too rooted; he had stayed put long enough to have certainties and he was seen as a "spokesman".[11]

Chaplin was a collier from the County Durham coalfield, a 'trade union secretary [who] worked with miners committed to political activism and self-improvement'.[12] His work is characterised by a fascination with social change and it carries a persistent 'exploration of the impact on working-class communities of the post-war settlement'.[13] Chaplin's *The Day of the Sardine* (1961) and his second Newcastle novel *The Watchers and the Watched* (published in 1962 and set in Elswick like Burn's text) both depict inner-city communities experiencing profound geographical and social fragmentation. The first book, for example, documents Arthur Haggerston's exploits as a teenager in mid-1950s Newcastle. He leaves school with few prospects and finds little satisfaction in the numerous unskilled, manual jobs in which he is briefly employed. Arthur seeks new forms of entertainment and self-expression through imported American youth culture: 'pictures twice a week, rolling round the milk bar [...] Saturday nights we'd go to some hop or other [...] We made a pretty dicey showing in our Saturday uniform – twills, platform shoes, wind-cheater and thin red tie'.[14] Such processes, the moment when industrial working-class cultural traditions rubbed up against an emerging youth culture, find expression in Burn's novel during the telling of Ray Cruddas's experience of this same period. In the mid-fifties, for example, Cruddas is told by the actress Diana Dors that he looks like someone who has 'come to read the meter' but by the end of the decade he has been swept along by the rhetoric of Harold Macmillan's infamous 'never had it so good' speech (153–154). Further, he has 'comprehensively Italian-Americanized his appearance and deregionalized his accent and become personable, prosperous, ochre-faced, slick' (112–113).

Along with the post-war realism of Chaplin, Burn's novel also evokes the North Eastern cultural representations of an earlier writer, Jack Common. Unlike Chaplin, however, Common left Newcastle for London at the age of twenty-five and worked on John Middleton Murry's literary journal, *The Adelphi*.[15] Despite a reputation, enhanced by his friendship with George Orwell, as the 'authentic' voice of the working class, it was not until 1951 that Common wrote his first novel, *Kiddar's Luck*. For this largely autobiographical work, he returned to the certitude of his birthplace and the scattered memories of his Edwardian youth. A significant thread can be drawn between Bobby Thompson's stage routine, which Cruddas now copies, and *Kiddar's Luck*. Through the process of autobiographical retrospection, Common merges traditional literary technique with 'qualities and features of popular oral cultural expression, ranging from the [...] traditions of repartee and kidding, through the idiomatic narratives of the raconteur and folk-tale teller, to [...] monologue recitation and stand-up comic turns'. What emerges, facilitated by the ironic and self-reflexive localised humour of Common, is a form of 'self protection and resistance [...] with a sense of mutual encouragement, solidarity and community'.[16] This is the same effect of Thompson's comedy and the appeal of Ray Cruddas's social club: humour acting as a form of protection against hardship and uncertainty, felt and shared collectively.

Chaplin and Common both spoke to a version of the North East often understood and represented through images of masculinity and industrial labour. 'Since the 1930s', writes historian Robert Colls, 'the dominant way of representing North-East birth and death has hung on the heroic image of the male worker in or out of a job'.[17] As I discuss in the next chapter on Anthony Cartwright, the figure of the industrial worker has played an influential role in the national imagination, often as a powerful social and political metaphor connected to nationhood and democracy; it is one which has been disproportionate to the numbers of actual industrial workers when compared to other forms of working-class work. When embarking on his writing career, Burn rejected such literary and cultural tropes often mobilised in figurations of the North-East working class and turned instead to the postmodern poetics of New Journalism, following a North American movement which included Norman Mailer, Tom Wolfe, and Truman Capote amongst its central protagonists. Emerging in the 1960s, this hybrid form combined 'fictional techniques with the detailed observation of journalism',[18] unsettling the conventions of both realist fiction and objective reportage. Its approach heavily influenced Burn's non-fictional works of true crime: his first book *Somebody's Husband, Somebody's Son: The Story of Peter Sutcliffe* (1984) and, later, *Happy Like Murderers: The Story of Fred and Rosemary West* (1998). While *The North of England Home Service* can be seen as a symbolic return to the concerns of social realism, namely socio-economic and cultural change as experienced by the working class, its style and form also speak partially to both the impulses of New Journalism and, more specifically, American postmodern fiction. Two references in the novel, for example, connect it intertextually to the latter and to the work of E.L. Doctorow and Don DeLillo, respectively.

The poverty balls held by members of Chicago and New York's high society at the start of the twentieth century, and described by Doctorow in *Ragtime* (1974), are Burn's direct inspiration for Cruddas's new business venture. Burn quotes almost verbatim from, but without reference to, a twelve-line passage found in *Ragtime*: 'Guests came dressed in rags and ate from tin plates and drank from chipped mugs. Ballrooms were decorated to look like mines with beams, iron tracks and miners' lamps' (68). Only the line 'according to accounts written at the time' vaguely refers to the source being *Ragtime* (published, as noted, in 1974).[19] It is this tampering with historiography and the play on what constitutes an objective historical source which marks out the postmodern tendencies in Burn's writing. Fredric Jameson has written of how Doctorow's 'narratives do not represent our historical past so much as they represent our ideas or cultural stereotypes about that past'.[20] *Ragtime*, on one level, uses the 'stockyard ball' phenomenon to emphasise the vast inequalities that were present in turn-of-the-century North America and to expose the absurdity and triviality of wealthy society's distasteful response to poverty. It also evokes a tradition popular amongst the middle- and upper-classes of dressing up as their servants,[21] and the balls are a disdainful pastiche of the horror and poverty suffered by the working class in Chicago's stockyards as depicted in Upton Sinclair's novel *The Jungle* (1906). It is one of the many snippets of American history which are reconfigured by Doctorow to craft what Jameson describes as 'the most peculiar and stunning monument to the aesthetic situation engendered by the disappearance of the historical referent'.[22] This is how we now understand history, therefore Doctorow presents it as such. Linda Hutcheon argues that, in *Ragtime*, it is nostalgia 'always ironically turned against itself – and us'.[23] In *The North of England Home Service*, the irony lies in the appropriation of cultural stereotypes by the very people whose history is being stereotyped. Again, there is a tradition being evoked here, one of dressing up or of working-class 'drag'. Rhian E. Jones has written of a cultural shift, tied in with neoliberalism's 'elision' and 'erasure' of class, from 'the nuanced and pluralistic articulation of identities to their appearance in a simulated or appropriated form, as stereotypes'. And she identifies a particular consequence of such a shift, one which expands on what I argued in the Introduction: that class has been declared dead under neoliberalism at the same time that it has been mobilised to justify inequality and to generate consent. Rhian E. Jones adds:

> Class, in particular, was reconfigured from an inherently political identity to one which could be temporarily occupied, communicated through signifiers which were increasingly abstracted, simplified, and stripped of meaning. Meanwhile, those who happened to be born with the same signifiers involuntarily bolted on were vanishing from public view, their place on the political and cultural stage taken by ersatz, commodified versions of themselves, in a process so seamless as to be sinister.[24]

So, there is an adoption of working-class stereotypes and caricatures at the same time as there is an increasing lack of representations of the working class in popular and political culture. Jones argues: 'This attempt to render the actual working class politically invisible, while their cultural artefacts were ironically adopted, sat uncomfortably with the lived experience of much of the country'.[25] And there is a link here with the notion of the 'chav' and 'chav-hate'; Owen Jones has noted how mocking the working class in the twenty-first century has 'become a fad among privileged youth'. 'At universities like Oxford', he writes, 'middle-class students hold "chav bops" where they dress up as this working-class caricature'.[26] While there is an element of this portrayed in Burn's novel (rich footballers and businessmen visiting Bobby's, for example), it is those who have close connections to the working-class community who are reduced to copying those representations which are part of the spectacular contemplation of capitalist society, what Debord describes as the 'externality of the spectacle', which appears not as the authentic gestures of lived experience but as the gestures which belong to 'another who represents them back' to the individual subject.[27]

An attempt to pursue history and identity through objects and images has also been the preoccupation of several characters in the novels of Don DeLillo. In *Underworld* (1997), the baseball hit to win the

National League pennant for the New York Giants against the Brooklyn Dodgers in 1951 becomes a fetishised piece of memorabilia; it transcends simple sporting significance to transform into 'a powerful symbol of the lost innocence of a pre-nuclear, pre-digitized world', according to Burn.[28] Importantly, this winning home-run ball was struck by Bobby Thomson, the namesake of the legendary Geordie comedian who, as explained, gives his forename to Cruddas's club. Both Bobbies represent what is perceived as a simple, more coherent past, a way of reclaiming something from within the shallow, incomplete subjectivity of the contemporary moment by re-engaging with the apparent certainty of a rooted, knowable, and stable history. In this way, they invoke a certain type of nostalgic mode which can be read in several contrasting ways. Nostalgia is often thought of as a way of dealing with and adjusting to social change, loss, insecurity, uncertainty, and doubt. It is provoked by a sense of longing but can also be read as a response to the contemporary, felt acutely at times of discontent, anxiety, and disappointment. Burn offers his own theory: 'Nostalgia, or homesickness, is no longer (perhaps never was) about the past but about felt absences or "lack" in the present'.[29] In *The North of England Home Service*, there is a personal search for a working-class identity which has become detached from the socio-historical conditions which formed it. Robert Hewison has drawn attention to the irony that, in a time of considerable deindustrialisation, there has been a strong 'nostalgia [...] for the industrial past'.[30] According to Colls: '[I]n the early 1980s, the North East died again, this time on a scale of manufacturing decline commensurate with, or even worse than, the 1930s'. He adds: '[S]o many people and places *used to be* that the region is hardly discussed without reference to what went before'.[31] In invoking the industrial past, one so formative to the regional identity of the working-class North East, 'the nostalgia subject may be involved in escaping or evading, in critiquing, or in mobilizing to overcome the present experience of loss of identity, lack of agency, or absence of community', argues Stuart Tannock.[32] For John Kirk, this links in with collective and individual memory. '[T]he political importance of class memory', he stresses, 'particularly in times of rapid change, cannot be underestimated'.[33] Importantly, nostalgia is predominantly associated with conservative, traditional, and regressive values but, as David James notes, there are 'multivalent manifestations' of what is a complex cultural condition often used as a novelistic trope.[34] Nostalgia can be a progressive structure of feeling, says Tannock, one which provides 'a valid way of constructing and approaching the past' by offering radical alternatives through an invocation of historical moments which, in turn, enables change amid the discontinuity of the present.[35] It can reveal the 'unrealized possibilities, unpredictable turns, and crossroads' embedded within modern history, Svetlana Boym has suggested.[36] Nostalgia is historically contingent, Boym argues; it is both released by and a reaction to changing conceptions and new understandings of space and time. Importantly, she identifies two tendencies within nostalgia: restorative and reflective. While the former 'attempts a transhistorical reconstruction of the lost home', the latter works at the contradictions and ambivalences located within the passage of time and allows for a more flexible, challenging comprehension of the historical past, often deferring or resisting a return home.[37]

In Burn's novel, the potential of nostalgia or the ability of the nostalgic subject to challenge and confront the dominant socio-economic formation is prevented by the way in which history is produced and consumed. Burn imagines a community which seeks a sense of continuity with its industrial, working-class roots in order to respond to the alienation of the contemporary moment. However, access to such a past is blocked by capitalism's re-packaging and re-ordering of history as a disabling accumulation of historical images. The nostalgic mode, as a form of political agency, has been appropriated and invested in by the market ethics of the very form of political economy from which the nostalgic subject has become alienated. Nostalgia, in this instance and when aligned with Boym's notion of its 'restorative' form, acts as a kind of failed utopia, reconfiguring a society which is no longer possible, a retreat and relief from 'the sources of anxieties, fears, and frustrations to which nostalgia is a response'.[38]

This process is exemplified by the ghostly presence of the aforementioned Bobby Thompson and the deeply nostalgic feelings his name evokes. He is a product of the interwar working-class culture famously described by Richard Hoggart as part of a tradition of 'cock-eyed fun',[39] one which finds humour in hardship, appreciates those who are 'rough diamonds but hearts of gold' and values 'not being stuck-up or a getter-on'.[40] According to Burn, the real-life Thompson had a 'style of comedy that was rooted in his own hard upbringing during the twenties and thirties' and he 'stayed the way he was, preserved in amber' (81, 83). This meant he was eventually left behind by the new age of commercial television in the mid-to-late 1950s and the increasingly powerful influence of American popular culture. In contrast, the socially mobile Ray Cruddas, writes Burn, 'looked up to date and in tune with the new feeling of youthful modernity and adventure that was supposedly about to sweep the country and had found its emblem in [...] Tommy Steele' (158). The alleged banality and shallow populism of this new pop culture, epitomised by 1950s teen idols such as Steele who looked to and imitated American musical styles, are what gave rise to Hoggart's cultural reservations. And the transition in popularity from the comedy of Thompson to that of Cruddas is the moment which Hoggart describes as the 'old forms of class culture' disintegrating, substituted 'by a poorer kind of classless culture'; Hoggart writes:

> At present the older, the more narrow but also more genuine class
> culture is being eroded in favour of the mass opinion, the mass

recreational product, and the generalized emotional response. The world of club-singing is being gradually replaced by that of typical radio dance-music and crooning, television cabaret and commercial-radio variety.[41]

It is this world of mass, light entertainment, of cabaret and variety, which Cruddas originally embraced in a London where social class apparently did not matter and when the 'commercial vernacular of consumer culture' was being deployed by those around him (160). Here we find one of many echoes of Colin MacInnes's novel of late-1950s London: *Absolute Beginners* (1959). Ray's girlfriend Pauline Reeves, a Soho showgirl and art student, is reminiscent of MacInnes's Suze – the ex-girlfriend of the text's unnamed teenage narrator. Pauline insists that the spirit of the time is best understood through the pop images of consumerism. 'What's needed', she tells Ray, 'is an approach which doesn't depend for its existence on the exclusion of the symbols most people live by' (160–161). Hoggart's dissection of what he memorably called the 'shiny barbarism' of the new mass arts, and the adverse effects on what he outlines as a resilient working-class culture, has been well-rehearsed as a critical argument.[42] What is significant in *The North of England Home Service* is Ray Cruddas's attempts, in the twenty-first century, at a return to a culture which fifty years earlier he had rejected. Even Hoggart noted that these 'old-fashioned' cultural values were 'increasingly coming to appear stuffy and probably laughable' in the 1950s.[43] 'How much of a decent local, personal, and communal way of life remains?', Hoggart asked. In the late fifties, he was adamant it could still be found in the speech, attitudes, and cultural forms of the working class: 'Working-Men's Clubs, the styles of singing, the brass bands, the older types of magazines, the close group-games like darts and dominoes'.[44] In the twenty-first century, Burn's novel finds an imitation of this personal and communal working-class life expressed through pastiche. And crucially, the young Ray Cruddas was historically representative of the emerging mass culture as explored in Part Two of Hoggart's book and yet, in the contemporary moment and as an older man, he is seeking a return to the 'stable' working-class culture as detailed in Part One. However, what both Bobby Thompson and the childhood memories (from the 1920s and 1930s) of Hoggart refer to is a working-class structure of feeling formed back in the interwar years: a time of significant political and social anxiety rather than the stable and safe past sought by the patrons of Bobby's and its adventures in restorative nostalgia.

As sociologist Bill Williamson has described, memories are a 'benchmark against which to measure the present and a powerful bond among those who share them'.[45] But historical memory is contestable and varied even though people often share a common history. Memory alters with social change; it creates different meanings and is used in a variety of ways in any given historical setting. The problem, in the nostalgic structure, is that the past can be used to legitimize all that went before. Or, on the contrary, it is used to mark the progress made by society, predominantly by those forces which are led by a distinct political logic. So what happens when collective memory becomes part of consumer society? Particularly if, as Boym suggests, such memory is one of the 'common landmarks of everyday life' which constitutes 'shared social frameworks of individual recollections'.[46] The simulation of an imagined working-class culture and communal history, as explored by Burn, can result in a fetishisation of the past and an aestheticization of place: two impulses which result in the pastiche of both cultural and historical forms and the draining of meaning. In the neoliberal present as imagined in *The North of England Home Service* there is no 'linear unfolding' or 'possible dialectic of history', as Jean Baudrillard has described the contemporary experience of a history on repeat.[47] The novel knowingly resists the construction of an unfolding present-day plot, a structure of progression and resolution, while refusing to sustain a contemporary focus; for example, the narrative regularly and abruptly switches back to the 1950s and the milieu of post-war London. Burn presents these distinct historical periods as two very different experiences of time and space, symbolic of the way in which the novel critiques how history and social change are understood and represented. Whereas the contemporary moment fails to generate new modes of authentic experience or knowledge, due to the commodification of history and nostalgia, Burn explores the dynamism and complexity of a new popular culture in post-war Britain, one in which the forces of an accelerated consumer society and the mass arts are beginning to emerge. According to Selina Todd, for the working class the 1950s was a 'paradoxical decade'. While many young people felt in a better position than their parents had been before the war, 'they weren't as well off as the advertisements and government rhetoric seemed to suggest – and they weren't sure that the gains they had made were here to stay', adds Todd. She suggests that Macmillan's 'never had it so good speech' fuelled concerns about insecurity and raised questions about what kind of society was being created. Macmillan 'called for a debate about whether full employment and a welfare state were really sustainable', says Todd. The message was that a free market economy could deliver more prosperity. 'It was an alluring message', she concludes, 'but one that condemned a very large number of people to a lifestyle maintained only through credit, uncertainty and fear'.[48]

For his first novel, Burn re-imagined the life of 1950s singing star Alma Cogan. The real-life Cogan was one of the most successful recording artists of the decade. She died in 1966 at the age of thirty-four. The Cogan of Burn's text, who acts as the first-person narrator, does not die but lives on into the late-1980s (the decade of the novel's setting), gently fading from the music charts and the gossip pages of the popular press until she is all but forgotten. Burn explores the undocumented world of a post-celebrity and the strange non-deaths of those figures who are immortalised by the memorabilia collectors and transformed by the ever-increasing power of technology. 'It seems that as long as you're in print or on film or a name on a buff envelope in an archive somewhere', writes Burn in *Alma Cogan* (1991), 'you're never truly dead now. You can be electronically colourised, emulsified, embellished, enhanced, coaxed towards some state of virtual reality'.[49] Cogan goes in search of herself through the detritus of her former life: stage dresses, publicity shots, rare demo tapes, for example. This leads her to the obsessive Francis McLaren whose prize possession is a recording of Myra Hindley and Ian Brady, the Moors Murderers, torturing one of their five child victims, Lesley Ann Downey. Playing in the background on the tape is Alma Cogan's cover version of 'The Little Drummer Boy'. Again, Burn is documenting what has also been a preoccupation of DeLillo's: how, in a 'thoroughly postmodern, dehistoricized' world, mass murderers and pop stars 'become nearly interchangeable figures in a culture of celebrity'.[50] Daniel Lea has noted how, in *Alma Cogan*, '[t]here is a direct correspondence between the actions of entertainers and murderers [...]: both achieve a kind of celebrity; both suppress their own personalities beneath a performative mask and both are owned by the public in a disempowering way'.[51]

In many ways, *Alma Cogan* is a companion piece to *The North of England Home Service* and Ray Cruddas is a male counterpart to Cogan. Both of these fading stars of light entertainment lose control over their own identity; their personalities have been created by the 'culture of celebrity' and have become a thoroughly public, media-owned artifice. Like Arthur Machin in David Storey's *This Sporting Life* (1960), who rebels against his casting as a celebrity ape, Cruddas is frustrated by being constantly viewed and judged by his fame, always on hand to perform and entertain. This even applies to how his mother perceives him: '*It's not me she's seeing* [...]', writes Burn, '*She's seeing the other Ray. The one off the telly. The one with his face in the papers. Well, maybe not in the papers so much any more*' (180).[52] As well as providing an example of the novel's humour (here employed through pathos and self-deprecation), this extract also reveals that there is a disconnection between how Cruddas views himself and how he is seen by others. His is an empty personality, any uniqueness or texture smoothed out by the banality of show business and a constant readiness to adapt or change in exchange for popularity. Debord has described the celebrity as 'the spectacular representation of a living human being', the 'opposite of the individual', someone 'well known for not being what they are'.[53] Both Cogan and Cruddas symbolise that first embracing of American pop culture in the post-war years, as well as providing a rare link with a disappearing working-class music hall tradition. And, in *The North of*

England Home Service, Burn describes, evoking Chaplin's figuration of such social and cultural change, the penetration of a brash and dynamic new way of living into fifties Britain: 'hamburger bars [...] starting to spring up all over; the visual crash and commotion, the roar and racket non-stop from neon-rise to neon-set' (149). London, and the late-night bars and cabaret clubs of Soho in particular, provides 'a rich density of living' and the city is described in vivid, compelling detail (149). It is such passages which suggest the text's social realist tendencies, in that they are interested in representing a changing social world amidst the emergence of new popular and cultural forms.

However, in these sequences, Burn employs the same indirect referencing as mentioned earlier in regard to Doctorow's *Ragtime*; he quotes, again not quite verbatim and without acknowledgement (although it is placed in quotation marks and Ray is described as having 'heard' this description), from MacInnes's *Absolute Beginners* to describe a Soho club in the late-1950s. As noted, this novel is a significant shadow text to *The North of England Home Service*. The following description of the real-life Mazurka or 'Ginnie's', as this small drinking club on Denman Street was known, is Burn's:

> The great thing about here is that no one, not a soul, cares what your class is, or what your income, or whether you're nobody or famous, or a boy or a girl, or bent, or versatile, or what you are so long as you can hold a drink and behave yourself and have left all that crap behind you when you come in the door. (151)

Compare this with a passage in *Absolute Beginners*:

> But the great thing about the jazz world, and all the kids that enter into it, is that no one, not a soul, cares what your class is, or what your race is, or what your income, or if you're boy, or girl, or bent, or versatile, or what you are – so long as you dig the scene and can behave yourself, and have left all that crap behind you, too, when you come in the jazz club door.[54]

Apart from altering the generic 'jazz world' setting to a drinking club, the only other noticeable change Burn makes is in the omission of 'race'. This is the first indication that the world he is describing is not quite the utopia of equality and freedom which is posited by the narrator of the earlier text he draws directly from. According to Nick Bentley, in his novel MacInnes 'projects a radical construction of community that incorporates differences in class, "race", gender and sexual orientations, and offers an alternative form of "community" to Raymond Williams's model'.[55] *Absolute Beginners* figures everyone on the Soho jazz scene as being 'on absolutely equal terms', as MacInnes's narrator has it.[56] The 1950s milieu described by Burn, however, turns out to be far less inclusive, as revealed by the qualification in the passage which follows his description of Ginnie's: 'In practice, of course, it actually wasn't the kind of place you could just walk into off the street unless you were with somebody who was already known there or you came with an introduction from a member' (151). One form of exclusion is explored by Burn through the introduction of James (or Jimmy) Li, a Guyanese champion boxer recently arrived in Britain from Jamaica on the Empire Windrush. Seeking to take advantage of what is described as 'a different kind of racial tension brewing' to that of the fascism of the 'Mosleyite thirties' (132), social unrest which culminates in the 1958 Notting Hill riots featured in *Absolute Beginners*, boxing promoter Jack Solomons hires Jimmy Li to fight a white boxer for a 'Black vs. White' promotion (132). This is at a time, writes Burn, when 'No dogs, no Irish, no Coloureds' was an 'easy punchline' for comedians across London (132). What Burn's text does, therefore, is trouble what Ian Haywood has described as the 'mythic' vision of post-war London in *Absolute Beginners*.[57] Alan Sinfield argues that *Absolute Beginners* suppresses the reality that 'the experiences of the boy were open to only the tiniest minority of young people'.[58] The 'boy' is the unnamed narrator who describes the jazz world, an emerging subculture, as being able to 'cut you free from other allegiances'. 'But subculture', Sinfield adds, 'is a response to class, gender and racial pressures, not an alternative to them'.[59] Crucially, MacInnes anticipated not only 'the fallacy of the classlessness of youth' but also 'the new journalism of the 1960s – fast-moving, welcoming the new, launching into superficially unpromising topics', as Sinfield has noted.[60] And his episodic formal style, paragraph-length sentences and quick movements in and through different narrative sites, is one which Burn shares.

The North of England Home Service depicts experiences which relate to a distinct historical place and time then, carrying both a geographical and temporal specificity to which the novel is drawn back. And it is this compulsion to deal with historical forces of change that also marks out the forms of realism which emerge in Burn's writing. Realism is not simply a matter of formal technique or content but a historical mode concerned with social and historical conditions. And as Brecht asserts, 'discovering the causal complexes of society' and 'emphasizing the element of development' are two key facets of the realist form.[61] Burn's novel is interested in the experience of, as noted, 'unrooted particulate individuals' as well as the processes which have precipitated what is figured as a distinct contemporary cultural condition. While 1950s London is seemingly vibrant, enabling, and alive with possibility, the text's obsession with it suggests, however, that the problems explored in the contemporary moment, the experience of being unrooted, can be traced back to this earlier period of social change and its emerging myths of equality and classlessness.

The text's continual cutting in and out of narrative episodes, much like the medium of radio which is the inspiration for the novel's title,[62] points to the way in which popular culture cuts back, forth, and across history. Burn is particularly interested in the submerged histories of post-war Britain, exploring what lies beneath the pop-nostalgia images of the period. Again, Jimmy Li is instructive here. Described as 'half West Indian and half Chinese' (128), he emigrates from the Caribbean onboard the Windrush looking, in part, to further his boxing career. The colour bar, which banned black boxers from fighting competitively and contesting British titles, ended the month the Windrush first docked, although Burn incorrectly states that it is still in place on Li's arrival (132). He originally lives in an underground Clapham air-raid shelter where he and his fellow Caribbean migrants are held, or rather hidden, after their arrival at Tilbury. What the colour bar and the treatment of these West Indian men and women represent are far from an equal, open Britain; it is one in which the processes of racialisation work to exclude, deny, and, literally in the case of the Clapham shelter, submerge those marked as outside of the nation state. *The North of England Home Service* subsequently charts Jimmy Li's journey into the streets of London's West End, onto boxing bills around the capital, to a fight with Welshman Boyo Morgan in which he suffers a life-threatening injury, and finally to a high-rise council flat in Birmingham. Compellingly, the plot of Li's life is one mirrored, although it takes different forms in each, by many of the characters in Burn's novel; first comes the move away from home and the severing of roots, then the embracing of a new culture and a new way of life, followed by a trauma or a period of uncertainty which results in the desire to return to a previous time of continuity and rootedness. Here is offered an alternative mode of engaging with history, in contrast to the way it is understood through the pastiche and hyperreality of heritage culture. The text provides an opportunity to connect what appear to be individual responses and disconnected experiences to connecting factors within British history: capital, empire, race, and class.

Both the natural and built environments also provide, in *The North of England Home Service*, tangible evidence of historical, political, and social change. 'The interpenetratedness of the life that had been lived underground for generations', writes Burn, 'and the modern lives currently being lived above ground was something that was constantly making itself felt' (46–47). Homes across the North East are evacuated due to gas leaks from the dormant collieries below and the local landscape is prone to collapse and subsidence due to centuries of mining. The historical legacy of industry acts as an everyday reminder of what this community has lost; deindustrialisation is here being experienced as an ongoing process, it is the insidious presence of a way of life that is now absent. In Burn's novel, the physical places in which the deindustrial present intersects with historical memory produce what Fisher has described as a key feature of contemporary culture: an excessive nostalgia, 'given over to retrospection, incapable of generating any authentic novelty'.[63] For example, Rusty Lane, the former mining village where Jackie Mabe lives, contains rows of old miners' cottages which have been joined by a modern development which features '"traditionalizing" elements' such as 'cast-iron foot scrapes, decorative cobbles, "Victorian" street lamps incorporating a make-believe flicker' (40). It is the kind of architecture, often allied with the gentrification of once industrial areas, which David Harvey describes as producing 'exactly the same serial monotony as the modernism [...] [it was] supposed to replace'.[64] It has no direct relationship to its functionality or historical moment. Neither do industrial relics (old railway sleepers and lumps of cheap coal) which are used to fuel the pyres of burning cattle during the mass culls of the foot-and-mouth crisis. These industrial-sized fires bring back strong memories for the local community:

> To them it was like a glimpse at the past – a welcome whiff of old industrial times and a last gasp of disappearing worlds. From the country the pyres sent a ghost smell of factory chimneys and booming heavy industries, smarting the eyes and furring the nostrils, like a million kettles left on to burn. (172)

There is a failure to engage with the present and the accompanying horrors of the crisis engulfing the agricultural landscape. And, crucially, we see an articulation of everyday trauma and suffering. The burning pyres do not represent the reality of the contemporary moment but rather evoke the insidious presence of loss, 'a ghost smell' of a seemingly once reliable industrial society with a distinctive physical character. They momentarily produce what Boym has described as '[c]ollective frameworks of memory [which] are rediscovered in mourning'.[65] And her notion of reflective nostalgia is instructive here. Both individual and cultural memories are being awakened, evoking a wistful response which 'cherishes shattered fragments of memory and temporalizes space'.[66] Importantly, this form of reflective nostalgia is troubled by Burn. The experience of remembering is not sketched as a positive or enabling reaction; the smoke from the fires smarts the eyes and furs the nostrils, literally blocking the senses and therefore preventing an understanding of what this cultural and collective memory represents, both in terms of the past and the present.

The North of England Home Service is an attempt to record and reflect upon social change, deindustrialisation, memory, and nostalgia while exploring the causes and consequences of such processes in relation to place, space, and class. In doing so, and as I have described, it shares some characteristics with the work of, amongst others, DeLillo. Burn interviewed the writer in his home city of New York in 1991. He wrote that DeLillo deserved the reputation as 'one of the most inventive, knowing voices in America' but described his prose as one which 'occasionally over-cooks'.[67] A decade later, and relayed in an article on US fiction written for *The Guardian*, Burn would complain of the 'incessant, pumped-up media yakkety-yak' of contemporary culture and the once definitive but now 'pale [...] stale and grating' American voice of contemporary US literature.[68] This experience is what triggered his symbolic return to the texts and language of David Storey, Alan Sillitoe, Sid Chaplin, and the British working-class literary traditions of post-war social realism. *The North of England Home Service* can be seen as a way of trying to reconceptualise both of these forms, not rejecting them outright but extending and manipulating tendencies in both. It is a methodology which demonstrates Burn's response to the challenge of trying to find critical distance from the cultural dominants of late capitalism while resisting the potential of being 'disarmed and reabsorbed'.[69]

As a novelist, critic, and writer, Burn resists easy categorisation, so it proves even more difficult to place his work within a literary history that often involves, as Dominic Head warns, 'drawing chronological lines in the sand'.[70] Such a historical mapping of the novel's progression suggests neat categories which not only give a false impression of singular development but also fail to account for the complex continuities in literary modes. Burn, rather, formulates what Andrzej Gąsiorek, in identifying a key feature of post-war British fiction, has described as: 'cross-breed narrative modes, taking what suits [...] from a variety of genres, and creating new forms that cannot easily be classified'.[71] In doing so, *The North of England Home Service* is able to present itself as a warning of the dangers of a commodified nostalgia, knowingly reproducing its failures, both formally and thematically, and providing a social critique of the fatal repetitions and historical forces which block the path to an authentic, progressive future. What is significant here is Burn's obsession with rootedness and 'free-floating individuals', especially when thinking back to his dismissal of Sid Chaplin as being 'too rooted' and 'a spokesman'. The experience of returning is a central and recurring theme throughout the text, particularly when this involves going back to a place that appears to offer familiarity and stability but which is, despite its apparent authenticity, something new and unfamiliar. Towards the end of the novel, Jackie Mabe watches as a procession of ducks land on the illuminated, translucent roof of a warehouse after mistaking it for a large expanse of water. He begins to notice, writes Burn, that the birds,

> far from being disconcerted by this new experience, were circling round and trying it a second, third, even a fourth time, until the entire flock, or so it seemed to Jackie, was joining in the game of dive-bombing the warehouse roof. (221)

Such a return, described in the novel as yet another type of Disneyfication, may initially be bewildering but those performing it begin to enjoy the novelty, much like the patrons at Ray Cruddas's social club. It shares much in common with a central feature of restorative nostalgia, as described by Boym: 'Never mind if it's not your home; by the time you reach it, you will have already forgotten the difference'.[72] In contrast, what Burn's own symbolic return to the once-familiar and seemingly-grounded realism of working-class regionalism reveals is not such a hedonistic embrace; rather, it signifies a process of working through form via and beyond the postmodern poetics of later American fiction in order to craft a new way of critiquing and understanding the neoliberal present with a rooted hybrid literary mode. This sense of returning to the primal scene of contemporary political realities is something explored further in the next chapter, in the work of Anthony Cartwright, a writer who shares Burn's obsession with working-class memory and with deindustrialisation as a historical condition fundamental to class experience.

Notes

1 This is Burn's own description; see Gordon Burn, 'Living Memories', *The Guardian*, 11 June 2005, www.theguardian.com/books/2005/jun/11/featuresreviews.guardianreview33. Burn's father worked as a paint-sprayer in Newcastle while his mother had a job in a department store in the city. They lived in a west end tenement and then a nearby council flat before Burn left for university. Bill Lancaster wrote in 2009, following Burn's death at the age of sixty-one, that the North East had been 'robbed [...] of its finest writer'. This was despite Burn residing in Chelsea, London for many years. See Bill Lancaster, 'Gordon Burn, 1948–2009', *North East Labour History Journal*, April 2010, pp. 172–177 (p. 172).

2 Ray Cruddas's surname comes from George Cruddas, a director at the former Armstrong's works in Elswick, whose name was also used for the Cruddas Park flats (again in Elswick) which were part of T. Dan Smith's modernist-inspired rebuilding of the city in the sixties. Therefore, the Cruddas name is evocative of the rapid political, social, and geographical changes experienced by Newcastle. It should be noted that the city is never actually named by Burn in his text but all geographical and historical indicators point to Elswick as the setting for the novel.

3 Bill Lancaster, 'Newcastle – Capital of What?', in *Geordies: Roots of Regionalism*, ed. by Robert Colls and Bill Lancaster (Edinburgh: Edinburgh University Press, 1992), pp. 53–70 (p. 63). Burn has described such processes, more recently part of a 'Blair and Camelot culture', as 'just another erasure in an area [the North East] whose history was full of erasures, wipings-out, disappearances'. See Gordon Burn, *Born Yesterday: The News as a Novel* (London: Faber and Faber, 2008), p. 143.

4 Gordon Burn, *The North of England Home Service* (London: Faber and Faber, 2004), pp. 69–70. References for further quotations taken from *The North of England Home Service* will be provided in parentheses.

5 Mark Fisher, *Ghosts of My Life* (Winchester: Zero Books, 2013), p. 14.

6 See Guy Debord, *Society of the Spectacle* (Detroit, MI: Black & Red, 1970).

7 Fisher, *Capitalist Realism*, p. 20.

8 During the 1940s and 1950s, Thompson was revered as the spokesman of the North East's working class. Known as the 'Little Waster', he would regale 'audiences with tales of wife trouble, debt and the dole' and became a popular figure on BBC northern radio transmissions such as *Wot Cheor, Geordie!* See Natasha Vall, *Cultural Region: North east England, 1945–2000* (Manchester: Manchester University Press, 2011), p. 32.

9 The inference is not that the character of Cruddas is anyway autobiographical. Rather, that Cruddas and his return to the North East are symbolic of the pull the region has on those born there. Burn has spoken of a 'North East state of mind' which is rooted in 'background, affinity – emotional belonging – and subject matter'. Burn quoted in Richard T. Kelly, 'North East State of Mind', *New Writing North Review*, November 2009, pp. 24–31 (p. 27). Kelly also notes how the ill-health and death of both of Burn's parents led him to spend more time in Newcastle, around the time of *The North of England Home Service's* publication.

10 See Gordon Burn, 'After the Flood', *The Guardian*, 15 November 2003, www. theguardian.com/books/2003/nov/15/featuresreviews.guardianreview10.

11 Burn, 'Living Memories'.

12 Christopher Hilliard, *To Exercise Our Talents: The Democratization of Writing in Britain* (Cambridge, MA: Harvard University Press, 2006), p. 116.

13 Ian Haywood, *Working-Class Fiction from Chartism to Trainspotting* (Plymouth: Northcote, 1997), p. 118.

14 Sid Chaplin, *The Day of the Sardine* (Leeds: The Amethyst Press, 1983), p. 120.

15 Common's editorial position during the 1930s at *Adelphi* allowed him to act as a patron to other working-class writers, building up networks between worker-writers in Newcastle, the literary classes, and the intellectual left in London. See Hilliard, p. 112, p. 131.

16 See Michael Pickering and Kevin Robins, 'A Revolutionary Materialist with a Leg Free', in *The British Working-Class Novel in the Twentieth Century*, ed. by Jeremy Hawthorn (London: Edward Arnold, 1984), pp. 77–92 (p. 79).

17 Robert Colls, 'Born-Again Geordies', in *Geordies*, ed. by Colls and Lancaster, pp. 1–34 (p. 19).

18 John Hollowell, *Fact & Fiction: The New Journalism and the Nonfiction Novel* (Chapel Hill: The University of North Carolina Press, 1977), p. 10.

19 The original passage:

> At palaces in New York and Chicago people gave poverty balls. Guests came dressed in rags and ate from tin plates and drank from chipped mugs. Ballrooms were decorated to look like mines with beams, iron tracks and miners' lamps [...]. (see E.L Doctorow, *Ragtime*, (London: Penguin, 2006), pp. 34–35)

20 Fredric Jameson, *The Cultural Turn: Selected Writings on the Postmodern, 1983–1998* by Fredric Jameson (London: Verso, 1998), p. 10.

21 See Todd, p. 53.

22 Jameson, *Postmodernism*, p. 25.

23 Linda Hutcheon, *Poetics of Postmodernism: History, Theory, Fiction* (London: Routledge, 1988), p. 89.

24 Rhian E. Jones, p. 2.

25 Ibid., p. 44.

26 See Jones, *Chavs*, p. 120. He comments that Prince William, 'one of the most privileged young men in the country', also attended a 'chav-themed fancy dress party' at Sandhurst military academy.

27 Debord, passage 30.

28 Burn named *Underworld* as one his books of the year in 1997, before it had been published in Britain. And in his book on footballers George Best and Duncan Edwards, he goes in search of the 'home-grown version of DeLillo's Marvin Lundy', finding a similar obsessive collector and trader of sporting memorabilia in Leslie Millman – an authority on Manchester United ephemera. See Gordon Burn, *Best and Edwards: Football, Fame and Oblivion* (London: Faber and Faber, 2006), p. 212; and Gordon Burn, 'Books: Books of the Year', *The Independent*, 29 November 1997, www.independent. co.uk/life-style/books-books-of-the-year-1296850.html.

29 Gordon Burn, 'The "English Disease"', *The Guardian*, 7 May 2004, www. theguardian.com/music/2004/may/07/1. A very similar description also appears in the novel: 'Nostalgia, or homesickness, is never about the past but about felt absences or a sense of something lacking in the present'. See Burn, *The North of England Home Service*, p. 86.

30 Robert Hewison, *The Heritage Industry: Britain in a Climate of Decline* (London: Methuen, 1987), p. 88.

31 Colls, 'Born-Again Geordies', p. 7, p. 24. Original emphasis.

32 Stuart Tannock, 'Nostalgia Critique', *Cultural Studies*, vol. 9, no. 3, 1995, pp. 453–464 (p. 454).

33 Kirk, p. 145.

34 David James, 'Introduction: Mapping Modernist Continuities', in *The Legacies of Modernism*, ed. by David James (Cambridge: Cambridge University Press, 2011), pp. 1–20 (p. 10).

35 Tannock, p. 461.

36 Svetlana Boym, *The Future of Nostalgia* (New York, NY: Basic Books, 2001), p. xvi.

37 Ibid., p. xviii.

38 Tannock, pp. 457–458.

39 Richard Hoggart, *The Uses of Literacy: Aspects of Working-Class Life* (London: Penguin, 2009), p. 117.

40 Ibid., p. 147.

41 Ibid., pp. 311–312.

42 Ibid., p. 170

43 Ibid., p. 169.

44 Ibid., p. 294.

45 Bill Williamson, 'Living the Past Differently: Historical Memory in the North-East', in *Geordies*, ed. by Colls and Lancaster, pp. 148–167 (p. 148).

46 Boym makes a key distinction between collective memory and national memory, the former 'suggests multiple narratives' while the latter invokes a 'single teleological plot'. Boym, p. 53.

47 Jean Baudrillard, 'The Evil Demon of Images and The Precession of Simulacra', in *Postmodernism: A Reader*, ed. by Thomas Docherty (Hertfordshire: Harvester Wheatsheaf, 1993), pp. 194–199 (pp. 194–195).

48 Todd, p. 211.

49 Gordon Burn, *Alma Cogan* (London: Faber and Faber, 2004), p. 152.

50 John N. Duvall, 'Introduction', in *The Cambridge Companion to Don DeLillo*, ed. by Duvall, pp. 1–12 (p. 7).

51 Daniel Lea, 'Trauma, Celebrity, and Killing in the "Contemporary Murder Leisure Industry"', *Textual Practice*, vol. 28, no. 5, 2014, pp. 763–781 (p. 767).

52 This quote is italicised in the text which places emphasis on the urgent need felt by Ray to explain the reality of his relationship with his mother to her nurse Marzena.

53 Debord, passages 60 and 61.

54 Colin MacInnes, *Absolute Beginners* (London: Allison & Busby, 2011), p. 83. To further confuse matters, it appears that Burn's novel has since been used in a book (first published in 2007) by the notorious gangster Frankie Fraser when describing the Soho scene in the 1950s. The details about Ginnie's and the eponymous former 'Windmill girl' who ran it, which appear in *The North of England Home Service* (p. 149), are repeated almost verbatim in Frankie Fraser, *Mad Frank's Underworld History of Britain* (London: Random House, 2012), p. 90. Fraser has written a number of books which pre-date *The North of England Home Service*, however, so this section may have been lifted from one of his own originally and also used by Burn. In either instance, it is an example of the potential complications and uncertainties surrounding historical narrative and the way that a writer may deliberately manipulate and subvert such a construction.

55 Nick Bentley, *Radical Fictions: The English Novel in the 1950s* (Oxford: Peter Lang, 2007), p. 250.

56 MacInnes, p. 83.

57 Haywood, p. 115. I understand this 'mythic' vision as being that of the narrator in *Absolute Beginners* and not that of MacInnes; Haywood seems to imply the latter.

58 Sinfield, p. 193.

59 Ibid., p. 194.

60 Ibid., p. 193.

61 Bertolt Brecht, 'Popularity and Realism', in *Aesthetics and Politics*, ed. by Theodor Adorno et al. (London: Verso, 2007), pp. 79–85 (p. 82).

62 The title is a reference to the BBC's northern output on its flagship national radio station, the Home Service, which became Radio Four in 1967. During the 1950s, the BBC was seen as having a significant role to play in protecting British culture by resisting an increasing Americanisation of cultural forms. Burn discusses this in 'After the Flood', *The Guardian*, 15 November 2003.

63 Fisher, *Capitalist Realism*, p. 59.

64 Harvey, *The Condition of Postmodernity*, p. 78.

65 Boym, pp. 54–55.

66 Ibid., p. 49.

67 Gordon Burn, 'Wired Up and Whacked Out', *The Sunday Times*, 25 August 1991, p. 36.

68 Burn, *The Guardian*, 15 November 2003.

69 Jameson, *Postmodernism*, p. 49.

70 Dominic Head, 'H. E. Bates, Regionalism and Late Modernism', in *The Legacies of Modernism*, ed. by James, pp. 40–52 (p. 41).

71 Andrzej Gąsiorek, *Post-War British Fiction: Realism and After* (London: Edward Arnold, 1995), p. 19.

72 Boym, p. 44.

3 Anthony Cartwright and the Deindustrial Novel
Realism, Place, Class

After completing two novels located a distance from but concerned with Thatcherism, Anthony Cartwright has spoken of how he felt compelled to complete his loose Dudley trilogy by shifting the focus further back than both the early-twenty-first century of *Heartland* and the 1995 setting of *The Afterglow*. The result was *How I Killed Margaret Thatcher*: a hybrid historical novel partially set in the 1980s. Cartwright says:

> I thought it was unfair to not try and deal explicitly with it because it is there in *The Afterglow* and *Heartland*, the impact of the eighties and Thatcher as a lurking presence. How can she not be? There was an element of tracing it back to that moment and saying, 'This is what it's about'.[1]

All of Cartwright's first three novels are about the impact of deindustrialisation on his hometown of Dudley in the West Midlands. They are interventions into debates concerning class, identity, gender, race, political agency, and neoliberal discourse. Here I provide a reading of how a contemporary British writer has sought to register change through what is an articulation of a specific working-class structure of feeling. This is captured by engaging with deindustrialisation as an ongoing process which, crucially, is the decisive experience in Cartwright's fiction. And the notion of such a historical condition being fundamental to class experience goes some way to explain why the third novel is drawn back to the 1980s and Thatcherism. The novels form a 'loose' trilogy because they overlap in a number of illuminating ways, specifically on place (Dudley), class (working), and in their range of recurring characters, but also because of their attempt to draw the connecting narratives back to the 1980s as a source site. Here there are compelling links to the other forms of writing about class looked at in this book: *GB84* and the enduring significance of Thatcherism; Sunjeev Sahota's work and the racialisation of class. But why focus on these three novels in particular when Cartwright has continued to write about Dudley and deindustrialisation in his later work?[2] And why does he 'end' this loose trilogy with the 1980s?

The 'profound reshaping of social life' brought about by Thatcherism, as it is described by Stuart Hall, involved the emergence of new processes which dramatically altered the lives of the British working class.[3] Crucially, realism is the mode with which Cartwright has responded to this period of deep and disorientating shift. According to Tony Davies, realism must not be understood simply as a matter of content and aesthetic practice but as a historical mode, one which is concerned with social and historical conditions and the 'lived class relations of capitalist societies'.[4] What is important here is Davies's insight about the realist form compelling and almost forcing the writer to reveal or articulate dominant forces and social relations; this task then is 'something not chosen or freely exercised but enforced', he adds, 'by circumstances beyond [...] [the author's] voluntary control'.[5] This chapter traces the shifts in and the development of form, from the social realism of *The Afterglow* through to ways in which *How I Killed Margaret Thatcher* pushes at the parameters of the realist mode. Such a tracking provides insights into both historical process and the difficulty of representation, examining how the novel as a form can give a tangible sense of neoliberalism and, in turn, provide enabling ways of knowing. Such difficulties in capturing the complexities of neoliberalism, what Adorno alludes to as the attempt to 'conjure up in perceptible form a society which has become abstract' as I noted in the Introduction,[6] mean for Cartwright a (re)turn to the seemingly recognisable and 'known' place of his hometown and the distinctive history of the Black Country.

Paul McDonald in *Fiction from the Furnace: A Hundred Years of Black Country Writing* draws attention to eight locally-born writers, from David Christie Murray and Ellen Thorneycroft Fowler to Francis Brett Young and Archie Hill, for whom this is a 'distinct region that has significance in their narrative world. It is not merely an incidental backdrop'.[7] Its history, adds McDonald, 'has been one of the most colourful and dramatic in England and, in this respect alone, [acts as] an ideal spur for the creative imagination'.[8] What McDonald locates in the tradition of such writing is both a celebration of and ambivalence towards the Black Country and Black Country identity. Thought of as its 'unofficial capital', Dudley played a central role when the area became the 'nation's furnace' during the industrial revolution.[9] A thirty-foot coal seam was one reason why large-scale manufacturing – steelworks, coal mining, iron foundries, and forges – prospered. Dudley was particularly noted for its position in the iron trade and, as Valentine Cunningham has said, it was this material which played a significant role in the 'manifestations of classic early English industrialism'.[10] According to Mike Wayne, industrialism has a powerful place, as 'a conceptual metaphor',[11] in the British political, social, and cultural imaginary; this is despite the industrial worker, in contrast to other working-class jobs in the service sector, forming 'a quantitatively smaller part of the economy as an occupation'.[12] Additionally, in the 1830s and 1840s, 'there was little enthusiasm for the industrial age from the working class, so appalling had its consequences been up until that point', Wayne suggests.[13] But a significant cultural significance came to be placed on industrialism in the early twentieth century, emerging out of the relationships between capital, labour, and liberalism and the development of a new society, forging new ways of thinking about British identity. 'There is a sense that the political maturation of the industrial organised working class is absolutely central', argues Wayne, 'to the prospects of developing a dem-ocratic society in which the majority had a say in the conditions which shaped their lives'.[14] Industrialism, therefore, has taken up an influential role in the British national imagination, despite and not because of the size of its actual material base in comparison to other forms of work and aspects of the British economy (finance and commerce, for instance). The working class and industry became a 'legitimate component part of national identity'.[15] And throughout most of the twentieth century, this potent conceptual metaphor meant that the industrial working class was seen to have an active role in shaping society. The demise of manufac-turing and of an industrial society was long, complicated, and uneven. What is significant in Cartwright's work is not only the historical weight of such a powerful political, cultural, and social metaphor as a presence but also the literal presence and absence of heavy industry in the lives and memories of many of his characters. Elsewhere, I have described how Cartwright, along with work by Catherine O'Flynn and Edward Hogan, explores the effect of the disappearance of industrial jobs on working-class subjectivity and how the often damaging mythologies sur-rounding such forms of work also 'undermine and erode contemporary notions of both male and female working-class identity'.[16] So, deindus-trialisation is a historical process which continues to be felt within the twenty-first century. For Raymond Williams, the term refers to a 'dam-aging and even frightening' process.[17] Crucially, he has said:

> [T]he society that is now emerging is in no sense 'post-industrial'. Indeed, in its increasingly advanced technologies, it is a specific and probably absolute climax of industrialism itself. What is often loosely meant is the declining relative importance of manufacturing [...]. The decline itself is real [...]. Yet at this stage it is necessary to insist that a decline in manufacturing is not a decline in 'industrialism', and certainly not in industrial capitalism.[18]

By 'at this stage', Williams means the early- to mid-1980s to which Cart-wright repeatedly, both imaginatively and politically, returns but, as I have argued in the book chapter cited above,[19] it is important to main-tain a concept of deindustrialisation which has a contemporary and con-tinuing relevance, as being part of what is now a later period of global capitalist development and, therefore, as part of a process of class making and reshaping. And as Wayne suggests, the image of the industrial worker has been a significant if shifting component part of British national identity; it has also contained and continues to evoke very specific regional inflections.

The fact that *The Afterglow* and the subsequent two novels in the Dudley trilogy were all published by Birmingham-based Tindal Street Press 'reminds readers', argues David James, 'of the local provenance of Cartwright's creative plight: the plight [...] to articulate pressing issues in an exceptional dialect that enriches the Black Country novel'. Comparing such an approach to that of Alan Sillitoe, James adds: 'This kind of imaginative appropriation of one's birthplace and community has proven to be a vibrant catalyst' for a successful writing career.[20] Cartwright's three novels are works of regional fiction in that they are written from within and about a specific, enclosed area of England, one which has been crafted into fiction by a writer native to that location. He is an insider writing about a place and class he knows first-hand, albeit from a now distanced position.[21] His novels are what Williams has described as 'doubly regional',[22] focusing on a specific geographical area and a specific class. James argues that contemporary regionalists, in 'honouring' earlier generations of social realists, can offer 'perspectives on community space that resonate with the experience of marginalization, inhabitation, and belonging worldwide'.[23] It is through such active renewal and revival of both realist and regional fiction, argues James, that the perceived limitations of these literary forms can be worked through. Crucially, Cartwright has lamented the deliberate dismissal of working-class writing as 'regional' and spoken of reclaiming the term as an oppositional or resistant force within neoliberal hegemony.[24] The labelling of a novel as 'regional' suggests that it depicts an area subordinate to the centralised power of a nation state. And, as Williams acknowledges, a singular class, singular region perspective can have difficulty in providing the necessary analysis of the 'fully developed class relations' inherent to a global capitalist society.[25]

James cites Pat Barker as the leading protagonist in the development of a reinvigorated British realist tradition, one which is able to get beyond such perceived impediments. As John Kirk has persuasively stated, Barker's mode of realism has seen 'the most sustained attempt to write working-class women into the novel'. This has not been by a return to what Kirk describes as the hierarchy of discourses which define 'classic realism', but rather the writing of individual, female characters who constitute a collective voice;[26] it is a modest yet significant adjustment of the realist mode rather than a radical departure. Barker's first novel *Union Street*, a title which conjoins two dominant features of twentieth-century working-class history: the union and the street, provides a demonstration of such a re-alignment. Seven separate sections tell the stories of seven women living in the same location. And such an adaptation of the realist mode, using multiple perspectives positioned within an enclosed class environment to explore socio-economic pressures, is replicated by Cartwright in *The Afterglow*. The novel deploys a strikingly similar formal structure to *Union Street*: eleven interlocking chapters portraying the lives of seven connected characters (four male, three female) to tell the story of a community. So, here is a significant enabling presence for Cartwright. This dialogical framework allows for the subtle gradations within a single social class to emerge, depicting the variety of struggles faced by the different yet connecting experiences of *The Afterglow*'s characters. These individual responses to and experiential understanding of the processes of historical change provide a way of mapping the wider shifts taking place within capitalism; and the disruptions to working-class life act as a manifestation of such socio-economic transformation. Cartwright's novels, like the work of Barker, depict what has remained and resisted in the face of a process of erasure and abandonment. This is expressed formally in the reshaping of, if not quite a complete break from, the linear narrative traditionally associated with realism. And the act of writing individual stories into an overlapping narrative helps to avoid a generalisation or the subsuming of working-class subjectivity.

Language and the crafting of a distinctive idiolect is one way in which Cartwright evokes this sense of a lived, varied class experience.[27] Kelman, who Cartwright acknowledges as an influence,[28] has described the ideological and political necessity of, when writing, entering 'into my own world [...] my own experience, my own culture and community'.[29] And the use of the Dudley idiom is one way in which Cartwright attempts to speak from within 'the lived-in, the everyday' experience of contemporary working-class life.[30] Not only do Cartwright's texts document a specific regional accent, they also explore the multi-accentuality of language in the deployment of characteristic Black Country words and phrases. Williams notes how dialect, which comes from the Greek for discourse or conversation, moved away from its original meaning of connoting variation; instead, it became a term to signify a culturally subordinate form to the standard or literary language.[31] So, there is a suggestion here that to write in dialect is to write about inferior and secondary concerns. Further, Tony Crowley describes Standard English (or the standard/uniform language of a given nation) thus:

[A] form of language [...] which lies beyond all the variability of usage in offering unity and coherence to what otherwise appears diverse and disunited. It is the literary form of the language that is to be used and recognised all over the national territory.[32]

Crucially, it involves the construction of a uni-accentuality, according to V. N. Voloshinov.[33] Additionally, Crowley argues that this is a 'search for linguistic unity and identity [...] founded upon acts of violence and repression: a denial of heteroglossia – discursive and historical – in favour of centralising, static forms'.[34] The use of the Dudley vernacular in his fiction is one way Cartwright challenges this sense of subordination. Jeremy Scott has noted: '[T]he dialect from which [...] idiolect is constructed is often imbued with ideological resonances relating to issues of class, region, culture – even nation'.[35] It is particularly significant then that Cartwright is utilising a tradition of fashioning into prose the distinctive linguistic features of the West Midlands voice. Poet Geoff Stevens has observed, in reference to his local community, that 'Black Country dialect verse is not something new, but part of our past and future culture'.[36] And McDonald has noted, in his study of such writing, how author Archie Hill adopted the demotic to work as 'an implicit contrast to the standard English rhetoric of authority; a resistance', challenging sites of power and sources of oppression.[37] This employment of 'linguistic otherness', as Valentine Cunningham describes it, can have an oppositional, class-based resonance; in the 1840s, for example, the period in which industrial fiction first emerges, this 'whole other world of namings, of discourse, in and of the industrialized areas, a proletarian lingo and dialect' which exists 'alongside the official rhetorics of Church and State' was seen as a 'challenging alternative living language'.[38] Cartwright's use of such 'linguistic otherness' acts as a source of resistance to dominant logic, as an enabling resource by allowing for self-definition, and it asserts a sense of working-class being; further, it is an experiential discourse which provides an affirmation of existence. Such an affirmation is registered in voice then, a move which is intimately linked to place.

What is formative in Cartwright's texts is the dramatic physical reconfiguration of a once sustaining and enabling landscape. The name Cinderheath,[39] which features in *Heartland* and *How I Killed Margaret Thatcher* as a fictional suburb of Dudley, gives a sense of what has happened to this industrial town; by conjoining a volcanic rock (cinder), and its connotations of fire and destruction, with the name given to infertile scrubland (heath), Cartwright implies a 'visibly altered place',[40] not only due to the historical workings of industry but also as a result of its violent collapse. And this notion of scorched earth, of not only as a barren wasteland but also as a deliberate act, is exacerbated by the increasingly insidious behaviour of the land itself. In *How I Killed Margaret Thatcher*, for example, houses have to be held up by scaffolding when '[t]hings started slipping into the old workings'.[41] This gives an enhanced feeling of drift and it connotes the experience of a way of life coming loose. A critical understanding of how trauma works provides one way to trace such forms of social change but, according to Antony Rowland, there has been an absence of a 'discourse of trauma and testimony in relation to Working-Class Studies'.[42] This is due to a general lack of understanding about working-class experience, he suggests, but also as a result of the nature of the trauma to which it relates. Following Lauren Berlant, Rowland uses the notion of trauma to describe the 'general atmosphere of suffering';[43] it not only relates to one-off, unexpected, and large events but also applies to the quotidian experience of the ongoing and ordinary which can be equally as insidious and disabling. This emphasis on everyday suffering, rather than trauma, is a more adequate way of describing twenty-first-century subjectivity, according to Berlant.[44]

Significantly, Cartwright's texts offer compelling contrasts between the more familiar sources of trauma (and its mass mediation) and the routine, mundane experience of, what Pierre Bourdieu has described as, ordinary suffering or la petite misère. For example, the horrors of the Bosnian War appear fleetingly on the television in the Wilkinson's home in *The Afterglow*, the events of 11th September 2001 act as a subplot to the narrative of *Heartland*, and *How I Killed Margaret Thatcher* is littered with images of violence (the Falklands War and the Iranian Embassy siege, for example). These large public sites of traumatic experience are figured as backdrops in the novels and it is the local and personal which are foregrounded throughout. Bourdieu has noted the creation within contemporary capitalism of multiple social spaces and 'conditions for an unprecedented development of all kinds of ordinary suffering'.[45] And one way in which writing about the working-class experience of deindustrialisation has attempted to articulate, or to see and understand, this has been through an engagement with the once ordinary but now haunting presence of the built industrial environment.

Risley is the only character in Cartwright's debut novel not given his first name in his chapter's heading. This not only effaces his identity, but also places the focus on his family surname, therefore on the people to whose history and way of life he cannot access. He reads his landscape thus:

> The train slid [...] past a row of disused factory buildings. The sun made the raindrops on the window sparkle. There was a beauty in these buildings, he thought, the corpses of outlandish beasts decomposing, rotting into the black ground; a beauty in the stillness of their hulks, holding shadowy light in their bellies; a beauty in their spent energy.[46]

It is a passage littered with oxymorons: 'shadowy light', 'spent energy'. And it is full of contrasts: the word 'beauty' features three times along with 'sparkle', 'outlandish', 'light', and 'energy'. These are all positive descriptions depicting life, value, and vitality. But there are also more sinister, disturbing descriptions: 'corpses', 'decomposing', 'rotting', and 'black ground'. It is a confusing landscape, one imagined through the sublime, the experience of an overwhelming sense of awe. And it is one that Risley cannot comprehend, hence the evoking of aesthetic rather

than political descriptions of his environment. In an attempt to overcome this, however, he begins to scale these 'hulks' or shells of industry. He climbs up a disused factory chimney to get a view of the town, gaining a sense of freedom, expression, and understanding. He is also recreating one of the few memories he has of his father: being taken up in a crane his dad worked on during the building of Merry Hill Shopping Centre which replaced Round Oaks Steelworks. It is a painful but also a positive act. Ultimately, Risley fails, falling to his death through a skylight in a factory roof: 'He threw his arms out to break the fall as he went through the glass. [...] He was upside down. [...] His feet were still working in mid-air, trying to find his step, but he was falling, falling'.[47]
This extended metaphor – a life turned upside down and collapsing – is deployed throughout the Dudley trilogy and it threatens to over-reach in *How I Killed Margaret Thatcher* (I return to this point below) but here it works to emphasise Risley's profound dislocation. Crucially, he has already been written off and demonised by the local community: there is a common presumption that he was on the roof to steal from the factory rather than as a result of his feeling of social detachment. However, Risley is providing an alternative perspective on a deindustrialised landscape which has increasingly become aestheticized by a growing number of contemporary photographers and urban explorers. Tim Strangleman, while arguing for a 'more generous critical cultural reading' of 'ruin porn', has noted how such a fetishisation of industrial ruination is in danger of ignoring the historical fact that such places are 'constructed and destroyed by capitalism and class interest'. The working-class are often excluded from the 'image-driven "coffee table" collections of industrial decay'; it is a 'selective obituary' of a landscape which 'ignores the people who once populated [it]'.[48] While Risley does provide an aestheticized description of Dudley's ruins, seeing 'a beauty in their spent energy',[49] his is an engaged and critical enquiry. This is not merely a setting, a backdrop; it is a constitutive part of the class experience.

In Cartwright's work the working-class family is destroyed (*How I Killed Margaret Thatcher*), posited as an important resource (*Heartland* and *The Afterglow*), and represented as the site around which the forces of capitalism are most strongly felt by women and articulated through female experience (*The Afterglow*). Mary Wilkinson in Cartwright's debut novel is central to this final observation and, like Risley, offers illuminating ways to read a working-class experience of contemporary capitalism. Although present throughout the text, it is in the penultimate chapter, headed simply 'Mary', where a greater sense of the strains and pressures placed on her are expressed; it is around this working-class mother that the forces of capitalism coalesce at their most oppressive and potent. She is the one who looks after everybody else and works to alleviate the familial problems caused by unemployment, depression, and illness, increasingly to the detriment of her own well-being. And it is the experience of these multiple sources working alongside and against each other, intersecting at key points, which shape female working-class subjectivity in the novel. Sheila Rowbotham has argued that it is through such an understanding of the way in which capitalist society works that resistance can emerge. She says: 'The contradiction which appears clearly in capitalism between family and industry, private and public, personal and impersonal, is the fissure in women's consciousness through which revolt erupts'.[50] *The Afterglow* explores such contradictions as they surface, through the narrative of Mary. Cartwright writes:

> That was what it was like; a feeling of something coming loose, hot, uncomfortable, scary. She fainted in the kitchen and nearly cracked her head on the table but instead landed across one of the chairs, her arms and legs sprawled.[51]

Agency plays a significant part here. Mary is the one who, as noted, works to keep the family together and she solves other people's problems before her own. What agency she has is focused on maintenance and the imperative of survival rather than revolt. Class is also a determining factor in her response to the destructive nature of capitalism; resistance, in the terms used by Rowbotham, is replaced by endurance.

The types of political action available to a working-class character such as Mary are suggested by the year in which *The Afterglow* is set: 1995. This places the text during the drift of the post-Thatcher period when John Major's Tory Party was in power. It was also the year which witnessed a significant moment in the history of the British Labour Party: the amendment of Clause Four. This 'famous socialist commitment', as described by Alistair Reid and Henry Pelling, was adopted by the party in 1918. It ran as follows:

> To secure for the producers by hand or by brain the full fruits of their industry, and the most equitable distribution thereof that may be possible, upon the basis of the common ownership of the means of production and the best obtainable system of popular administration and control of each industry or service.[52]

In his first conference speech as Labour leader in 1994, Tony Blair declared his intention to re-write Clause Four and abandon its political aims. A year later, a new passage of the constitution was approved by the party which spoke of 'common endeavour', 'true potential', and 'a spirit of solidarity, tolerance and respect',[53] rather than 'common ownership' and the 'control of each industry'. It, symbolically at least, gave birth to New Labour and was the culmination of a 'process of renewal' which 'modernisers' within the party instigated following the election defeat of 1983.[54] The change to Clause Four meant a shift to the right, the embrace of free-market economics, and an attempt by Blair to alter the Labour Party's appeal: the more positive and progressive aspects of social liberalism were aligned with, and in some ways integral to, the regressive and damaging impact of economic liberalism. The notable absence of the Labour Party, the labour movement, and the historical structures of collectivism in *The Afterglow* can be read as an indication of what this ideological retreat represented for the deindustrial working class. While Mary remembers a time when the institutions of the working-class movement, notably the Labour Club,[55] played a role in her life, her current situation is bereft of such a cultural and political expression of a wider system of collective support. This became more prominent following what Wayne argues was a specific change of focus in New Labour's policymaking agenda: 'the culture of the industrial working class was displaced in favour of the elite strata of the professional "creative class" working within the cultural industries themselves, a move that helped detach the Labour Party from its historic class roots'.[56] Satnam Virdee has described how the socialist Labour left in the 1980s built a strategy which placed due emphasis on class but did not see it as the only form of oppression. It was able to draw together a range of intersectional responses to Thatcherism, around 'the totemic figure of Tony Benn' and maintaining class struggle as a guiding principle, in order to 'find the best political solutions to defend the diverse but complimentary concerns of workers, racialised minorities, women, gays and peace activists against the ravages of an unrestrained capitalist and conservative offensive'.[57] New Labour's embrace of economic liberalism and dismissal of class as being of no contemporary relevance placed little, if any, emphasis on such alliances and the important forms of collective, collaborative responses they made possible. As I discussed in the Introduction, the damage done to the working class and New Labour's abandonment of such communities in conjunction with its commitment to broadly maintaining the economic and political project of neoliberalism created the conditions for a reactionary response to begin to gain traction and support. The rise of the far right and its targeting of working-class communities disowned by New Labour, as figured by Mary's experience in *The Afterglow*, takes a central role in Cartwright's second novel.

Although set ostensibly in June 2002, *Heartland* moves across numerous moments in that year and the preceding one, using short sections to shift back, forth, and across historical time. It is a formal structure utilised to convey the complex and complicated processes which feed the variety of activities of and responses to the far right. The use of multiple perspectives, which form a fragmented community, places the focus in the novel onto the intersections of race and class. The character of Adnan is instructive here. As a British Pakistani, certain expectations, predominantly racist ones held by sections of the white community, are placed upon him. He is excluded from the national community (the imagined community of Britain), as well as his working-class community in Dudley, and singled out as having conflicting and antagonistic social and cultural 'values'. It is from such exclusion that he rebels, leaving his hometown to forge a new sense of self. He assumes a blank identity, from which he can determine his own future and, consequently, resist the projection of racist ideology forced on to him, as the constructed 'other', on which far-right extremism partially thrives. Again, Cartwright's construction of family is also important here. Adnan's parents came to Britain from Pakistani-controlled Kashmir. Their three children take very different approaches to formulating British Muslim identities. In rejecting his, Adnan is constructing a form of defence which results in an understandable avoidance of, rather than a challenge to, the racism of which he is a victim. Tayub adopts a more direct approach to such oppression, embracing, to the growing concern of his family, Islamic extremism. The eldest son Zubair, in a third, alternative response, pursues another path, structured around his young family, his job as a lawyer, and his social life embedded within Dudley. All three characters demonstrate the complex intersections of race, class, and religion in modern Britain. What *Heartland* attempts to do is draw out the similarities between this family's concerns and the wider, multi-ethnic working-class community of Cinderheath. Like Tayub, Jim Bayliss's son Michael becomes involved, as a young white teenager, in another type of extremism in the form of gang culture, which is a response to the volatile uncertainties of the contemporary moment. Importantly, Zubair and a member of the British National Party (BNP) are shown performing the same parental commitments (taking their young children to the cinema, for example); this seemingly ordinary act challenges assumptions, predicated on the fear of difference, which ignore the reality of shared interests. So, the novel is drawing attention to what Paul Gilroy has described as the 'liberating sense of banality' through which it is able to dispel and challenge the construction of race based on the social imposition of difference.[58] This is a central theme of the book then: an engagement with the complexities of community and the intersection of and class as a site of structural inequality. The site of an abandoned steel plant is mooted, in the novel, as the location for a new mosque. This is jumped on by the BNP which is seeking, by fielding a candidate in the local government elections, to exploit a sense of anxiety and uncertainty within the multi-racial and multi-faith Cinderheath community. Crucially, *Heartland* maps three important developments: (1) the vacuum left by New Labour's move right; (2) the lack of an inclusive, intersectional class politics; (3) the fragmentation of the labour movement more generally.

Steven Fielding has suggested that Cartwright's novel is unusual in being a twenty-first-century fictional representation of formal politics which focuses on 'complex contexts' and features a politician working for the common good rather than individual gain. Fielding argues: '*Heartland* has a Labour councillor [Jim Bayliss] seek re-election in a working-class town undermined by decline and riven by ethnic tension. Cartwright has the reader empathize with the councillor's various dilemmas'.[59] It is this last point about empathy which I wish to pick up on. And, as a way into offering a different analysis to that of Fielding, it is worth quoting at length the following extract from *Heartland*:

> Jim became a councillor in 1979, against the prevailing mood. He thought he was doing his bit for Cinderheath, Dudley, England, the Labour movement, the working class. He'd noticed people using the term 'working class' again lately, hadn't heard it for years. Blair had got things right in that respect as well as many others: how could there be a Labour party when there was no Labour left for it to represent? It had to become something else. There were jobs now, of course. The big losses had all come twenty-odd years ago, but it was hardly the same – jobs for cleaners and security men, shop work and mobile-phone sales [...]. Even the call centre jobs were going to Bangalore. This was his town's position in the new world order.[60]

Despite emerging out of the traditions of the labour movement, the councillor embraces the political vision of New Labour. This ostensibly means abandoning class as a form of contemporary political and social analysis. I read *Heartland* as not empathetic with the challenges facing politicians such as Jim, as Fielding argues, but, rather, as a text which exposes the problems created by a departure from class and a lack of understanding of how class works. Jim is symbolic of this problem. He is unable to respond to the profound political, social, and historical shifts which have occurred following the neoliberal turn or to comprehend class as a broad, shifting, material category. As Stuart Hall has detailed, the dynamics of global capitalism continue radically to alter the composition of class. Neoliberalism has resulted in a recomposition which 'is transforming the material basis, the occupational boundaries, the gender and ethnic composition, the political cultures and the social imagery of "class"', according to Hall. Importantly, however, such recomposition 'is not in the least synonymous with disappearance', he adds.[61] Jim recognises that the Labour Party 'had to become something else' but this, as Hall argues, required a new approach to class rather than a full-scale withdrawal from a class-based critique of capital. *Heartland*, as an intervention into this debate, figures the New Labour abandonment of the working class, a social and political distinction which to Jim's mind is a relic of another era, as one of the causes of the fractured structure of feeling which the text locates.

Cora Kaplan has written of how New Labour moved away from class terminology so as to avoid the 'possibility of alliances between different disruptive collectivities'.[62] The party sought to align class exclusively

with the figure of the male, unionised, industrial worker, or 'Old Labour', and therefore consign it to the past. 'New Labour's virtual ban
on thinking or speaking of class relations, or class agency, or class as
a still meaningful category of analysis', adds Kaplan, '[...] has, as its
corollary, the deliberate emptying out of the affect that attached to the
history of old solidarities and conflicts'.[63] Similarly, and while acknowl-
edging the positive impact of multicultural discourse,[64] Francis Mulhern has drawn attention to the ways in which a subsequent focus on
multiculturalism, and the form of liberalism it emerges from, fails to
challenge the conditions (capitalism) which often cause and contribute
to exclusion and oppression. He says: 'The promotion of culture as a
defining social relation has tended to obscure the articulations of ethnic
and class formation'.[65] In *Heartland*, the working class are portrayed as
divided by race, religion, and ethnicity. Such binary formations, when
positioned within a single class perspective, shift political debate away
from the inequalities of capitalism, argues Owen Jones; the focus, rather
than being on the problems caused by the uneven balance of wealth
and power under neoliberalism, is on racial division within the working
class. And the intersection between race and class, at which the most
destructive forms of inequality (prejudice, hatred, and oppression) are
often located, is lost through a process of divide and rule. As Jones
suggests, 'linking the problems of working-class communities to their
ethnic identity, rather than to their class [...] encourages the idea that
working-class people belonging to different ethnic groups are in competition with each other for attention and resources'.[66] Further, Daniel
Trilling in *Bloody Nasty People*, his book on the BNP and the far right,
notes how social inequality continued to rise after 1997 and the election
of Blair's New Labour government. Importantly, when the mainstream
political debate has shifted onto such economic disparity, it is discussed
in 'terms of race, rather than class' and this suits the far-right doctrine
of fringe parties like the BNP.[67] 'While New Labour's chief ideologues
promoted the idea that class divisions were no longer relevant', comments Trilling, 'working-class people of all races were feeling the sharp
end of the New Labour project'.[68] This sense of abandonment is felt
acutely by the Cinderheath community in *Heartland*, some of whom
turn to alternative social forms: political extremism, for example, or
an entrenched nationalism. David Harvey has noted how 'a disposable
workforce', when alienated by the dynamics of neoliberalism, 'inevitably turns to other institutional forms through which to construct social
solidarities and express a collective will'. This is partly a result of the
stripping back of the 'protective cover' of, for example, welfare capitalism and the 'social dislocations' which have ensued.[69] Further, Cartwright has spoken of a 'very typical divide-and-rule policy' which he
believes has 'helped destroy working class communities'. There is also
a tradition of right-wing, working-class support in the West Midlands.

'The picture is complicated', Cartwright has observed, before adding, in regard to writing about Dudley. 'And that [right-wing tradition] has to be in there'.[70] As Virdee has mapped, Enoch Powell and a 'racializing conception of English nationalism built around a white identity',[71] which I return to in Chapter Six, has historically gained significant traction in the West Midlands. Notably, such working-class support has been uneven and inconsistent.[72] Socialist activists, forging a white, Asian, and black working-class formation, responded in productive and powerful ways to the racisms of the New Right: the Indian Workers Association and Jagmohan Joshi in the West Midlands, for instance.[73] New Labour's failure to build an inclusive, intersectional class politics to challenge the rise of the right presented the far right with an opportunity to reactivate the violent traditions of Powellism but in new forms.

The BNP, Trilling argues, sought to intervene at, and exploit from within, the level of local politics by attempting to craft a softer, neighbourly public image. This became a targeted strategy of the party during the late-1990s when Nick Griffin, who became leader in 1999, sought a break from the overtly fascist 'street movement' approach, rooted in the National Front (NF) which splintered to become the BNP, by creating 'new presentational techniques' that would 'insinuate [the party] into local politics'.[74] Rather than the explicitly violent tactics of the NF, Griffin proposed a new communication policy which would be formulated upon a concept of community politics.[75] This 'public-facing discourse' would conceal the political extremism of the BNP's internal doctrine which 'remained as racist as it ever was'.[76] Organising grocery deliveries to households, running a taxi service for pensioners, and leading day trips for youngsters are a selection of the increasing number of local activities, exclusively aimed at white people, in which the party became involved; setting up, running, and financing community football teams was another.[77] *Heartland* has such a development at its centre: the BNP providing money along with organisational and public support to Cinderheath Sunday FC.

So, *Heartland* works at the contradictions of capitalism which can often lead to or produce responses predicated on extremism. 'Societies that promise equality, freedom and democracy', argues Trilling, 'yet preside over massive inequalities of wealth, are breeding grounds for racism'.[78] In the Black Country, such economic disparity is felt and understood through what has been lost. On the morning of the election, when the Labour Party defeat the BNP by sixty-four votes to retain the Cinderheath seat, Jim Bayliss fantasises about delivering a speech in which he urges people to think of the old steel works as a 'place of hope'. He adds: 'Hard, hard work. Industry. Endeavour, eh? The ability to pull yourselves up. Together. To work together'.[79] The councillor is grasping for some understanding of what the old symbols of the labour movement represent. However, in doing so he stumbles over his words and is, ultimately, unable to find a positive meaning in the rusting gates of the abandoned site. 'It wasn't really a place of hope', he concludes, '[i]t was a cenotaph'.[80] Despite his attempts to help the community, Jim has become detached from it and he is unable to inspire or speak for the working class as a multi-ethnic, multi-racial formation. The title of the novel recalls the history of the Black Country as not only playing an integral part in the industrialisation of Britain but also as the home of the people for whom the Labour Party was first created. In Cartwright's novel, the fear is that it will become another type of heartland, one where far-right extremism and the BNP can flourish. Jim Bayliss's narrow victory holds this threat off but it is only a temporary success. And a draw between Cinderheath Sunday FC and Cinderheath Muslim Community FC means that a Sikh team, the Gurdwara, win the league title on the final day of the football season, narrowly denying the BNP another symbolic victory. However, as Trilling asserts, racist doctrine will continue to find outlets where inequality and social abjection persist. What *Heartland* suggests, in documenting the aftermath of an abandonment of class politics, is that there needs to be a primary focus on class and its intersections with race in order to formulate a truly inclusive way out of the trauma of neoliberalism.

In contrast to *Heartland* and *The Afterglow*, *How I Killed Margaret Thatcher* is a text which pushes more explicitly at the parameters of the realist register. Cartwright has spoken of the problems he faced when trying to articulate a distinctively working-class experience of Thatcherism within the confines of the novel form. 'I did think about all sort of different approaches and structures', he has revealed. 'I thought about writing a realist novel but as if Thatcher was still Prime Minister, a novel with more of a dystopian vision'. Ultimately, the resulting text is not as firmly in the social realist tradition of the previous two, admits Cartwright: 'it's edging towards something else because how do you convey what happened effectively?'.[81] Ostensibly, what he has produced, therefore, is a hybrid historical novel, a form which presents its own unique set of problems and sites of potentiality. According to Georg Lukács, the historical novel is a literary mode which should provide 'a clear understanding of history as a process, of history as the concrete precondition of the present'.[82] Tony Davies's notion of realism as a historical mode is again useful here: it is a form through which it is possible for a novel to 'stand in some acknowledged and organic relation to the struggles [...] of the exploited classes'.[83] In Lukács's formulation, this emerges through an exploration of the underlying social and historical processes of a given period of time which often lead to a 'deep disturbance of the social or [...] the more personal life'.[84] Crucially, in Cartwright's work, it is the third novel which attempts to reveal the under-currents at source, connecting and in turn critiquing the previous two texts to form what Lukács describes as a 'total historical picture'. Lukács argues that such totality 'depends upon a rich and graded interaction between different levels of response to any major disturbance of life'.[85] Taken as a whole, this is what the Dudley trilogy attempts or has been compelled to do following Cartwright's commitment to depict working-class life following the neoliberal transition; and the social and historical conditions, along with the accompanying contradictions and causalities, have shaped the mode adopted by this contemporary British writer.

In *How I Killed Margaret Thatcher*, Sean Bull's granddad Jack holds on to a dogged faith in the democratic values of the British political system and the post-war social contract; however, his son Johnny believes in direct political action, calling for a workers' revolution and backing the miners during their industrial strike of 1984/1985. Despite their differences, the former has imbued the latter with a belief in socialism and provided him with a language of capitalist critique. During a heated discussion (and disagreement due in part to Jack's latent racism) about the inner-city riots of 1981, and the injustices of a capitalist society, Johnny says to his father: 'Yow've said yerself iss unfair. Yer tode me how unfair it is. From each according to his ability to each according to his need. Yow taught me that'.[86] This vision of a fairer, equal society not only seems to exclude female agency ('his ability', 'his need'), however, but also has taken on a more desperate pitch than the triumphal tone in which it has traditionally been adopted. Only when a 'higher phase of communist society' has been achieved, wrote Marx, 'can the narrow horizon of bourgeois right be crossed in its entirety and society inscribe on its banners: From each according to his ability, to each according to his needs!'[87] For Marx, this saying encapsulates the meaning and practices of communism; it is the proclamation of a new type of society, one without the inequality and oppression of class structure. In *How I Killed Margaret Thatcher*, it has become less a proud symbol of socialist ambition and more a desperate attempt to formulate a response to the bewildering dynamics of Thatcherism. Significantly, it is once again from within the family that a reply to the social and historical conditions of capitalism evolves. And in its framing of communal debate and discussion, the novel is part of a wider cultural engagement, on the left, with the discourse of political action and class struggle. In Cartwright's novel, both Jack and Johnny, during their often fractious discussions, warn of the destruction Thatcher will cause to the working class of the West Midlands but neither fully comprehends the potency and subsequent impact of Thatcherism. The novel is particularly effective at exploring the foreboding sense of helplessness felt by the working-class community. But, tellingly, it is left to the contemporary narrative of Sean, with a distance of three decades, to map an understanding of deindustrialisation:

> It was what you'd do, I suppose, if you had a plan, if you set out to destroy a place: close the big works first, one by one, create waves

that spread out from their closing, factory after factory, shop after shop; later on the brewery, the rail yard [...] a whole town was disappearing, caving in.[88]

On first reflection, there appears to have been a common sense to what happened ('It was what you'd do, I suppose'), however, the crucial phrase is 'if you had a plan'. As already noted in the discussion of *The Afterglow*, deindustrialisation and the neoliberal turn are figured as deliberate and co-ordinated attacks against the working class. This was a systematic and concerted mobilisation of socio-historical forces and one which, formally, realism strains to contain. For example, notably violent episodes, heavy in a symbolism which is at risk of developing into melodrama, are compellingly suggestive. A near-fatal fall by Sean at the opening of the novel is one such event; another is the death of his father. After losing his job at the local steel plant, Francis Bull takes to removing abandoned machinery from dormant factories. Disturbed by the police, he slips on a blade from one of the machines and bleeds to death at home, too frightened to go to the hospital. Sean finds him in the bathroom. 'I stand there and look at him, can't move, stand looking and looking', writes Cartwright. 'They killed him. They killed him'.[89] This particularly gruesome death has echoes of Risley's in *The Afterglow*. And, again, there is a recognition that this is part of something wider, part of an attack on the working class, in the line 'they killed him'. But there is a danger that such a violent and severe conception of Thatcherism detracts from its nuances and from the neoliberal turn more broadly.

In this regard, D. J. Taylor has described how fiction writers face 'the great difficulty' when focusing on Thatcher, and more broadly the 1980s, of 'pinning down someone so divisive, so self-evidently larger than life and yet at the same time so indisputably real, in a form as open-ended and provisional as the novel'.[90] Similarly, yet with an important emphasis on the doctrine rather than the individual which Taylor fails to make, Louisa Hadley and Elizabeth Ho describe Thatcher 'as a powerful personality and an equally powerful obstacle that occludes and forecloses an engagement with the political and social conditions of Thatcherism that continue to affect the present'.[91] Added to this is a further danger: that such figurations of the 1980s can only operate at the surface level of pop-cultural objects which, in turn, offer a detached nostalgia rather than a critical intervention into the decade. As Lukács has warned, 'history is far more than costume and decoration, it really determines [...] life, thought, feeling and behaviour'.[92] So, here are two problems which arise when seeking to address Thatcher and Thatcherism. A third is the figuration of the evil individual; the deceptive comfort this provides through the seemingly physical and singular manifestation of a disparate and complex political ideology can be disabling. One way in which twenty-first-century writing has sought to deal with all of these inter-connected issues is by placing Thatcher at the periphery of the narrative, notably through the inclusion of some of her most memorable political proclamations. For example, Cartwright's text and Damian Barr's memoir *Maggie & Me* (2013) insert a quote from Thatcher's extensive repertoire at the beginning of each chapter while Hilary Mantel does the same at the beginning of her short-story 'The Assassination of Margaret Thatcher' (2014). This seems to reveal a belief that the 'truth' of Thatcherism lies in her public utterances. However, in *Maggie & Me* they merely become another 1980s artefact in a nostalgic text littered with pop-cultural references. And in Mantel's text, the device plays more of a functional role: a transcript of what Thatcher said on the steps of Downing Street during a key moment in the Falklands conflict provides historical specificity to Mantel's story.[93] Cartwright places his selection of Thatcher quotes separately from the rest of the narrative and therefore sets up a juxtaposition of the political and the personal, between rhetoric and experience. It is a similar device used more convincingly by David Peace in *GB84*, as discussed in Chapter One. It is less effective in Cartwright's novel but there does momentarily emerge a disconnection between Thatcher's words and what is being experienced by the working class. This helps shift the focus onto neoliberalism and away from Thatcher as the evil individual, and it is an attempt to define working-class experience from within rather than having it described, and its meanings dictated, from without. One of Thatcher's quotes in Cartwright's novel reads: 'I am very anxious about the West Midlands because I recognise that the people there think they have suffered'.[94] The key word here is 'think'. They have merely misunderstood the situation, according to the former Prime Minister, they have not thought about it properly and comprehended the reality; they have not fully accepted the everyday 'common sense' of neoliberalism. As a counter to this, the novel articulates a specific working-class structure of feeling and it is one which emerges from beyond the individual figure of Thatcher. The central plot device around which the novel revolves, a nine-year-old boy's fantasy of killing the Tory leader (again another feature which brings into question the realist tendencies of the text), reveals the futility and absurdity of a belief that stopping one individual will defeat Thatcherism and reverse the set of social and political forces it has unleashed.

Cartwright's trilogy, followed by two further novels centred on working-class life, represents a sustained attempt to write class into the twenty-first-century British novel. Here are three novels which track class as a historical process, one felt and experienced as having material and economic implications. Joe Kennedy, when discussing Cartwright in his 2018 book *Authentocrats*, warns against some of the ways in which class has been discussed since the Brexit vote. 'Doesn't the insistence on provinciality and, by implication, whiteness and indigenousness (and, for that matter, maleness) merely strengthen the idea that class is a cultural category more than it is a material one?', he asks, during an analysis of

Cartwright's *Iron Towns*.[95] This is a very real danger and one skilfully examined by Kennedy, and discussed in my Introduction, as the crafting of a conservative, authentic, working class with 'legitimate concerns'. But that is not the image of the working class constructed across Cartwright's first three novels, with a focus on female working-class experience in *The Afterglow*, on the multi-ethnic, multi-racial community of Cinderheath in *Heartland*, and the attempt to figure new ways to understand Thatcherism and deindustrialisation in *How I Killed Margaret Thatcher*. Kennedy argues that Cartwright 'rails against the "social divide" between the capital and the provinces from the perspective of a writer loaded with cultural capital who only belatedly counsels against the "ignoring" of Not London'.[96] On the contrary, however, the loose Dudley trilogy is not a belated response, it represents a long process of tracking social and historical change as a dialectical process which accelerates at certain points, rather than being a simple case of cause and effect. And the social divide is understood as social inequality, not represented by the perceived differences between a metropolitan elite and a 'left behind', 'provincial' working class but symbolised by the material inequalities of class, exacerbated by the processes of deindustrialisation and the destruction wrought by neoliberalism. Cartwright's Dudley trilogy marks the end of Part One and what has been a mapping of deindustrialisation as a social and political process; the first three chapters have engaged with historicising figurations of what are conceptualised as the dynamics of capital. Part Two and the final three chapters will now shift that focus to examine ways in which the processes of demonisation released by such dynamics have been imaginatively and powerfully worked through by novels from Ross Raisin, Jenni Fagan, and Sunjeev Sahota.

Notes

1 Phil O'Brien, 'An Interview with Anthony Cartwright', *Contemporary Literature*, vol. 56, no. 3, Autumn 2015, pp. 397–420 (p. 416).
2 In 2016, Cartwright published *Iron Towns* which was quickly followed by a novella in 2017 titled *The Cut*. The former novel re-imagines the West Midlands through an evocation of historical myth and is centred around football and industrial memory. It is not set in Dudley whereas *The Cut*, written as a response to the EU Referendum, sees Cartwright return to his hometown for a fourth time. It covers much of the same ground as the first three Dudley novels, briefly mentioning Luke from *The Afterglow* and featuring the Clancey family. See *Iron Towns* (London: Serpent's Tail, 2016); *The Cut* (London: Peirene Press, 2017).
3 Hall, *Hard Road to Renewal*, p. 2.
4 Tony Davies, 'Unfinished Business: Realism and Working-Class Writing', in *The British Working-Class Novel*, ed. by Hawthorn, pp. 125–136 (p. 130).
5 Ibid., p. 129.
6 Adorno, 'Reading Balzac', pp. 122–123.
7 Paul McDonald, *Fiction from the Furnace: A Hundred Years of Black Country Writing* (Sheffield: Sheffield Hallam University Press, 2002), p. 5.
8 Ibid., p. 2.

9 Ibid., p. 7, p. 2.
10 Valentine Cunningham, '"In the Darg": Fiction Nails the Midlands Metal-worker', in *British Industrial Fictions*, ed. by H. Gustav Klaus and Stephen Knight (Cardiff: University of Wales Press, 2000), pp. 36–53 (p. 38).
11 Wayne, p. 159.
12 Ibid., p. 164.
13 Ibid., p. 157.
14 Ibid., p. 164.
15 Wayne, p. 166. Wayne argues that Britain's 'industrial identity remained a significant if troubled and increasingly embattled part of its economy and identity right through to the 1980s, when under Thatcherism, de-industrialisation set in with a vengeance' (pp. 9–10).
16 Phil O'Brien, 'The Deindustrial Novel: Twenty-First Century British Fiction and the Working Class', in *Working-Class Writing: Theory and Practice*, ed. by Ben Clarke and Nick Hubble (London: Palgrave Macmillan, 2018), p. 242.
17 Williams, *Towards 2000*, p. 94.
18 Ibid., p. 93.
19 O'Brien, 'The Deindustrial Novel, pp. 231–232.
20 David James, 'Relocating Mimesis: New Horizons for the British Regional Novel', *JNT: Journal of Narrative Theory*, vol. 36, no. 3, 2006, pp. 420–445 (p. 433).
21 Cartwright is now based in London. See O'Brien, 'An Interview with Anthony Cartwright', p. 398.
22 Raymond Williams, 'Region and Class in the Novel', in *The Uses of Fiction: Essays on the Modern Novel in Honour of Arnold Kettle*, ed. by Douglas Jefferson and Graham Martin (Milton Keynes: Open University Press, 1982), pp. 59–68 (p. 66).
23 James, 'Relocating Mimesis', p. 432.
24 O'Brien, 'An Interview with Anthony Cartwright', pp. 407–408.
25 Williams, 'Region and Class in the Novel', p. 67.
26 Kirk, p. 160, p. 147.
27 I use the term idiolect here to refer to the individual voice of Cartwright's characters, constructed through the accent, grammar, and cadences specific to the Dudley dialect.
28 See O'Brien, 'An Interview with Anthony Cartwright', p. 406.
29 See James Kelman, *'And the Judges Said...' Essays* (London: Secker & Warburg, 2002), p. 40.
30 Ibid., p. 37.
31 Raymond Williams, *Keywords: A Vocabulary of Culture and Society* (London: Fontana Press, 1988), p. 105.
32 Tony Crowley, *Standard English and the Politics of Language* (Basingstoke: Palgrave Macmillan, 2003), p. 84.
33 Voloshinov argues that it is in the multi-accentuality of signs (the multiple meanings of words) that the 'last glimmers of life' and the dynamics of class struggle are to be found. He adds: 'The ruling class strives to impart a supra-class, eternal character to the ideological sign, to extinguish or drive inward the struggle between social value judgments which occurs in it, to make the sign uni-accentual'. See V. N. Voloshinov, *Marxism and the Philosophy of Language* (Cambridge, MA: Harvard University Press, 1986), p. 23.
34 Crowley, p. 8.
35 Jeremy Scott, *The Demotic Voice in Contemporary British Fiction* (Basingstoke: Palgrave Macmillan, 2009), p. 10.

36 Geoff Stevens, 'Black Country Dialect Poets', *The Blackcountryman*, vol. 5, no. 2, 1972, pp. 43–44 (p. 44).

37 McDonald, p. 98.

38 Valentine Cunningham refers specifically to Disraeli's shock at reading such 'linguistic otherness' as recorded by the British Government's Children's Employment Commission of 1842, a report into living conditions in the Midlands which formed part of his research for *Sybil* (1845). See Valentine Cunningham, 'In the Darg', p. 49.

39 Heath is a suffix common to the West Midlands: there is Cradley Heath as well as Wall Heath, Kings Heath, and Balsall Heath. Further, this technique of renaming is also calling on a tradition within Black Country writing; writers like Ellen Thorneycroft Fowler and Francis Brett Young, for example, used names for towns which 'suggest parallels with real places'. See McDonald, p. 37.

40 Raymond Williams, 'The Welsh Industrial Novel', in *Culture and Materialism: Selected Essays* (London: Verso, 2005), p. 222.

41 Anthony Cartwright, *How I Killed Margaret Thatcher* (Birmingham: Tindal Street Press, 2012), p. 168.

42 Antony Rowland, *Poetry as Testimony: Witnessing and Memory in Twentieth-Century Poems* (London: Routledge, 2014), p. 100.

43 Ibid., p. 100.

44 See Lauren Berlant, *Cruel Optimism* (Durham, NC: Duke University Press, 2011).

45 Pierre Bourdieu, et al., *The Weight of the World* (Stanford, CA: Stanford University Press, 1999), p. 4.

46 Anthony Cartwright, *The Afterglow* (Birmingham: Tindal Street Press, 2004), p. 155.

47 Ibid., p. 166.

48 Tim Strangleman, '"Smokestack Nostalgia," "Ruin Porn" or Working-Class Obituary: The Role and Meaning of Deindustrial Representation', *International Labor and Working-Class History*, vol. 84, 2013, pp. 23–37 (p. 25, p. 29).

49 Cartwright, *Afterglow*, p. 155.

50 Sheila Rowbotham, *Woman's Consciousness, Man's World* (Harmondsworth: Penguin, 1973), p. xv.

51 Cartwright, *Afterglow*, p. 226.

52 As quoted in Alistair J. Reid and Henry Pilling, *A Short History of the Labour Party* (Basingstoke: Palgrave Macmillan, 2005), p. 37.

53 Ibid., p. 181.

54 See Laybourn, pp. 150–151; Reid and Pilling, p. 181.

55 See Cartwright, *The Afterglow*, pp. 214–215.

56 Wayne, p. 176.

57 Virdee, p. 150.

58 Gilroy, p. xxxviii. The radical potential of everyday banality is problematised, however, by a similar and equally convincing description from Renni Eddo-Lodge of how racism works: 'It looks normal. It is pedestrian. It is unquestioned. It's just a part of the landscape, you might walk past it every day'. See Eddo-Lodge, p. 132.

59 Steven Fielding, *A State of Play: British Politics on Screen, Stage and Page, from Anthony Trollope to The Thick of it* (London: Bloomsbury, 2014), p. 242.

60 Anthony Cartwright, *Heartland* (Birmingham: Tindal Street Press, 2010), p. 51.

61 Hall, *Hard Road to Renewal*, p. 5.
62 Kaplan, p. 100.
63 Ibid., p. 100, p. 101.
64 Mulhern applauds multiculturalism as 'an unprecedented attempt to acknowledge and embrace the historical fact of a multi-racial society'. He adds: 'It has been an important, if sometimes ambiguous, favouring condition of the struggle against racism'. See Francis Mulhern, '*Culture and Society*, Then and Now', *New Left Review*, vol. 55, 2009, pp. 31–45 (p. 41).
65 Mulhern, p. 41.
66 Owen Jones, p. 103.
67 Daniel Trilling, *Bloody Nasty People: The Rise of Britain's Far Right* (London: Verso, 2013), p. 145.
68 Ibid., p. 141.
69 Harvey, *A Brief History of Neoliberalism*, p. 171.
70 O'Brien, 'An Interview with Anthony Cartwright', p. 415.
71 Virdee, p. 116.
72 Virdee notes that less than a decade after Powell's infamous 'Rivers of Blood' speech, 'parts of the organized working class had undergone a dramatic, organic transformation in their political consciousness' and 'moved towards a more inclusive language of class that could [...] also encompass racialized minority workers' (p. 135).
73 See Virdee, p. 119 and Ramdin, pp. 408–409.
74 Trilling, p. 75.
75 Arun Kundnani, writing in 2014, noted how the English Defence League (EDL) has since replaced the BNP by building upon but also reversing some of these changes enacted by the BNP under Griffin. Notably, EDL figurehead Stephen Yaxley-Lennon (Tommy Robinson), is a former BNP member. Kundnani writes:

> In the last few years, the BNP's organizing capacity has been severely reduced, firstly by the leaking of its membership list and secondly by the financial burden of defending itself against a legal challenge to its racist membership policy. But these tactics targeted the messenger, not the message, allowing others to pick up where the BNP had left off. As it turned out, the EDL was well placed to do so. It had not organized as a conventional party and had no formal members, so it was less vulnerable to the tactics that had been partially effective against the BNP. (Arun Kundnani, *The Muslims Are Coming! Islamophobia, Extremism, and the Domestic War on Terror* [London: Verso, 2015], p. 244)

76 Trilling, p. 71, p. 76.
77 Ibid., p. 75.
78 Ibid., p. 206.
79 Cartwright, *Heartland*, p. 260.
80 Ibid., p. 260.
81 O'Brien, 'An Interview with Anthony Cartwright', p. 416, p. 417.
82 Lukács, p. 18.
83 Tony Davies, p. 128.
84 Lukács, p. 56.
85 Ibid., p. 46.
86 Cartwright, *Thatcher*, p. 139.
87 Karl Marx, 'Critique of the Gotha Programme', in *Selected Works* by Karl Marx and Friedrich Engels (London: Lawrence and Wishart, 1968), pp. 319–335 (pp. 324–325).
88 Cartwright, *Thatcher*, p. 67.

89 Ibid., p. 214.
90 D.J. Taylor, 'La divine Thatcher: How Novelists Responded to Maggie', *The Guardian*, 19 June 2015, www.theguardian.com/books/2015/jun/19/margaret-thatcher-1980s-how-novelists-responsed.
91 Louisa Hadley and Elizabeth Ho, '"The Lady's Not for Turning": New Cultural Perspectives on Thatcher and Thatcherism', in *Thatcher & After: Margaret Thatcher and Her Afterlife in Contemporary Culture*, ed. by Louisa Hadley and Elizabeth Ho (Basingstoke: Palgrave Macmillan, 2010), pp. 1–26 (p. 4).
92 Lukács, pp. 76–77.
93 Damian Barr, *Maggie & Me* (London: Bloomsbury, 2013); Hilary Mantel, 'The Assassination of Margaret Thatcher', in *The Assassination of Margaret Thatcher: Stories* by Hilary Mantel (London: 4th Estate, 2014), pp. 203–242.
94 Cartwright, *Thatcher*, p. 173.
95 Kennedy, pp. 107–108.
96 Ibid., p. 107.

Part 2

Resisting Demonisation

4 Ross Raisin and Class Mourning
Masculinity, Work, Precarity

Ross Raisin's 2011 novel *Waterline* takes up a significant position in this book. My reading of it, which begins Part Two of *The Working Class and Twenty-First-Century British Fiction*, brings together the concerns of the previous chapters – class struggle and industrial action (Chapter One), nostalgia and class memory (Chapter Two), deindustrialisation and trauma (Chapter Three) – and provides a transition to the notions of social abjection and the intersections of class, race, and gender which I explore more extensively in Chapters Five and Six. It is a novel in which the central character Mike Little traverses 'a hostile, alienated geography where community has ceased to exist and only "the economy" remains', according to Alan Warner's review.[1] Mick's diminutive surname connotes the effect of this development: his life, identity, and sense of self reduced to very little. He is a former Glaswegian shipbuilder, a man made homeless by the forces of deindustrialisation, workplace disease, and the disintegration of his community. So, in some ways it appears to be specifically about white, male, industrial working-class experience. But much of its value lies in the way such a narrative intersects more expansively with gender, race, and precarity through a thematic engagement with the uneven developments of neoliberalism. I begin by positioning *Waterline* in relation to James Kelman, an enabling presence in Raisin's work, before examining the novel's engagement with the Upper Clyde Shipbuilders Work-In of 1971/1972 (a primal scene of neoliberalism), left-wing melancholia, trauma, and shame as forms of working-class masculinity, the destructive legacies of class patriarchy, the racialisation of labour, the precarity of migrant work, and the making of a global working class. A move through these connecting themes plots a way forward to the concerns of the concluding two chapters, drawing together the pressures specific to class experience in order to illuminate an understanding of how class stigma has evolved into the form it takes in twenty-first-century Britain.

Raisin is an English writer who has turned to the traditions of contemporary Scottish fiction in order to write about a working-class experience of neoliberalism. This is not only in terms of voicings and language, using James Kelman as a model to write in the demotic, but also as a source of subject matter and narrative focus. Mick Little evokes the tradition of working-class militancy on the River Clyde and the sense of community and class identity which built up around the shipyards in industrial Scotland's central west belt. A third-person narrative aligns itself closely with Mick by way of flashbacks, dreams, day-dreams, and memories. These personal moments of recollection, at times actively sought but also repressed by grief, lay stress on the collective experiences of the workers and their community. They are brief anecdotes of ship launches and militant action, of family life, and an active social milieu. Mick's memories are populated by people but the present is barren, devoid of human contact or support. After he is made redundant from his job as a plater in the shipyard, he is employed as a taxi driver, his wife dies and he spirals into a cycle of mourning and depression, and then works briefly in London before becoming homeless on the streets of the English capital. By grounding the narrative in the distinctive cadences and intonations of Glaswegian, Raisin's use of language in *Waterline* is reminiscent of much of Kelman's work: his first novel *The Busconductor Hines* (1984) in particular, and, for its evocation of Clydeside, *Kieron Smith, Boy* (2008). Clipped words ('da' for 'dad' and 'no' for 'not'), the use of 'weans' for children, 'messages' to describe the shops and groceries, the deferred deployment of 'but' and 'just' to give sentences an abrupt end, all of these linguistic registers used by Raisin can also be found in Kelman's writing. It is a style which places the text within the community it depicts. And it is similar to an approach which in many ways has defined Kelman's career. In his essay 'Elitism and English Literature, Speaking as a Writer', he sarcastically describes how 'received wisdom' demands that an author 'go and write a story, whatever story you want, but do not use whatever language is necessary. [...] Write a story wherein people are talking, but not talking the language they talk'.[2] Kelman's challenge to such assumptions is a method to which Raisin has been drawn; in a striking echo of Kelman, he told *The Telegraph*: 'Each character has a particular language from a specific place and it's very necessary to use that language [...]. It's dishonest not to, and odd not to, and irresponsible not to'.[3]

So, *Waterline* demonstrates a commitment to write about and from not only the margins but also the everyday and the ordinary; it is part of what H. Gustav Klaus has defined in Kelman's writing as an 'egalitarian strategy to avoid anything that would present vernacular voices as inferior'.[4] And, as discussed in Chapter Three, it is a commitment Cartwright shares. However, the different approaches taken by Raisin and Cartwright are also instructive. Whereas the language of the latter's third-person narrator is in Standard English and his characters speak in the accent and dialect of Dudley, crucially without the use of speech marks in order to present both as equivalents, Raisin has Glaswegian direct discourse intertwine with sections of third-person narration. For example, the following extract describes a young shipyard apprentice (Joe) looking out over Clydeside from his high-rise flat:

> From up on the seventeenth storey, the view's a beauty. [...] Joe doesn't much look out at these things though. If he's looking out, it'll be at Ibrox. The ground's a few minutes' walk from the multi just. [...] This morning but he's having a see out the window'.[5]

It is through the use of free indirect discourse that *Waterline* articulates the urban Scots which Joe, Mick Little, and the hybrid narrative voice share: the use of 'a beauty', 'just', and 'but' are all registers which point to this distinctive demotic. The above passage also evokes the community out of which this voice emerges: industrial working-class Glasgow. And it is suggestive of what Kelman has described as 'trying to get down to that level of pure objectivity. This is *the* reality here, within this culture'.[6] Therefore, Raisin has been directly influenced by the Scottish writer in terms of accessing contemporary working-class experience and subjectivity through the deployment of a specific hybrid form of narrative discourse but it is also in its subject matter that *Waterline* suggests further comparisons to Kelman. One central strand of the text concerns the legacy of industrial capitalism and, in particular, industrial disease: Mick's wife Cathy dies from lung cancer (mesothelioma) contracted from exposure to asbestos on Mick's overalls which she would wash at the end of each working day. This is very much Kelman territory. He has worked with and spoken on behalf of the charity Clydeside Action on Asbestos.[7] I shall return to these connections when looking at Cathy's experiences in more detail below but it is worth noting here that Raisin shares this sense of political commitment with his Scottish counterpart. And this relates back, once more, to language. While commenting on his research into the intonations and cadences of urban Scots, Raisin has spoken of his involvement with Clydebank Asbestos Group. 'I made a real effort to get it right [...]', Raisin has said. 'By listening to people, simple as that. I interviewed them about asbestos, shipbuilding'.[8] His novel engages directly with the history and legacy of industrial male and female working-class experience and how these are felt and understood in the twenty-first century.

The narrative in *Waterline* is intermittently traced back, from the present, to the days when the streets around the Clyde were 'mobbed with hundreds of workers starting out for the day shift' (9). Tellingly, it is to a specific and illuminating moment in the history of working-class political struggle that Mick Little repeatedly returns: the Upper Clyde Shipbuilders (UCS) Work-In. Again, this is Kelman territory: geographically, socially, and politically. In 1971, following decades of deliberate and managed decline on behalf of the British Government, the Conservative

Party, led by Edward Heath, sought the closure of the four yards which made Upper Clyde Shipbuilders: Govan, Linthouse, Scotstoun, and John Brown.[9] As a reaction to the impending closure of the shipyards, and the potential loss of thousands of jobs, the shop stewards, led by Jimmy Reid, Jimmy Airlie, and Sam Barr, organised a working occupation. This involved taking the yards over, re-employing laid-off workers, and continuing to build ships in a radical move to prove that there was a viable and economic future for shipbuilding on the River Clyde. The communities in which the yards were located almost exclusively relied on this industry and, therefore, had a significant amount to lose from liquidation. The response of the work-in, which lasted for sixteen months, was part of what became a wider movement to challenge the 'loss of control over the economy, the destruction of existing industry and the erosion of the most crucial political gain of the post-war period, the right to work'.[10] The actions of the shipyard workers, supported locally by a strong working-class community base, eventually persuaded Heath to perform a U-turn and provide thirty-five million pound in government assistance to save three of the four yards: Govan, Linthouse, and Scotstoun. A separate yet significant incentive package was also provided to American company Marathon Oil to buy John Brown. The work-in is an important but often over-looked moment in post-war British history. It made international news throughout 1971 and 1972, receiving support from the likes of John Lennon and Yoko Ono,[11] and saw Jimmy Reid elected Rector of Glasgow University.[12] Crucially, it gave Heath his 'first major defeat at the hands of the working class', which along with the miners strikes of 1972 and 1974, culminated in his party losing the General Election of 1974.[13]

The year of *Waterline's* publication marked forty years since the start of the work-in and it is a historical event which repeatedly flashes up in the text and in Mick Little's memory.[14] Mick remembers it thus:

> When the work-in was starting [...], everybody heard about it. That's how it succeeded. Everybody joining together to support them – the miners, the Dutch, the Beatles – there'd been eighty thousand on the march through Glasgow. Eighty thousand! And, as well, they were actually building something then, they weren't striking, they were actually keeping the work going, how could anybody argue with that? (120–121)

There is a significant emphasis on the plural here: 'everybody' (used twice), 'they' (three times), 'them', and 'anybody'. And it is a memory full of people, 80,000 in this instance, and of positive and productive political action. Mick and his fellow workers are performing an act of defiance and, importantly, what is thought of as common sense: 'how could anybody argue with that?', for instance. This is not part of the logic of capital which will eventually see the yards shut down as part of a project of deindustrialisation. Further, the work-in as a social and political response emerges out of a profound sense of belonging felt by shipbuilders like Mick. This is indicated in *Waterline* by the repeatedly vivid descriptions of a life lived on Clydeside:

> [T]hat sense of the river always being there, around him, inside him. The sheer thrill of a ship on its stocks, grown from just a few small pieces of metal, walking toward it each morning and seeing that it was bigger, looking like it was parked there at the end of the street, looming over the end tenement. He can mind exactly the feeling of it. (97)

Again, there are similarities with the work of Cartwright here: the significance of the industrial landscape figured on an immense and sublime scale. But what is also important is the sense of self that this particular form of industry provides. It literally becomes Mick; the River Clyde is 'inside him', it defines who he is. And therefore, the dismantling of much of this landscape erodes Mick's identity and working-class subjectivity. But it continues to resonate with who and what he identifies as; he is still able to 'mind exactly the feeling of it'. Whereas, the UCS Work-In represents the working class affirming the right to work and exercising a powerful agency, the option to choose and to control is denied Mick in the present moment. So, why does *Waterline* repeatedly return to such a powerful and evocative memory of successful working-class political action? Whereas a novel such as *GB84* documents a symbolic defeat, what does a past yet momentous victory reveal about working-class agency in the twenty-first century?

It is the emphasis on the subjunctive element (the 'what if') intrinsic to the UCS Work-In which makes its inclusion in *Waterline* compelling. Raisin's novel explores the structural dynamics behind Mick Little's fall into homelessness; it adopts realist tendencies to depict his once stable domestic life (partly idealized by Mick, albeit through flashbacks) and there is due emphasis placed on his experiences on London's streets. The inclusion of the UCS Work-In within the narrative is not essential to such an approach; Mick could have worked at any number of yards or docks and during different time periods. Therefore, its presence is important for a number of reasons: it allows for a greater stress to be placed upon what life used to be like for Mick's Glaswegian community; it also suggests what political power the working class were once able to generate while raising hopes and doubts around the possibility of doing so again. In *Waterline*, the spirit of Clydeside in 1971/1972 is strongly evoked but it remains, for the likes of Mick at least, a distant and fractured part of historical memory. Finally, it also has a significant if largely unacknowledged role in the formation of a nascent neoliberal logic which developed into Thatcherism. Keith Joseph, one of Margaret Thatcher's closest allies in the Conservative Party, selected the UCS dispute as the first case study in 'industrial intervention' for the Centre for Policy Studies, a right wing think-tank Joseph set up alongside Thatcher in 1974 to promote neo-liberal economics. According to John Foster and Charles Woolfson, the think-tank was part of the 'meticulous preparation for a far more brutal and coercive use of state power against the working class'.[15] So here, in a sense, is a primal scene of neoliberalism. And Jimmy Reid's belief in the power of the working occupation as a response to such a mobilisation of right-wing agency was particularly prescient; he insisted that the forces of state and capital organised against the work-in sought to 'decimate communities and cast thousands of workers on to the dole queue and blight the future of the younger generations, forcing social upheaval and people leaving communities in search of their future'.[16] Subsequent attempts to curb union power were part of a wider neoliberal doctrine sought to deregulate, privatise, and remove state involvement from the heavy industries as part of a dynamic move towards deindustrialisation.

Mick meets the closure of the yards and the waves of redundancies, first experienced by himself at Clydebank and then later at Govan, thus:

> I am a shipbuilder. That right, eh? So what are ye now that the ship-yard has copped its whack and the job is away? I am a shipbuilder. Once a shipbuilder, always a shipbuilder, and all that tollie they'd told theyselves. No just the jobs that went, but the life. Ordinary life, it was gone; it had to be admitted. Himself a culprit. One of the worst. He wouldn't let go. Couldn't cope with the idea that things had changed. (89)

There is an assumption that if he repeats 'I am a shipbuilder' enough times then it will be true. Again, the novel provides access to Mick's thinking through the adoption of free indirect discourse. And what this formal approach is able to reveal are the doubts in his conceptions of selfhood: 'That right, eh?'. He is having this conversation with himself. And, crucially, Mick registers his own culpability. He describes himself as a 'culprit': an offender, a participant in his own demise. This suggests an internalisation of neoliberal logic, something examined throughout this book as a form of victim blaming which textual figurations of class are able to question and resist. In *Waterline*, it is the dismantling of the Clyde yards and with it their working-class communities which initiates Mick's decline; and the death of Cathy brings to the surface everything that he has lost. Further, the success of the work-in is now viewed with incredulity. He looks back on a time when his fellow worker and former shop steward Bertie used to stand 'up on his brazier with a hundred black squad around him, he'd have the whole yard in his spell' (69); but later: 'Hard to believe, looking at it now – at Bertie, old and trembling – that they'd won' (70). The self-assurance and confidence Mick once felt within a collective, working to produce some of the world's most famous ships, has been replaced by the precarious, anonymous nature of the service industry; he now drives a taxi for a living.

Whereas figures such as Bertie provide an everyday reminder of the shipyards, there is also a significant structure on the Clydebank skyline which evokes the industrial history of the area: the Titan Crane of the John Brown yard. Two textual figurations of the crane suggest illuminating ways of reading the deindustrial landscape: one is from *Waterline*, the other from a poem by Brian Whittingham which features in *A Rose Loupt Oot: Poetry and Song Celebrating the UCS Work-In*.[17] In the latter, titled simply 'The Titan Crane', Whittingham writes of 'ghosts of sprouting hulls [...], a shrill horn piercing the air and [...] spectres stampeding towards the gates'.[18] These are recalled by two former shipbuilders who visit the crane, now a tourist attraction which 'sits beside the empty dock'. The vista from the 150ft-high platform offers a 'bird's-eye view of desolation', 'a barren panorama of rubble and nothingness'[19] For Whittingham, the crane acts as an apposite signifier:

> In the jib's machine room
> the gears and wires and wheels
> of the once mighty crane
> are still and silent and dead.[20]

The accumulative effect of 'and' (used twice) enhances the sense of industry and movement which is evoked in the second line. This technique is then repeated in the stanza's concluding line but, in contrast, it is deployed to connote a grinding, haunting halt. An emphasis is placed on how one has replaced the other: there is now a disabling inertia where there was once enabling activity. And the familiar has become unfamiliar; a symbol of the industrial Clydeside is now a spectral, mocking figure.[21] It is the latter which is evoked by Raisin's novel: the crane as a cruel joke. He writes of Mick:

> He's heard about the crane. Turned into a visitor centre. He's seen it lit up pink and red at night [...]. [T]hey were talking about putting a restaurant in the jib and making it revolve. [...] It was part of a project to represent the industrial heritage of the area. A revolving pink restaurant. (5)

History has been turned into spectacle as capitalism absorbs and guts it of its core. The Clyde waterfront on which the crane sits has been renamed Glasgow Harbour and transformed from a site of production into one of consumption: there are 'twinkling new apartment blocks' and a 'dry ski centre' (8). It is what David Harvey has labelled 'Disneyfication [...] coupled with gentrification'.[22] And the absurd pink revolving restaurant and ski centre are '[n]ew forms of niche consumerism and individualised lifestyles' which are 'built around a postmodern style of urbanisation'.[23] The new 'Harbour' symbolises the attempted gentrification, so prevalent under neoliberalism, of a working-class area. And the visitor centre is part of capital's safe packaging of history, transforming the complex past and present into a sterile heritage product; further, it is eliding the violence, struggle, and hardship experienced by the working class.

The wider redevelopment is one of the many forms of capital accumulation by dispossession. 'The transformation of cultures, histories [...] into commodities for sale', writes Harvey, 'entails dispossession both past and present of human creativity'.[24] Crucially, whereas the plan for the Titan Crane appears as a cruel joke played on the working class of the area, Mick returns the mockery with a quip of his own: 'if all you're looking out on is puddled wasteland every direction – [...] pigeons roosting and crapping over the rusted fabrication sheds – it isn't going to make your mozzarella parcels taste much better, is it?' (5). This takes the description offered by Whittingham's poem of 'desolation', 'rubble and nothingness', which is matched by Raisin's invocation of a 'puddled wasteland' and 'rusted [...] sheds', and reclaims partial control over it through the use of humour. In this way, Mick disrupts, momentarily at least, the broader project of gentrification. Kirsteen Paton has noted how gentrification 'is used as part of urban policy to "gentrify people", that is, to make their subjectivities and behaviours more congruent with the neoliberal principles of the economy'.[25] Mick resists such conditioning, exposing the incongruity of this form of 'regeneration' by deploying a parallelism of his own: comparing the façade of 'civilised' dining with the bleak reality of deindustrialisation.

In London, Mick is drawn to a similar deindustrial landscape. Raisin writes: 'One thing is for sure: they don't like you sitting down in this city. [...] They don't want you staying put; they want you rushing about' (143). The capital is a dehumanising place, an environment within which he has to be continually on the move. There is a notable absence of free public space. The few options are places such as shops, pubs, and cafes which are available only to a fee-paying public. Mick gravitates to the riverside and a derelict Battersea landmark: 'And right there on the opposite bank, the genuine shocking sight of a massive red brick power station [...]. A kind of peacefulness about things here' (148). This site offers some sense of security in an otherwise disorientating landscape, and he achieves a fleeting mental stability from being near such a spectral symbol of industry and labour. But the enormity of the decommissioned Battersea Power Station also offers unsettling memories of his home city and its gentrification. Raisin writes:

> One thing that must be admitted: it's bloody big. When did they close it? Who cares, what does it matter? It doesn't. Probably the

Milk Snatcher but. We don't want power stations, what we want instead is more apartment buildings. (158)

Again, there is the physical and metaphorical enormity of industrial ruins: the sheer scale of them demands attention. And 'Milk Snatcher' refers to Margaret Thatcher who infamously, as Education Secretary in 1971, scrapped universal free school milk. This is one of *Waterline's* many oblique references to the former Prime Minister, who is a haunting rather than a decisive figure in Mick's memory. It is the landscape itself which provides greater insight into historical, social, and political change. And the comparison between Battersea and Glasgow Harbour is here explicit: a former industrial site which once provided thousands of jobs transformed by global capital into a twenty-first-century prestige destination. The coal-fired power station ceased production in 1983 and proposals to convert it into an indoor theme park based upon Britain's industrial heritage later collapsed. Shops, offices, and luxury homes have since been built in and around the once derelict structure with prices ranging up to more than six million pound for a penthouse apartment. The closure of such sites is figured in *Waterline* as depriving the working class of a livelihood while the subsequent regeneration excludes a local community often in need of jobs, affordable homes, and public space.

The landscape in *Waterline* is notably deindustrial but, crucially, there is still industrial work; it is not post-industrial. Two of the four sites which were formerly part of the Upper Clyde Shipbuilders remain, albeit in a drastically reduced capacity. Raisin describes these as 'the shipyards, what's left of them' (8). And this is a Glaswegian landscape in which everything points to the yards, 'the streets that run straight lines toward the river' (8). The novel imagines what these streets were like at the height of shipbuilding on the Clyde: 'The noise of boots on the road, the hooter about to sound up the way and signal the start of work [...] the whole black squad marching on up the road' (9). This scene is then compared with the present moment and a strategic break created by the start of a new paragraph emphasises how different the experiences are for a couple of young apprentices heading to the riverside: 'A different story the now. Two lads in blue overalls walking through the empty streets like a pair of convicts who've just survived the end of the world' (9–10). So, this is a landscape haunted by ghostly figures: the Titan Crane as discussed above and the seemingly dissonant presence of a pair of apprentices. These young men are imbued with a sense of what this landscape represents. 'Their fathers and grandfathers have shown them enough photographs [...] how it used to be' (9), writes Raisin. It is a second-hand memory of the same streets but looked at from the perspective of the deindustrialised present; once reliable and familiar sights and sounds are now unfamiliar and strange. And it is through such emotive recollections that *Waterline* engages with trauma. According to Roger

Luckhurst, traumatic memory exists as 'a half-life, rather like a ghost, a haunting absent presence of another time in our time'.[26] The traumatised subject often seeks solace in residual images: partial or left-over memories which form part of traumatic memory. 'Trauma, in effect, issues a challenge to the capacities of narrative knowledge', says Luckhurst. 'In its shock impact trauma is anti-narrative, but it also generates the manic production of retrospective narratives that seek to explicate the trauma'.[27] Such experiences, as they relate to the industrial working class in *Waterline*, are embodied in the elliptical evocations of the history of the Clydeside which repeatedly puncture the contemporary setting of Raisin's text. They are memories which will not be repressed. In comparison to Anthony Cartwright's engagement with everyday suffering, this is a traumatic experience released by a single, hugely significant event: the death of Mick's wife. And, further, it is a form of trauma which emerges through the lived processes of mourning.

'Mourning is commonly the reaction', Sigmund Freud has said, 'to the loss of a beloved person or an abstraction taking the place of the person, such as fatherland, freedom, an ideal'.[28] Mick's mourning is a reaction to the death of his wife Cathy ('a beloved person') but he also laments the loss of his 'fatherland' (Scotland and specifically, Glasgow), the 'freedom' provided by employment in the shipyards, and the working-class 'ideal' of the right to work. These are experiences which are all explored through traumatic memory. Luckhurst has described how this, in turn, can disrupt an individual's sense of self: '"[T]he traumatic event is persistently re-experienced" – through intrusive flashbacks, recurring dreams, or later situations that repeat or echo the original'.[29] In *Waterline*, images of Cathy cleaning his overalls encroach on Mick's dreams. There are also flashbacks of the yards and his previous spells of unemployment and day-dreams about famous ship launches and social gatherings. These recollections all confuse his sense of reality, his identity collapsing under this weight of uncertainty. And they disrupt a possible understanding of the present. Further, Mick borders on the state of melancholia, during which there is a 'disorder of self-esteem',[30] precipitated by a private and public loss. Here is a figure through which both individual trauma and collective trauma are explored; the latter described by Kai Erikson as 'a blow to the basic tissues of social life that damages the bonds attaching people together and impairs the prevailing sense of communality'.[31] But the blame Mick attributes to himself is a mixture of working-class male pride, shame, and the neoliberal mantra that personal failure is a result of personal failings. Again, this relates to Freud's description of melancholia as 'an extraordinary reduction in self-esteem'. Referring to his patients, Freud writes that, with melancholia, the individual feels 'worthless, incapable of functioning and morally reprehensible, he is filled with self-reproach, he levels insults against himself and expects ostracism and punishment'.[32] In comparison, Mick feels as though he has failed as the head of the household to provide for and protect his family. He blames himself for Cathy's death and absconds to London, unable to face the reality of a life in Glasgow without his wife. But as *Waterline* explores, it is unemployment and industrial disease which have created such a personal crisis, one which has been experienced on a profound scale in Mick's working-class community. And this moves the blame away from the neoliberal self and onto the dynamics of industrial capitalism. For example, the local cemetery in Glasgow provides macabre evidence of the alternative 'industrial heritage' of the Clyde shipyards. When Mick is seen by one of the graveyard staff attending to Cathy's grave, Raisin writes:

> That whole length of path is lined with the names of yardmen, copped their whack before their time. A whole shop floor under that lawn, he'd heard the registrar say a while back, and it would be true enough, except that so many of them are the wives and weans. (21–22)

This is a very different type of yard to the ones which made Clydeside. And it is an experience which is in stark contrast to the lifestyle choices now available at Glasgow Harbour. In an analysis of Beatrix Campbell's *Wigan Pier Revisited: Poverty and Politics in the 80s*, Ian Haywood has noted that, according to Campbell, 'working-class women have always been the true repositories of the proletarian condition'.[33] This is played out to devastating, literal effect in *Waterline*. Cathy Little supports her husband during the work-in, his spells of unemployment, and his decision to move to Australia and England to find work. And like the 'wives and weans' in the above extract, she was exposed to the asbestos used in the shipyards. Not only is this exposure due to the patriarchal structures of the working-class family, and the pressures placed upon her as a working-class woman, but also the actions of Scottish capital and the Clyde shipping magnates. According to Kelman, the latter 'knowingly and cynically exposed tens of thousands of Clydeside workers to one of the deadliest substances known to humankind'.[34] But as *Waterline* asserts, it was not simply 'Clydeside workers' who were exposed but whole families. Raisin's novel is engaging with the destructive legacies of working-class patriarchy and industrial disease as well as with the ongoing campaign for recognition of and justice for mesothelioma victims.

In contrast, the presence of the UCS Work-In provides a seemingly more positive evocation of working-class history. However, in the present moment – the early-twenty-first-century setting of the novel – to what extent does Raisin's novel, to use Walter Benjamin's phrase, fan or set alight a 'spark of hope in the past'?[35] Benjamin's concept of history is useful here, not least because for Mick the working occupation of 1971/1972 is a memory which he attempts 'to seize hold of [...] as it flashes up at a moment of danger'.[36] This raises significant questions around what uses such a memory can have. There is a danger here of what Benjamin labelled left-wing melancholy in his 1931 essay of the same name.[37] It is one which Wendy Brown has described as 'left traditionalism', of seeking solutions to contemporary problems through out-dated political assumptions and positions.[38] Brown echoes Stuart Hall's assessment: that the left must address capitalism as it is today and, therefore, seek to understand its relentless, evolving dynamics. Brown writes that a failure to do so could leave the left 'caught in a structure of melancholic attachment to a certain strain of its own dead past, whose spirit is ghostly, whose structure of desire is backward looking and punishing'.[39] Crucially, for Mick in *Waterline* the disabling processes of mourning and melancholy relate not only to a very personal loss but also the longing for a type of political action which in the past has resulted in victory. There is an important difference here to Benjamin and Brown's conceptions of left-wing melancholy, a concept which relates specifically to an obsession with defeat on the left rather than a victory such as the work-in.

Immediately following the flash of memory concerning the working occupation described earlier, when he remembers how 80,000 marched through Glasgow, Mick is drawn back to his present-day situation in an airport hotel on the outskirts of London. Raisin writes: 'A strange kind of work-in it would be if they tried that here, scrubbing lavvies that haven't been sat on, plates that no food has touched' (121). For Mick, the past provides a form of solace and pride but it does not supply him with a way of addressing the problems of the present. Rather, this disjuncture allows the novel to explore the contemporary working-class experience of a distinctive form of neoliberal capitalism.

Mick becomes part of a sectionalised, non-unionised workforce at an airport hotel where he is employed as a kitchen porter. When the housekeepers congregate in the staff room to discuss their grievances concerning a change in work and pay conditions, he joins the meeting out of a mixture of curiosity and solidarity:

> He claps with them. It feels good, being part of it. At the same time
> but, there's a sense of being cut off, all of them, cut off. They're
> clapping in a basement and there's nobody else here. It's hard no to
> think how small they are. (120)

Such a profound feeling of powerlessness is a manifestation of the difficulty facing this contemporary working class of being able to place its oppressor. Hence, the comparison between the boss, who sacks the staff for holding an unauthorised meeting, and Margaret Thatcher: 'She stands there just, the arms folded, triumphant, the Iron fucking Lady' (129). Again, there is a danger here, as detailed in the last chapter, of placing the blame onto a caricature of one identifiable villain. However, the emphasis in such passages is not on a mythical individual but on a profound sense of being 'cut off' which, tellingly, is reflected by the physical landscape in which this precarious form of employment takes place. The hotel is located amongst a 'great tangle of carriageways and multi-storey car parks' (104); it is a confusing space which, much like the industrial landscape in Glasgow, plays a constitutive role in terms of working-class subjectivity. What the passage reveals is a lack of agency; this contemporary working class is unable to orchestrate a challenge to a system that treats the workers as disposable and replaceable. In this way, the airport hotel staff, who work long hours on temporary, hourly-paid contracts, are members of what Guy Standing has defined as the precariat. He usefully identifies the defining features of such a 'new' class formation: a profound lack of protection against dismissal, accidents at work, changes to contracts, extensions to working hours, and aggressive management. Therefore, the lack of agency comes from a deliberate attack on workers' rights and trade union organisation. Jan Breman argues that due emphasis is not placed on such attacks by Standing who downplays the extent to which the crusade for "flexibility" has aimed not just to cheapen the price of labour but drastically to weaken its capacity for collective action. Entrenching artificial distinctions between different fractions of the working class is not the way to overcome this.[40]

So there is a significant risk here; the precariat is not a separate class and must be considered as part of the working class. But the way Standing describes labour in the twenty-first century does prove useful when reading *Waterline*. He identifies 'anger, anomie and alienation' as inevitable consequences of neoliberalism's approach to the labour market, in that it creates 'a society that has made "flexibility" and insecurity cornerstones of the economic system'.[41] Such 'flexibility' also makes it easier for both capital and the neoliberal state to mobilise against workers, who in both *Waterline* and the novels of Sunjeev Sahota are migrant workers buffeted by the market and by shifting definitions and notions of 'illegality'. The acceleration and expansion of precarity has been an essential part of global, neoliberal capitalism. In Chapter Six, I return to look at how this plays out within the service industry – where service is a form of servitude akin to Mick's job as a taxi driver – but it also finds a significant resonance in the experience of migrant workers in Raisin's novel.

In *Waterline*, globalisation is one reason given for the closure of the Glasgow yards; the Scottish shipbuilding firms are unable 'to keep up with the Japanese and the French and the Germans' (65). Crucially, the workforce that Mick Little momentarily joins in London is comprised of the 'global precariat'. The kitchen porters are predominantly from Africa, the housekeepers from South America, and the chefs and receptionists from Eastern Europe. It is a division of the workforce along lines of race, gender, and ethnicity; it is an example of how 'power relations within the collective labour process are distributed among different social groups' and how 'capitalists use the power of social differences to their own utmost advantage' according to Harvey.[42] One of Mick's colleagues in the kitchen is Dia, an accountant in his native Ghana. Raisin writes:

> Dia asks him about Scotland and Mick begins telling him about the yards [...]. It's surprising, in fact, how much he knows already. He knows all about the big boats that were made on the Clyde, which probably goes to bloody show what dark part some of these ships they made had to play in people like Dia's history. Mick realizes he doesn't know if Ghana has a coastline even. Pretty bloody ignorant, really, but he doesn't ask. (116)

Much of Glasgow's wealth in the eighteenth century was founded on the slave trade. The city provided a direct shipping route from the banks of the Clyde to the Caribbean and America. And Glaswegian merchants earned immense wealth by trading with plantations worked by African slaves.[43] These links to Africa can also be traced through the history of the British Empire: many black sailors, often from Sierra Leone and therefore British colonial subjects, made Glasgow their home and married white Scottish working-class women. 'Black people had lived and worked in the port area of the city for a number of years', notes Satnam Virdee, during an analysis of the racist riots on the Clyde in 1919. 'Against a backdrop of rising unemployment, many white seamen branded the "coloured" seamen as unfair economic competition'.[44] Such racism was both exploited and supported by some socialist Clydeside leaders, namely Manny Shinwell of the Independent Labour Party,[45] as well as actively challenged and 'vigorously opposed' by others on the left, specifically Arthur McManus (of the Socialist Labour Party) and John McLean (British Socialist Party).[46] Mick's friendship with Dia raises his consciousness of a wider historical, internationalist struggle then, as well as of the present-day inequalities, conditioned by gender, race, and ethnicity, inherent within the labour market. But what it also draws attention to is that while the shipbuilding communities which built up around the Clyde benefitted from British imperialism, one legacy of such heavy industry has been the oppression of other communities and nations elsewhere as well as a complicated history of working-class racism and anti-racism within Scotland.

Compellingly, what the workforce in the London hotel points towards is one of the many contradictions of neoliberal capitalism: the need for migrant labour at the same time as the crafting of a myth concerning the parasitic immigrant. Imogen Tyler has identified what she has called a 'liberal paradox': 'the opening up of international borders to flows of capital and the simultaneous "damning" of states and regions against "undesirable" migrants from the global South'. Crucially, this relates to 'a migratory pull which is paradoxically fuelled by market demands for cheap unregulated migrant labour in the global North'.[47] The abject figure is something addressed in greater detail in the following two chapters; here, however, the crafting of such a figure to justify the inequality of contemporary capitalism, eliding the contradictions in its construction, is important to consider when analysing Mick's experiences as a member of the migrant labour force and, later, as a homeless person on London's streets.

A term which is often deployed to describe such fluid class formations as a singular and identifiable group is the underclass. John Kirk argues that it is a highly dubious phrase used to serve particular ideological interests.[48] Further, John Welshman has shown how such a description of the working class emerges during periods of economic instability or restructuring, high levels of unemployment and poverty, and a growing sense of alienation;[49] crucially, it has often been part of a 'conservative analysis of the causes of social problems and their solutions'.[50] Further, it is a specific stereotype deployed to describe a group of people as a 'race' rather than a 'class'. As discussed further in Chapter Six, 'race' is both socially and politically constructed; it is, as Paul Gilroy explains, deployed to perform 'elaborate ideological work' in order 'to secure and maintain the different forms of "racialisation" which have characterised capitalist development'.[51] The construction of 'race' as it connects to notions of the 'underclass' is not always predicated on skin colour or ethnicity. But, it is a term which attempts to essentialise a diverse set of people. Again, Tyler is useful here: 'It is because the underclass are imagined as a *race* and not a class that poverty and disadvantage can be conceived as not economic or even properly political issues, but as a *hereditary condition*, a *disease*'.[52] Underclass as a concept is a discursive phenomenon, one used 'not to define the marginalised, but to marginalise those it defines'.[53] It serves to place a group of people outside the constructed norms of society. As Tyler has argued, it 'describes an adjunct class divorced from the body politic proper'.[54] Raisin's novel figures this class experience as being a product of capitalism and specifically neoliberalism, rather than as a result of personal issues, failings, or a 'hereditary condition'. And, crucially, by tracing the shifting conditions of Mick Little's life, the text illuminates the way in which class distinctions evolve and shift; in the present moment, Mick is a member of the anonymous 'underclass' but he has also been part of the industrial working class, the unemployed, the precariat, and the migrant workforce. All of these stages in his life are connected and are conditioned by the dynamics of capital.

Tyler notes that if the 'lumpen', in Karl Marx's terminology, is 'the abject of the proletariat', then 'the feral underclass are the abject of neoliberal subject-citizens'.[55] *Waterline* draws attention to how such an abject is constructed and marginalised by adopting multiple perspectives throughout the narrative. Consequently, there are numerous instances in the novel when Mick is seen through the eyes of others. He is a 'tramp on the pavement' according to a teenage boy (202), a 'homeless man' with a 'crazed look on his face' to a civil servant (157), and described as drunk, bruised, and agitated by a volunteer from a homeless charity. The last of these, Martin, depicts Mick and his friend Keith, who Mick meets in a hostel, thus:

> They have come down from Glasgow, possibly together, although it has been quite difficult to build a clear picture. One of the men, Mick, keeps quiet while the other, Keith, is obviously the one that does the talking for them both. They have no plans, and nowhere to go, that much is clear. (209)

By using a third-person narrator, the difficulty of understanding from an external perspective how these two men have ended up on the streets is emphasised. And the use of Standard English adds to this sense of an exterior viewpoint being unable to articulate the experience of another who does not use such language. What *Waterline* does as a narrative is 'build a clear picture' from the interior and through the adoption of a voice (urban Scots) which is closer to the experiential understanding of its central character. Further, the outsider perspectives reveal the assumptions placed on those made abject by capitalism. Kelman has spoken of a dominant tradition within literary fiction of never giving an internal voice to working-class individuals, only to those who describe them. 'You only ever saw them or heard them', Kelman says. 'You never got into their mind. You did find them in the narrative but from the outside, never from the inside, always they were "the other"'.[56] There is an element of Raisin's novel 'othering' Mick through the adoption of intermittent descriptions of him as a 'tramp' which puncture his own narrative. Warner argues that such a formal construct is one which distinguishes Raisin's writing from Kelman's. 'This is a conceit that Kelman would never countenance', says Warner, 'a breach of the character's existential consciousness which confirms some greater and abstract hierarchy'.[57] Jeremy Scott has noted that in a novel such as *How late it was, how late* (1994), 'there is, ostensibly, *no* controlling and dominant narrator, and for [Kelman] this is the only ideologically acceptable mode of authorship'.[58] In *Waterline*, a sense of the hierarchical is evoked but, importantly, Raisin uses it to disrupt the inscription of value onto Mick which is being performed by the presence of exterior voices. For example, the civil servant, an advisor in the Department for Business, who is wary of Mick's 'crazed eyes' is described as 'a fat man in a suit'. 'He's kidding on he can't see him but', thinks Mick. '[...] Go on, ye cunt, look at me. Think I give a fuck, eh?' (149–150). The novel, through its narrative structure, is undercutting and resisting any potential 'othering' of a working-class character like Mick by (quite literally) returning the gaze back onto those who contribute to such processes while also drawing attention to how the abject figure is constructed. A similar reversal is performed when Mick first meets Keith, a fellow Glaswegian to whom he gives the nickname Beans due to the latter's rant about the hostel's breakfast: 'How can somebody like that look at him and think – aye, there's a guy that's on my wavelength? No point dwelling on it but. Probably a headbanger' (156). Mick, in this instance as the one who inscribes negative value on to another, is incredulous that Keith sees him as an equal. However, the pair quickly become friends, based partially on shared experiences pertaining to class, gender, and ethnicity, and they form a bond that acts as a protection from the uncertainty of London. And, crucially, it is through the character of Keith that the violence of the streets is explored. Asleep on a park bench with Mick, he is attacked and set on fire. Raisin writes: 'He's alive but. [...] Mick pulls off the shreds of his jacket and his shirt, [...] takes off his own coat and rests it on top, lying down beside him, his hands stinging' (193). This incident alters the dynamic of the relationship between the two men: the fact that he is able to help Keith gives Mick some sense of agency again.

Towards the end of the novel, in what could be read as a 'happy' ending, Mick finds a flat and is reunited with his family through a missing persons charity; the penultimate chapter describes him going to buy a present for his grandson who he has been invited, by his son Robbie, to visit in Australia (although it is left unclear if he goes or not). One review of *Waterline* complained that 'the upward turn towards the end feels merely unconvincing as opposed to welcome relief'.[59] And this upturn does risk dealing with homelessness as a temporary problem, one with a simple solution, rather than a long-term issue which can only be addressed through the complex processes at work. And it evokes a type of sentimentality which Raisin has explicitly stated he wished to avoid.[60] As Michael Denning has noted in his study of the American Dime Novel, 'the happy ending was a sign that all was right in the world, that everything worked out in the end'.[61] But, Denning argues, such endings can also be more complex than suggesting mere conformity or convention. He suggests that 'the suspicion of happy endings is often taken too far'.[62] The unhappy ending also needs to be approached with caution, Denning suggests; in relation to 'a certain bourgeois "realism"', he notes, they 'are often simply the conventions of an aesthetic of slumming, static depictions of degradation'.[63] Mick's narrative ends in the novel's penultimate chapter with a hesitantly hopeful scenario: the possible trip to Australia. In contrast, the final chapter suggests a more disturbing conclusion. A homeless man is described as lying asleep, quite probably dead, on a beach. The description of this unnamed man suggests that it is Keith

(Beans): 'a dirty red woollen hat pulled down over his face, which is bruised and bloodshot, a pink scar running down his cheek and neck and under his coat' (262). The seaside resort is also anonymous. Importantly, this final chapter, unlike all of the previous forty-two, is unnumbered. Together with the unnamed body on the beach in an unspecified location, this adds to a sense of Keith being overlooked, ignored, another person lost and excluded. And this is implied in the movement of the runner, through whose perspective Keith is seen: 'He stops, just for a moment, and then begins again into a jog' (262). Raisin has spoken of how such a perspective was what he wanted to disrupt through the narrative of Mick:

> It was always going to be about homelessness and grief, but I started off with a specific idea: how a person becomes more and more distanced from the world they inhabited, to the point where the world around them no longer views them as an individual but as a type. But I wanted to make sure that person is very much always an individual in the narrative.[64]

What the ending draws attention to is that not everyone is in a position to resist such abjection; while Mick escapes his life on the streets, his friend Keith seemingly succumbs to the extreme risks of being forced to live in such a way; he is not allowed, by the societal structures in place, the opportunity to 'escape'.

The resistance of Mick, and equally of *Waterline* as a text, to a neo-liberal inscription of negative value onto the working-class individual provides an illuminating link to the work of Jenni Fagan and Sunjeev Sahota. Mick is aware that contemporary capitalism, in order to dismiss him as a social abject, inscribes a specific meaning to him:

> Only if he accepts that he is part of this, that he belongs here, will he be done for. Because if he does that, then there'll be no control over it, and he may as well throw in the towel. (159)

Mick is striving to regain a sense of control which has been taken from him, and in this he shares a response with the central characters of *The Panopticon, Ours are the Streets*, and *The Year of the Runaways*: an ability to name, place, and resist the forms of class oppression and inequality which dramatically shape life in twenty-first-century Britain.

Notes

1 Alan Warner, '*Waterline* by Ross Raisin – review', *The Guardian*, 13 July 2011, www.guardian.co.uk/books/2011/jul/13/waterline-ross-raisin-review.
2 Kelman, '*And the Judges Said*', pp. 64–65.

3 Genevieve Fox, "'I Wanted to Be Truthful and Authentic': Book Club Interview with Ross Raisin', *The Telegraph*, 2 December 2011, www.telegraph.co.uk/culture/books/bookclub/8930921/I-wanted-to-be-truthful-and-authentic-Book-Club-Interview-with-Ross-Raisin.html.

4 H. Gustav Klaus, *James Kelman* (Plymouth: Northcote, 2004), p. 15.

5 Ross Raisin, *Waterline* (London: Penguin, 2011), p. 8. References for further quotations taken from *Waterline* will be provided in parentheses.

6 Kelman quoted in Klaus, *James Kelman*, p. 7.

7 See James Kelman, 'A Note on the War Being Waged by the State against the Victims of Asbestos', in *Some Recent Attacks*, by James Kelman (Stirling: AK Press, 1992), pp. 59–63.

8 See Fox, *The Telegraph*, 2 December 2011. Raisin thanks Clydebank Asbestos Group in his acknowledgements at the back of *Waterline*. See Raisin, p. 263.

9 In *Waterline*, Mick is a former employee of John Brown in Clydebank, a yard internationally renowned for building the Queen Mary, Queen Elizabeth, and the QE2. Also, James Kelman is from Govan.

10 John Foster and Charles Woolfson, *The Politics of the UCS Work-in* (London: Lawrence and Wishart, 1986), p. 210.

11 Ibid., p. 204.

12 Reid became a prominent public and political figure. His inaugural speech as Rector concerning alienation was famously published in its entirety in the *New York Times*. See Carol Craig, *The Tears that Made the Clyde: Wellbeing in Glasgow* (Argyll: Argyll Publishing, 2010), p. 300.

13 Foster and Woolfson, p. 380.

14 Again in his acknowledgements, Raisin thanks Jimmy Cloughley who was on the UCS Work-In's organising committee. See Raisin, p. 263.

15 Foster and Woolfson, pp. 401–402.

16 Ibid., p. 227.

17 *A Rose Loupt Oot* features a collection of songs and poems written and performed in support of and to commemorate and celebrate the work-in. It is an attempt to resist the historical erasure of the work-in by seeking to explore 'how relevant to today's struggles similar broad alliances are'. It was collated not only to mark the achievements of the shipyard workers but also to look 'beyond the often prosaic and messy details of political action to its potential, its promise, its "hidden hert o' beauty"'. See David Betteridge, 'Introduction', in *A Rose Loupt Oot: Poetry and Song Celebrating the UCS Work-in*, ed. by David Betteridge (Middlesbrough: Smokestack Books, 2011), pp. 21–31 (p. 23, p. 30).

18 Brian Whittingham, 'The Titan Crane', in *A Rose Loupt Oot*, ed. by Betteridge, p. 120.

19 Ibid., p. 119.

20 Ibid.

21 Two other poems in *A Rose Loupt Oot* figure the Titan Crane more positively. Jim Aitken's 'Clearances: a Diptych' describes it as a 'memorial', 'proud' and inspiring, while Danny McCafferty's 'Fresh Chapter: The Titan Crane, Clydebank' speaks of it as protecting the town, providing 'stubborn hope', '[u]nbroken and unbowed'. See *A Rose Loupt Oot*, ed. by Betteridge, p. 125 and p. 129 respectively.

22 Harvey, *The Enigma of Capital*, p. 131.

23 Ibid., p. 131.

24 Ibid., p. 245.

25 Kirsteen Paton quoted in Tyler, 'Classificatory Struggles', p. 501.

26 Roger Luckhurst, *The Trauma Question* (Abingdon: Routledge, 2008), p. 81.
27 Luckhurst, p. 79.
28 Sigmund Freud, 'Mourning and Melancholia', in *The Penguin Freud Reader*, ed. by Adam Phillips (London: Penguin, 2006), pp. 310–326 (p. 310).
29 This refers specifically to the first set of symptoms identified by the American Psychiatric Association concerning Post-Traumatic Stress Disorder. As Luckhurst notes, 'the second set of symptoms suggests the complete opposite: "a persistent avoidance of stimuli associated with the trauma" that can range from avoidance of thoughts or feelings related to a general sense of emotional numbing to the total absence of recall of the significant event'. See Luckhurst, p. 1.
30 Freud, p. 311.
31 Erikson quoted in Luckhurst, p. 10.
32 Freud, p. 313.
33 Haywood, p. 143. Campbell also warned of the dangers of 'epic nostalgia' within the socialist tradition, particularly concerning heavy industry, which often ignores the 'weary labours of women'. Campbell quoted in Haywood, p. 144. See Beatrix Campbell, *Wigan Pier Revisited: Poverty and Politics in the 80s* (London: Virago, 1984).
34 Kelman, *Some Recent Attacks*, p. 2.
35 Walter Benjamin, 'Theses on the Philosophy of History', in *Illuminations* by Benjamin, pp. 253–264 (p. 255).
36 Ibid., p. 255.
37 Walter Benjamin, 'Left-Wing Melancholy', in *Selected Writings Volume 2, 1927–1934* by Benjamin (Cambridge, MA: Harvard University Press, 1999), pp. 423–427.
38 Jodi Dean has argued that Brown misreads Benjamin. Dean says: 'Brown suggests a Left defeated and abandoned in the wake of historical changes. Benjamin compels us to consider a Left that gave in, sold out'. Jodi Dean, *The Communist Horizon* (London: Verso, 2011), p. 171.
39 Wendy Brown, 'Resisting Left Melancholy', *boundary 2*, vol. 26 no. 3, 1999, pp. 19–27 (p. 26).
40 Jan Breman, 'A Bogus Concept', *New Left Review*, vol. 84, November/December 2013, pp. 130–138 (p. 132, p. 138).
41 Guy Standing, *The Precariat: The New Dangerous Class* (London: Bloomsbury Academic, 2011), p. 24.
42 Harvey, *The Enigma of Capital*, p. 104. In Harvey's reading of neoliberalism, according to David Roediger, 'race sits outside of the logic of capital'. As I detailed in the Introduction, it is my assertion that race must be viewed as a construction of social difference which it is also necessary to understand as a part of the logic of capital. See Roediger, p. 19.
43 As Patricia Horton has noted, 'Scotland's identity is inextricably bound up in the history of empire'. Quoting the Irish writer Fintan O'Toole, she adds that the country's 'heyday' 'occurs "in the nineteenth century – the supreme *British* century – in the era of Queen Victoria and David Livingstone, of industry and empire"'. See Patricia Horton, *Trainspotting*: A Topography of the Masculine Abject', *English*, vol. 50, Autumn 2001, pp. 219–234, (p. 227).
44 Virdee, p. 81.
45 Ibid., pp. 81–82.
46 Ibid., p. 83.
47 Tyler, *Revolting Subjects*, p. 93.
48 Kirk, p. 20.
49 John Welshman, *Underclass: A History of the Excluded, 1880–2000* (London: Hambledon Continuum, 2006), p. xx.

50 Ibid., p. xx.
51 Gilroy, p. 35.
52 Tyler, *Revolting Subjects*, p. 188. Original emphasis.
53 Hartley Dean and Peter Taylor-Gooby quoted in Welshman, p. xxi.
54 Tyler, *Revolting Subjects*, p. 184.
55 See Tyler, *Revolting Subjects*, pp. 185–186.
56 Kelman, 'And the Judges Said', p. 63.
57 Warner, *The Guardian*, 13 July 2011.
58 Scott, p. 93.
59 Gregor White, 'Book Review: *Waterline*, by Ross Raisin', *Daily Record*, 30 September 2011, www.dailyrecord.co.uk/news/local-news/book-review-waterline-ross-raisin-2735498.
60 See Fox, *The Telegraph*, 2 December 2011.
61 Michael Denning, *Mechanic Accents: Dime Novels and Working-Class Culture in America* (London: Verso, 1987), p. 212.
62 Ibid., p. 212.
63 Ibid.
64 See Fox, *The Telegraph*, 2 December 2011.

5 Jenni Fagan and the Revolting Class

Gender, Stigma, Resistance

Jenni Fagan's debut novel *The Panopticon* centres upon the first-person narration of Anais Hendricks, a youngster who, after being taken into care at birth, has lived in fifty-one different locations by the time she is fifteen.[1] Her story is told in the demotic voice of contemporary, working-class Edinburgh through an episodic yet mainly linear narrative punctured by flashbacks, dreams, and hallucinations. The novel begins with an alleged attack by the narrator on a police officer; this is slowly revealed as Anais struggles to remember where she was on the day of the assault. It is a Kelmanesque search for knowledge which mirrors her ongoing exploration of selfhood. This chapter critiques the ways in which Fagan's text, through a female working-class protagonist, challenges the making of the class abject. It will engage with Imogen Tyler's work on class stigmatisation to analyse what I identify as two sites of class resistance in *The Panopticon*: (1) opposition to the processes of abjection and demonisation; (2) defiance of the corrective and coercive processes of liberal, middle-class logic.

Tyler has written of the need to broaden 'traditional' concepts and understandings of class to allow for an analysis of how and by what means individuals and groups are stigmatised or made abject. She argues that class describes the problem of structural inequality in capitalist society; further, class is mobilised as a means to justify or validate economic and social disparities. Neoliberalism therefore uses class, through a process of naming, to stigmatise marginal groups, acting as a 'form of governance' legitimising 'the reproduction and entrenchment of inequalities and injustices'.[2] Tyler takes issue with, as I do in this book's introduction, the way in which social stratification models commonly adopted in sociological studies involve slotting people into pre-determined categories. 'What stratification research often "forgets"', she adds, 'is that it is actively engaged in the formation and establishment of the class hierarchies that it describes'.[3] Class is a 'relational concept', Tyler points out, and studies of class and inequality must 'pay heed to the power of naming, the symbolic violence of classifications and the performative effects of classificatory practices'.[4] Such a focus on the processes of class naming allows for an analysis of how the poor, the vulnerable, and the excluded are routinely stigmatised by a system of social classification.

This is a dynamic which involves not only the struggle for identification but also a struggle against the ways in which neoliberalism figures and mobilises class.[5] Tyler is primarily concerned with those 'surplus' populations, as described by French philosopher Georges Bataille, who are figured as moral outcasts, dismissed as unequal and 'scum': classes of people who are, paradoxically, classless and omitted from mainstream political and social life.[6] Fagan's novel engages directly with such exclusionary methods of naming; Anais and her peers in the care system are branded at various points as chavs, feral, a sexual and physical threat, a waste of taxpayers' money, a drain on state resources, a danger to the public, repeat and unrepentant offenders, and destined for a life in prison. Such methods also add to larger processes through which these youngsters become invisible and are ignored, dismissed, and dehumanised. And the novel's title refers to a place in which they are subjected to such forms of control: an old panopticon building located in a small village in south Edinburgh used as a care home for young offenders. Therefore, the writings of Jeremy Bentham and Michel Foucault offer a logical yet illuminating departure point because of the use of a panopticon as both a location in the text and as a symbol of coercion and control.

Bentham's panopticon was designed to allow for the clear and constant surveillance of a large number of people from one dominant position. A central watchtower, strategically positioned in the middle of a circular wall of cells, meant those housed in this late-eighteenth-century prison were made visible and could be viewed at all times; according to Bentham, a philosopher and social reformer, it would facilitate a 'new mode of obtaining power of mind over mind, in a quantity hitherto without example'.[7] Further, it was a way of, what Foucault has described as, reducing 'the number of those who exercise [power], while increasing the number of those on whom [power] is exercised'.[8] The development of the idea for such a structure is identified by Foucault as part of a longer historical process of distinguishing between the 'normal' and the 'abnormal', a system of 'binary division and branding'.[9] Allowing for 'measuring, supervising and correcting', it was a disciplinary mechanism employed to 'characterize, classify, specialize [...] along a scale [...] around a norm [...] and, if necessary, disqualify and invalidate'.[10] Crucially, panopticism (which translates, originally from Greek, as 'all-seeing': pan-optic) carries a dual function: to 'brand' and to 'alter'.[11] And in Britain it was a form of architectural design used on at least two occasions on prisons for women. A wing in the female prison of England's Lancaster Castle was based on Bentham's model; in Scotland, Robert Adam, who knew Bentham, designed the Bridewell, Edinburgh's own panopticon: one of its sections was described as being built 'for those unfortunate females labouring under disease, which renders it prudent to separate them from the mass of society'.[12] The Bridewell on Calton Hill was a product of the Scottish Enlightenment and it carries compelling similarities with the care home in Fagan's novel.

Anais Hendricks is labelled as 'abnormal', 'disqualified' from society, and subjected to corrective methods which seek to engender 'normal' behaviour. However, she recognises and refuses the class stigma forcefully attached to her while also challenging and refuting the reforming doctrine of 'progressive' thinking. Such resistance is expressed through Anais's first-person narration of the story. Momentarily disrupting her narrative is a report written by Angus, one of the staff from 'The Panopticon'. Inserted verbatim directly into the novel, and read by Anais, it details how the teenagers in the care home refuse certain namings or official and bureaucratic terminology which attempt to describe and determine who they are. They reject 'Cared-for Young People' because to imply that they are looked after is 'taking the piss' or a mockery and young people sounds 'shite' or not true to how they think of themselves. They also reject 'clients' because that suggests some agency and decide instead to use 'inmate' because they believe that they are in 'training for proper jail'. Further, Anais uses the popular 'lifer' because she and her fellow 'inmates' have always been in the system and think they will remain in it through to adulthood.[13] Written in Standard English and italicised in the text, Angus's report temporarily dislodges the narrative of Anais to reveal both how the system of coercion operates on a semantic level and why it is rejected by those it seeks to describe and control. The 'official' language of the state appears strange and anachronistic compared to the urban Scots of Anais and her friends. It is defamiliarised and, in turn, challenged and destabilised. As Angus notes: 'the reality is that up to seventy per cent of residents leaving care do end up either in prison, or prostitution, mentally ill, or dead' (220). This merely confirms what Anais already knows: 'We're just in training for the proper jail. Nobody talks about it, but it's a statistical fact. That or on the game. Most of us are anyway – but not everybody. Some go to the nuthouse. Some just disappear' (8). Again, there is a marked contrast here, on this occasion between the ways in which the same eventualities are differently described: prison/proper jail, prostitution/on the game, mentally ill/the nuthouse, dead/disappear. Only in the last of these is there a significant difference: Anais is drawing attention to how many of those in the care system 'disappear' rather than die; the suggestion being that they are non-entities and inconsequential. They have been, to return to Foucault, 'disqualified' from 'normal' society. Further, Anais's overall account speaks more directly to the lived experience of a life in care and, stripped of formality, it suggests in starker terms the inevitability of the four options available. A fundamental problem highlighted by the novel is that nobody talks to those like Anais who are branded and excluded. 'It's amazing what the social work dinnae ask', reflects Anais:

> They dinnae ask about the terrible baldness of the moon, they dinnae ask about rooms without windows or doors – and they sure as shit

dinnae ask about flying cats. I bet they didnae ask Isla what her dreams are as a mum. They didnae ask me about blood in an empty bath, and they didnae ask about what Teresa was gonnae do when she got out that bath – she was gonnae curl up with me and watch a movie. We were gonnae make microwave popcorn. (96)

What is important here is the relentless build-up of negatives: seven instances of dinnae/didnae which indicate what the social workers are not interested in, dismiss, or over-look. They overwhelm the three references to positive action which follow: 'gonnae do', 'gonnae curl up', and 'gonnae make'. And it is the thwarting of these which reveal the cause of many of Anais's problems. Teresa is her adopted mother who was murdered when Anais was eleven. This single, violent act denied her the love and security which a home and the simple acts of familial bonding – watching a film, eating food – provide. But a systematic neglect and an institutional inability to engage with the specifics of her experiences, a process of enquiry lost beneath stigmatisation and the positing of established yet destructive pathways out of care, means that Anais's behaviour is understood, by those in 'the social work', as a product of her own personal failings rather than as a result of the care system itself or the social and historical conditions from which it emerges.

The various methods of naming, emanating from institutional procedures as well as through social and political discourse, are part of a wider system of labelling, or 'branding' to use Foucault's term, which mobilises and provokes certain assumptions and prejudices. These are predicated on the way the youngsters from 'The Panopticon' look and dress and how they are seen to perform the labels attached to them. It is this aspect of naming or imagining which carries with it, in Fagan's novel, a distinctive class element; and it is one which is registered by Anais. When she meets John, a fellow resident at the Edinburgh care home, she predicts how he would be viewed within society: 'most people would just think he looked like a radge, but when you see him up close, and look at him – not his trackies or that – he's graceful. He just is' (66–67). It is because of what he wears, his tracksuit as an indicator of his class, that he is assumed to be a 'radge'. It is both an adjective and noun associated predominantly with the east of Scotland, a term which connotes, according to the *Oxford English Dictionary* (*OED*), an 'extremely angry', 'enraged', 'wild', 'violent', 'mad', and/or 'crazy' individual. 'Radge' is used repeatedly in Irvine Welsh's *Trainspotting* to describe a variety of different characters, many of whom fit the *OED*'s definitions.[14] And yet, as a noun, the dictionary also describes how radge can stand simply for 'a person'.[15] Crucially, Anais looks beyond John's 'uniform', as she describes tracksuits (185), in order to appreciate just that: the person. It is in recognising this form of class making and then destabilising it which enables *The Panopticon* to probe 'those forces that strip people of their human dignity and reproduce them as dehumanized waste, the disposable dregs and refuse of social life'.[16] Tyler argues that those who are made abject 'become fetishistically overdetermined and publicly imagined and represented in excessive, distorted and/or caricatured ways'.[17] So, it is through fabrication and repetition that such conceptions evolve into everyday language, and therefore continue to reproduce class stigma and act as constitutive parts of a wider neoliberal doctrine. The figure of the chav has been central to these contemporary social and political processes; it has been part of a mainstream political retreat from class and a refusal to engage with class as the foundational inequality of capitalism. Owen Jones argues that class denial is a key part of neoliberalism. 'The expulsion of "class" from the nation's vocabulary by Thatcherism and New Labour', he says, 'has ensured minimal scrutiny of the manifestly unjust distribution of wealth and power in modern Britain'.[18] But just as class has been rendered insignificant, class hatred has been mobilised to explain and justify increasing levels of inequality. According to Tyler, it has been the 'mediating agencies of popular culture, newspaper journalism, television and the Internet which transformed New Labour's symbolic abjection of class into the figure of the chav'.[19] And, as Rhian E. Jones notes, although it has been a 'multivalent and unstable signifier', in the twenty-first century chav has settled into a specific stereotype connoting 'an idle, stupid and semi-criminal underclass' characterised as '"cheats", "scroungers", "workshy" and "feckless"'.[20] Importantly, Anais undercuts the formulation of what purport to be common understandings; it is the type of shaping and crafting, attempting to construct the chav as 'a knowable figure',[21] which she rejects when describing her friend as 'graceful'.

The media obsession with, and its contribution to the creation of, the chav as a figure of class hatred transcends national boundaries within Britain because it speaks directly to social class concerns rather than to questions of nationhood. And, specifically, the chav is mobilised as a figure of disgust upon which to direct fears emanating from the evolving formations of twenty-first-century capitalism. Such social abjects are created to 'do the dirty ideological work of neoliberalism', argues Tyler. They are the 'material scapegoats for [...] social decomposition' and a way of redirecting concerns about insecurity and precarity in order to generate consent for neoliberal policy.[22] Fagan's novel disrupts the fabrication of such consent by directly counteracting the stigmatisation of the marginalised. This challenge to class naming is vividly and violently expressed in the novel when the staff and residents at The Panopticon embark on a day trip to a loch in the Scottish countryside. Anais, Shortie, Isla, and Tash are sailing on the water when they encounter a boat driven by a group of 'posh lassies':

'Chavs!' the blonde lassie says loudly. Her pals snigger. Shortie slows down paddling and turns right around. 'What the fuck did you say?'

Isla's still smiling; she kisses Tash on the cheek and grins happily [...]
'Oh my God, it's lesbo chav'. The blonde nods towards Isla. 'Fucking
ugly one at that', her pal adds. I stand up – paddle in my hand. 'It's
angry chav!' her pal laughs. 'You should watch your fucking mouth,
She'll kick your stinking cunt right intae next fucking week – ya
skanky bitch'. Shortie's livid. (211)

An initial one word description ('chavs') of the youngsters, accompanied
by an exclamation mark to emphasise its potency, is shouted 'loudly'
in order to draw attention to those from The Panopticon; it is a verbal
branding deployed to warn others on the loch (owned by the father of
one of the 'posh lassies'). Part of the reason why Anais and her friends
(and John, as already described) attract such abuse is because of the way
in which their bodies are inscribed by certain assumptions and expectations. 'Chavs' is deployed to mark the four youngsters out as different;
it is part of their 'young-offenders aura [...] children-in-care aura' which
figures them as abnormal and out of place (193). To a greater extent
than with John's male body, the labelling of the female body in this way
enables a multiple set of attributes to be fixed and evoked. Gender is
particularly significant here, in that it intersects with class to produce
numerous, interlocking inscriptions which are employed to label, define,
and stigmatise. This is demonstrated in the passage above by the accumulative effect achieved by the different descriptions of chav – first
'lesbo chav', then 'ugly' chav, and finally 'angry chav' – which itself is
indicative of the flexibility of this specific form of class stigma. Further,
it mirrors the lumping of connecting insults into one apparently easy-to-
identify figure while reflecting the multiple sites of oppression mobilised
against the female, working-class body.

The chav often relates specifically to the figure of the young white
working-class woman and the suggestion of 'an inability to "correctly"
perform femininity': a caricature employed to perpetuate stereotypes of
undesirable femininity, 'sexual promiscuity', 'non-traditional behaviour',
an 'aggressive lack of deference, and refusal of traditional family and
community hierarchies'.[23] It is part of a creation of revolting bodies,
a myth crafted to serve distinctly political (and oppressive) aims, and,
as Rhian E. Jones argues, imagined behaviour which, neoliberal logic
concludes, 'must be politically penalised'.[24] Central to 'chav-hysteria'
has been the figure of the chav mum which Tyler suggests is 'produced
through disgust reactions as an intensely affective figure that embodies
historically familiar and contemporary anxieties about sexuality, reproduction and fertility and "racial mixing"'.[25] Significantly, Shortie and
Anais immediately recognise the abuse directed towards them and reject
it. It is a form of class hatred which carries with it a stigma predicated
on a perceived departure from 'traditional' notions of sexuality (hence,
'lesbo chav') and heteronormative family structures (Isla kisses Tash following their symbolic marriage on a loch island). The association of

such stigmatisation with motherhood also resonates with the experience of Isla, who has two young children placed with foster parents, and it is significant that Shortie and Anais stand to protect her, both physically and verbally. Through Anais as narrator, an empathetic portrayal of Isla, as someone with complex personal issues, is provided by the novel to counteract the simplifications perpetuated by the chav myth. But this response on the loch to such attacks also operates on a more direct level: the warning 'watch your fucking mouth' is an attempt to block off the cycle of repetitive verbal discourse which creates the demonised figure of the chav.

Back on dry land, Anais and Tash wander off from their group to seek revenge on the 'posh lassies', who they subsequently assault and rob while smashing up their camper van. On one level, the youngsters from The Panopticon are performing the set of coded characteristics which have been attributed to them: violent, an aggressive lack of deference, an inability to fulfil imposed heteronormative notions of femininity. As Tyler has noted, class stigma shapes how marginalised communities think about themselves, speak of their experiences, and 'perform' their abjection;[26] they can become that which they are described as. Negative namings, however, also provide something to resist, to 'push against', according to Lisa McKenzie.[27] While hostility and abuse, in the forms of contempt and class hatred, 'are both externalised and internalised' by those on the receiving end, they raise the 'potential of working-class resistance to discursive practices of othering'.[28] As Rhian E. Jones has argued, positive approaches to such representations should 'engage with what they find as they find it, if necessary taking ownership of externally-imposed narratives, occupying them, inverting them'.[29] So, while the confrontation on the shores of the loch risks compounding the chav stereotype, it also provides an opportunity to respond to such processes of abjection. However, Fagan's novel does not directly narrate the violent revenge enacted by Anais and Tash; it is manoeuvred out of sight and, instead, suggested through the descriptions of the other young women as having black eyes and bloody noses (215). In a text which does not hesitate to depict extreme brutality, such a choice is compelling. The novel, by performing such a move, implies that it is a worthy reaction from the teenagers but one which needs to be controlled and managed for fear that its political potency may be hindered by its association with physical force. Challenges to both the chav label and the wider formulation of an apparent underclass are a crucial part of the social and political response to neoliberalism. Coupled with a resistance to the discourse of negative namings, the actions of Anais and Tash on the loch side do allow for a comprehension of the consequences of social abjection. However, the text itself appears uncertain as to how far sympathetic understanding will extend if these young women are to be seen performing their own abjection.

Beverley Skeggs has identified how a contesting and enabling source of value has been a significant part of the lives of working-class women: those who are 'marked by the symbolic systems of denigration and degeneracy' and 'positioned by but also [contest] the symbolic systems of historical inscription to generate alternative systems of value'.[30] In Fagan's novel, such 'alternative systems' emanate from the network of friendships which emerge between those in care. Prior to the altercation on the water, Anais, Shortie, Isla, and Tash take refuge on an island in the middle of the loch. 'This is great – we are conquerors', thinks Anais, 'maybe I could name it Anais's island. Or, island El Radgio' (202).[31] This taking of land is an attempt to claim a space, both physically and metaphorically, in which to define a different set of values. As noted, it is also a place owned by another class, and is therefore an act of social reappropriation and public reclamation. Significantly, it is an all-female space, in Eve Kosofsky Sedgwick's use of the term it is a homosocial space.[32] And it is one in which there is an opportunity to discuss and share experiences of the inequalities and oppressions of patriarchal society while formulating dreams of a positive future.[33] As noted above, Isla and Tash marry on the island with Shortie performing the service and Anais making the ring. Symbolising the construction of a competing societal structure to that which they have fled, this act of defiance to heteronormativity, an affirmation of female sexuality and same-sex relationships, is empowering. 'I'm smiling, cos the two of them look so young and happy', reflects Anais, 'and it makes me hopeful. I dunno for what, like – just hopeful' (208). By shaping their own social conditions, the four young women are able to craft an enabling resource through which they, rather than society, determine who they are and what roles they adopt or perform. They are populating a site of their own choosing, conquering as Anais describes it, and this makes them optimistic and, momentarily at least, able to see beyond the historical determinism of the care system: 'I'm smiling', 'this is great', 'just hopeful' are all positive terms which trouble the attribution and branding of labels such as 'angry', 'ugly', and 'feral'. An active resistance to such inscriptions also destabilises the sociological categories into which individuals are assumed to neatly fit. And this provides a significant challenge to what Tyler calls the 'lumpen history of the underclass'.[34]

As discussed in the previous chapter, the 'value' of the underclass is its flexibility as a 'lumping device';[35] a whole host of personal and social issues which emanate from structural inequality are described and dismissed as 'immoral and unrespectable' through the mobilisation of such a short-hand term.[36] Skeggs details how this form of classification, a concept or description of the working-class poor which has periodically been reinvented since the late-nineteenth century,[37] shapes 'disparate discourses of familial disorder and dysfunction, dangerous masculinities and dependent, fecund and excessive femininities, of antisocial behaviour, and of moral and ecological decay'.[38] It is a term adopted to distinguish between the deserving and the undeserving poor and, as already argued, to mark people out as being divorced from the body politic. However, as Tyler observes, 'pejorative class epithets, whatever ideological project they serve, do not describe existing classes of people'.[39] Along with a rejection of the ways in which the discourses of capitalist logic create and produce social abjects, Anais is representative of a refusal to accept a normative model and continues to challenge directly conceptions of how she should behave, act, and perform.

Fiona McCulloch has described *The Panopticon* as a 'contemporary Scottish gothic tale', one which is 'symptomatic of post-devolution Scotland's journey towards cosmopolitical autonomy'.[40] Anais's 'defiance of state expectations' is not read by McCulloch in class terms but rather as a response to 'her internalised inferiority and otherness' which is 'psychogeographical'; she, as a symbol of the need for Scottish independence, is resisting 'an Anglocentric mechanism of state control'.[41] 'The stateless Scottish nation's desire for autonomy from its confinement as England's binary other parallels Fagan's demonised orphan's desire for liberty from faceless power', concludes McCulloch.[42] My reading of the novel, as performing a double movement of class struggle, contests the construction of such a binary which excludes and omits the dynamics of class and classification. Positioning oppressor (England) against oppressed (Scotland) in a simplistic formulation fails to address the ways in which class is felt, lived, and experienced *within* Scotland. As Aaron Kelly has argued, Scottish devolution, for example, did 'not rid Scotland of poverty, racism, patriarchy, sexism and so on'.[43] And there is little to suggest that achieving Scottish independence would automatically do so either. Rather, as Kelly says of devolution, it offers 'a national forum in which these issues may be tackled or for that matter a national framework wherein they may be perpetuated'.[44] So, whereas independence from England (and from the United Kingdom) could provide a way of tackling inequality through self-determination, it does not necessarily follow that the lives of those branded, like Anais, as social abjects would drastically and instantly improve without an engagement with class division. Chris Bambery has observed that 'Scotland is scarred by a deep divide' in terms of social and economic inequality.[45] Fagan's novel engages with these issues by refusing, in contrast to McCulloch's reading, a homogenous national voice. And this relates back to the urban Scots deployed by Fagan. As Jeremy Scott argues, 'the voice of the Scottish working-class constituency has been suppressed not only by the "colonial" ambitions of the England-dominated British project but by the economically dominant groups within Scotland itself'.[46] Anais's Scotland is significantly divided along class lines and she directly and consistently denies both her positioning by what she identifies as the liberal middle-class and the expectations placed upon her; it is a resistance to the kind of imposed class stereotypes which have also been mobilised to 'explain' the Brexit vote, as I discussed in the Introduction.

Central to the class dynamics in Fagan's novel is the relationship between Anais and her social worker Helen Stevenson. 'Do-gooders are vomit-worthy', says Anais,

> They think if you just inhale some of their middle-classism, then you'll be saved. Helen's like that. She thought that what I really needed was homeopathic tongue-drops. She said I should take them if I ever felt like I was getting angry. What she really didnae like, though, was that I wouldnae stick tae the uniform. No hair extensions, no tracksuits, no gold jewellery. That really pissed her off [...] She wanted a case that was more rough-looking. More authentic. (185)

As previously noted, the 'uniform' is read as a signifier of class and, in particular, evokes certain expectations which are placed upon Anais. 'No hair extensions, no tracksuits, no gold jewellery' reads as if it were a public sign to warn off the undesirable and undeserving, designed to draw the boundaries of acceptability. Here, the novel inverts such a reading: Anais is the one who decides what is 'acceptable'. And by not 'sticking' to the uniform, suggesting that the way she looks is ever-changing and multivalent, she is destabilising the fabricated notions on which class stigma is predicated. Helen expects Anais to perform a certain way in order not only to define herself as different from her 'client' but also to generate value for herself from their relationship. Their association will make Helen appear 'cutting-edge' in front of her 'posh pals', Anais remarks (185). Such a binary is based upon an inscription of fixed value, a process which allows for a figure of class hatred such as the chav to be identified and ridiculed. However, Helen's expectations emanate from a desire to reform and rehabilitate and it is Anais's recognition and rejection of this motive which symbolises the novel's dismissal of what are superficial responses to structural inequality. In liberal approaches such as Helen's, class is not viewed as describing the foundational inequality of capitalism but rather as a life choice, one which can be remedied by inhaling some 'middle-classism'.

It is in its challenge to the futility of liberal, middle-class thinking that *The Panopticon* suggests a comparison with Irvine Welsh's *Trainspotting*.[47] Specifically, it is from their respective refusals to be easily assimilated by the 'liberal reader' that an illuminating comparison emerges. Alan Sinfield describes *Trainspotting* as 'rebarbative'; its language, its depiction of violence and prejudice, and its intrusion into high culture all act as impediments to the middle-class reader. Further, 'Renton's claim for heroin addiction as an assertion of the free human spirit stretches the liberal imagination'.[48] And 'literary' readers, Sinfield argues, are prevented from supposing they can readily assimilate Scotland and working-class

Edinburgh.[49] The significant correlation with Fagan's novel is that both texts directly challenge any notions of easy access into the lives of those marked out by society as the underclass. In *The Panopticon*, Anais poses a problem which Helen is charged with solving. The latter character is symbolic of a wider response directed towards those individuals who are unable or refuse to conform to perceived norms. And it is a response, predicated on what are identified as liberal values, which also finds expression in the coercive aims of the panoptic approach to correction. Anais is quick to make this connection to the panopticon where she resides: 'My social worker said they were gonnae make all the nuthouses and prisons like this, once. The thought of it pleased her, I could tell. Helen reckons she's a liberal, but really – she's just a cunt' (10–11). This echoes Foucault who has described how Bentham 'presented the famous Panopticon as a procedure for institutions like schools, factories, and prisons'.[50] Further, the identification, by Anais, of liberal thinking with the history of Bentham's panopticon is particularly illuminating. And she disturbs the conception of value in such bourgeois ideology by conflating the seemingly positive word 'liberal' with 'cunt'. That the novel is written from Anais's perspective, using her own language, is significant here; Fagan has revealed:

> I basically ripped it apart [...]. Cut it in half, rewrote it in the first person, in Scottish and it just settled. [...] It just didn't work [in Standard English] and I decided I had to rewrite it from her [Anais's] voice because me trying to be an author was getting in the way of the story. The thing that was important was who this character was and as soon as I began to allow her to speak it came to life.[51]

The deployment of 'cunt', particularly when it is used to undercut conceptions of 'liberal', would not have had the same effect had the novel adopted a third-person narrator speaking in Standard English. The reclaiming of 'bad' language as a form of speech, rather than symbolising the 'lowness' of those who use it, acts to disrupt notions of a civilised society. This can be seen in Anais's attack on Helen, as a symbol of the Scottish care system, whose 'liberal' attitudes are undermined; and it is through 'offensive' language – 'she's just a cunt' – that the hierarchies of power within which Anais is seemingly trapped are challenged. Further, in drawing attention to the historical development of social control within Scotland, her character troubles the binary set up by McCulloch that Anais is representative of a rejection of England's 'neoliberal stranglehold of Scotland' and of Anglocentric 'neoliberal panoptical power'.[52] As with Welsh's *Trainspotting*, the setting of Edinburgh is significant here.

Both novels explore the social divisions within the city, the processes of marginalisation which are part of the conception of what Kelly has referred to as the 'two prevailing and hegemonic constructions of Edinburgh – bourgeois Edinburgh and tourist Edinburgh'.[53] Hence, Kelly argues, there is a double process of class exclusion: firstly, by the 'economic inequalities of capitalism [...] and secondly, within a nationalist paradigm [...] the concomitant tourist culture of Scotland as a national heritage site'.[54] Both of these versions of Edinburgh are part of the same historical process which classifies, approves, disqualifies, and invalidates. And it is a development which both Welsh and Fagan trace back to the Scottish Enlightenment. Foucault has noted how the Enlightenment 'discovered the liberties' of individual freedom and progress while also inventing 'the disciplines'.[55] The latter was part of what Welsh has described as 'the real cost of the Scottish Enlightenment', the mechanisms of social control and marginalisation which meant Edinburgh became, Welsh says, 'the first city to render most of its citizens invisible'.[56] Further, and as Skeggs makes clear, 'the generic model of "the individual" [...] is founded on discourses of Enlightenment rationality, which [...] exclude women'.[57] Jeremy Bentham's panopticon was a product of this period of philosophical, cultural, intellectual, and scientific development; it was 'an important aspect of the European Enlightenment' according to Janet Semple, and a project which grew from its ideals as well as from 'evangelical Christianity and *laissez-faire* economics'.[58] It was designed to house those marked out as the criminal and undesirable members of society, to reform such individuals, and to impose punishment for non-conformity. Bentham argued that every such prison or penitentiary house should have 'three distinguishable purposes': to act as 'a place of safe custody', 'a place of safe labour', and as a 'hospital – a place where sickness will be found at least, whether provision be or be not made for its relief'.[59] Foucault described it in starker terms: 'a laboratory; it could be used as a machine to carry out experiments, to alter behaviour, to train or correct individuals'.[60] This chimes with Anais's experience of The Panopticon. 'In all actuality they grew me – from a bit of bacteria in a Petri dish', she asserts. Here, the processes of abjection are being felt by Anais at the level of private consciousness; she compares herself to bacteria, therefore to dirt and waste. It is yet another example of Anais being excluded and rejected. She explains this conception of herself as being part of an elaborate 'experiment'; it is a paranoid fantasy, acting as a sub-plot in the novel, in which shadowy patriarchal forces, operating from The Panopticon, control and manipulate her. Fagan writes: 'An experiment, created and raised just to see exactly how much, fuck you, a nobody from nowhere can take. It's funny having nothing – it means there's fuck-all to lose' (31). Further, Anais believes that she is both an experiment and is being controlled by *the* experiment which can see all and everything, 'every minute [...] of every fucking day' (34).

It is through the 'experiment' sub-plot that Fagan's novel adopts elements of magic realism, collapsing and problematising the boundary between Anais's imagination and her experiences of an identifiable contemporary world. McCulloch makes an important observation here, insisting that Anais's obsession with the experiment should not be dismissed as 'drug-induced paranoia' but rather be appreciated as a 'very astute political and philosophical point about contemporary society'.[61] However, McCulloch's singular identification of the experiment with the state, ostensibly the Anglocentric neoliberal state, is dubious. Anais's experiences of being created, constrained, and excluded are not exclusively a product of 'state expectations'.[62] Her experience is one of defying social control not only as it links in with other forms of discipline and authority – the care system, the police, school, for example – but also through the way in which she is excluded by the networks of community within Scotland. Her unwanted presence on the loch is one such example; another is the reaction of the local residents living near to The Panopticon. 'I bet there's petitions to close this place down already', reflects Anais, 'there'll be people from the village writing letters tae their MPs. Mr Masters is right. He told us all about it in history – communities dinnae like no-ones' (6). Anais is a 'nobody from nowhere' and a 'no-one', excluded by the way in which she is negatively inscribed by society and, crucially, from the accepted norms within Scotland; be they neoliberal, middle-class, or local. She is not simply the symbol of a stateless Scotland; rather, she is akin to a failed citizen, a form of neoliberal citizenship which I also critique in the next chapter on Sunjeev Sahota.

Anais's double exclusion is felt at a very local level: the nearby (Scottish) village's opposition, for example. Anais remarks that the residents write letters to 'their' MPs, not to 'her' (or 'our' or even 'the local') MP, indicating how she and those in the care home are denied a voice within the processes of representative democracy. And it is also her class which they are afraid of. 'They've got a campaign down the village tae get this place shut already', Anais tells John later in the novel. 'They're worried we'll fuck their children. Contaminate their bloodline' (63). Fears of degeneration and a rupture to the traditional class structures of this local community are what motivates such opposition. The children are figured as a disease and a source of pollution, a foreign body. And this is part of a wider system of order and constraint which the panopticon itself encapsulates. Foucault has argued that, much like capitalism, panopticism:

> arranges things in such a way that the exercise of power is not added on from the outside, like a rigid, heavy constraint, to the function it invests, but is so subtly present in them as to increase their efficiency by itself increasing its own points of contact.[63]

It is in this way that the labelling and altering tendencies inherent within the panoptic system permeate throughout wider society, repeating such processes in order to arrange, divide, and delineate. What Anais represents is a challenge to the perpetuation of such dominant logic. 'I am not an experiment', she affirms:

> I am not a stupid joke, or a trippy game, or an experiment. I will *not* go insane [...] I am not an experiment. If I keep saying it, I'll start believing it. I have to try. I am *not* an experiment. It doesnae sound convincing. It sounds stupid. (186)

She repeats what becomes a mantra four times ('I am not an experiment') and by rejecting the notion that the 'experiment' exists, even though it 'sounds stupid' and unconvincing to say so, she is refusing to be told by others who and what she is.

As already noted, it is through Anais's rebuke to middle-class intervention that a direct challenge to what Sinfield describes as the 'liberal reader' is made. A range of professionals (Anais's social worker Helen, Eric the student working at the care home, the chairwoman on the youth offending panel) embody an apparently humanitarian approach to discipline and reform. They are imbricated within a structure which purports to help young people such as those in The Panopticon while at the same time protecting 'civilised' society from them. But, in a reversal of the way in which she is classified by such structures, Anais offers her own counter narrative:

> Authority figures are broken, and they're always bullies [...]. Teachers, shrinks, pigs, staff, they all do the same, and so does life, without being able to think about who I would have been – if I'd actually got to be me. I wouldnae have been this. This was a mistake. (101)

Anais is reclaiming control over her own sense of selfhood; she is once again refusing to be dictated to. And by describing the systems and individuals who enact this oppression, *The Panopticon* draws attention to the means through which they make and condition those 'abjects' whom they seek to reform; these systems and individuals are a constitutive part of the process. The negative namings deployed by Anais, for example: 'broken', 'bullies', and 'mistake', act to disrupt and resist a hierarchy of power relations which works to divide and exclude. And Anais is seeking to expose what such systems of exclusion reveal about the motivation behind the actions of supposedly liberal intervention. 'I'll spend eternity drooling down my chin', concludes Anais, 'while Erics do their theses, then fuck off to have lives with houses and kids and gardens and holidays and cars and dreams' (79). Fagan disturbs the formation of what is posited as heteronormative behaviour under capitalism. Firstly, Eric is figured as one of many – note the pluralisation of his name by Anais – who will continue to observe and intervene. Further, this role within authority allows such individuals to participate within society: 'houses and kids and gardens and holidays and cars and dreams'; the repeated use of 'and' transforms what are relatively normal aspects of everyday life into excessive forms of exclusion. And whilst Anais suffers, the 'Erics' continue to accumulate possessions and positive experiences. Therefore, Fagan's text interrogates what such a construct is predicated on by exploring the systems and processes of social inequality.

Anais fights back, she rebels against and resists the imposition of class names and the structures of oppression and reform. The final movement of class struggle comes with an attack on The Panopticon itself. Anais describes how she picks 'up a glass bottle – lighting the rag with a match', adding:

> It catches [...] I raise the lit bottle [...] and launch it – up, up [...] they are chanting, smashing, punching [...]. The whole surveillance window shatters, and I see them – turning on their fucking tails – the experiment, for a fraction of a fucking second: exposed'. (319)

The panopticon's high, central watchtower gives the illusion of power.[64] In shattering the glass of the tower, Anais is destroying the fabric of the 'faceless gaze';[65] she is making the invisible, momentarily at least, visible and fracturing the symbolic, central facet of disciplinary power. Importantly, this is a collective effort: an alliance between Anais and the rest of the young children in the care home who have been classified as revolting but who themselves, in response, revolt. The final act of *The Panopticon* is not, however, the attack on its namesake but, rather, Anais's escape to France.

She boards the Eurostar for Paris and the novel ends as her train pulls out of London. Anais repeatedly fantasises about living in Paris and by having her flee to the French capital, the novel is in danger of succumbing to the narrative conventions which it otherwise works to destabilise; as discussed in the previous chapter, they are conventions which Ross Raisin also plays with in *Waterline*. Fagan's novel denies easy access into the lives of those marginalised as the underclass within twenty-first-century Britain. In concluding with Anais embarking on a train journey to Paris (although it is unclear if she arrives), the narrative, at the final moment, risks becoming one of escape from rather than of resistance to political discourses of abjection; it is in danger of no longer acting as a challenge but rather a comfort through the act of transhistorical resolution and the gaining of individual freedom. However, a closer reading of the Paris episode which places it within the wider dynamics of the plot complicates such a consoling and 'happy' ending. 'Teresa ate cakes from the French pattiserie [sic] when she was depressed', remembers Anais of her adoptive mother:

> She'd sit in her bed, in a kimono, drinking gin and reading. Sometimes I think she's still here, but she's not. Pat has the ashes, and me

and Teresa never did make it tae Paris. We had the passports ready and everything. She's so dead, it's more than a full stop. (88)

So, for Anais, Paris relates to the trauma of Teresa's murder and losing the one stable presence in her life. It is significant that the event is so final: 'it's more than a full stop'. The pain she feels is ineffable and language proves inadequate as a means through which to describe the death of her adoptive mother. So, there is an awareness here of the limitations of narrative to explain Anais's situation. And the clichéd idea of Paris which she regularly evokes throughout the text is figured as an unrealistic fantasy rather than an achievable and enabling possibility; rather, it signals the impossibility of being allowed to imagine anything else. The dream of France reveals not resolution but, rather, the socio-historical realities of Anais's experiences. She has to construct another world in order to cope with the uncertainties, oppressions, and inequalities of the present. And Paris represents the final coping mechanism, a way of refusing negative inscriptions of value and of resisting the pathways into adulthood laid out before her. But it does not address the reality of her abjection or the causes of it.

Tyler has highlighted the problems with a mode of resistance which involves becoming invisible and of escaping, of taking flight. What her research with and into those individuals who are made abject by neoliberal discourse reveals is that, for many, the conditions for a liveable life involve being able to lay down roots, to feel safe, to create a family and home, to belong to a community, and to have some sense of a (better) future.[66]

In part, Anais is revolting against the denial of such conditions, ones which she longs after even within the confines of the care home. 'I cannae believe I've been in The Panopticon for over two months now', she reflects. 'It almost feels like home, cos of, like, Shortie, and Isla, even Angus, and the roof. It's a long time since I've wanted to stay anywhere' (239). This comment is made, however, at the beginning of what becomes a particularly violent sequence in the novel: Tash is missing presumed murdered, Isla is found dead in her cell, Shortie is attacked by some local children, and Anais is raped by a gang of five men. This horrific attack is filmed and uploaded onto the internet; it represents yet another type of social control enacted by the patriarchal structures in place. It has been orchestrated by Anais's boyfriend to pay off his debts and is figured as the ultimate expression of panoptic society: the webcam and the anonymous power it symbolises standing in for the central watchtower.[67] Further, this is how patriarchy works: disciplining and forewarning those whom it targets and oppresses. Anais's final act in the novel does not represent the flight simply from an 'Anglo neoliberal stranglehold', as McCulloch claims, but is also a result of and predicated on trauma and traumatic experience. In bypassing class, McCulloch argues that the challenge to Scotland, in a 'post-referendum homecoming', is to 'remedy its own dispossessed alterity'.[68] But this is not exclusively a nationalist issue; the focus needs also to be on the performance and projections of 'alterity' or otherness *within* Scotland. Crucially, *The Panopticon* resists a homogenous national voice by exploring how class, as a material inequality of capitalism, operates in a Scottish context. What this allows for is the text to expose how neoliberal capital and class work across a range of intersectional sites; it is a powerful dynamic, one which I will now examine in the sixth and final chapter of this book.

Notes

1 Fagan, born in Livingston, grew up in the Scottish care system and has spoken about drawing on this experience to write *The Panopticon*. See Jenni Fagan, 'I Went From Growing Up In Care To Being A Best Selling Granta Author – By Jenni Fagan', *Marie Claire*, 30 August 2013, www.marieclaire.co.uk/blogs/544200/i-went-from-growing-up-in-care-to-being-a-best-selling-granta-author-by-jenni-fagan.html; Alan Bett, 'Poetry in Image: Jenni Fagan on taking *The Panopticon* to the screen', *The Skinny*, 13 January 2015, www.theskinny.co.uk/books/features/poetry-in-image-jenni-fagan-on-taking-the-panopticon-to-the-screen

2 Tyler, *Revolting Subjects*, p. 8.

3 Tyler, '*Classificatory Struggles*', p. 499.

4 Ibid., pp. 499–500.

5 Tyler, *Revolting Subjects*, pp. 16–17.

6 Ibid., p. 19.

7 Jeremy Bentham, 'Panopticon; or, the Inspection-House', in *The Works of Jeremy Bentham*, ed. by John Bowring (Edinburgh: William Tait, 1838–1843), pp. 39–66 (p. 39).

8 Michel Foucault, *Discipline and Punish: The Birth of the Prison* (London: Penguin, 1991), p. 206.

9 Ibid., p. 199.

10 Ibid., p. 199, p. 223.

11 Ibid., p. 199.

12 Hugo Arnot, *The History of Edinburgh, from the Earliest Accounts, to the Year 1780 [...]: With an Appendix* (Edinburgh: Thomas Turnbull, 1816), p. 544.

13 Jenni Fagan, *The Panopticon* (London: Windmill Books, 2013), pp. 219–221. References for further quotations taken from *The Panopticon* will be provided in parentheses.

14 Irvine Welsh, *Trainspotting* (London: Vintage, 2004), p. 65 and p. 75.

15 See 'radge, *adj.* and *n.*2', *OED Online*, Oxford University Press, www.oed.com/view/Entry/266773.

16 Tyler, *Revolting Subjects*, p. 140.

17 Ibid., p. 10.

18 Owen Jones, p. 248.

19 Tyler, *Revolting Subjects*, p. 163.

20 Rhian E. Jones, p. 13, p. 12.

21 Tyler, *Revolting Subjects*, p. 165.

22 Ibid., p. 211.

23 Rhian E. Jones, p. 76, p. 18.

24 Ibid., p. 18.

25 Imogen Tyler, 'Chav Mum Chav Scum', *Feminist Media Studies*, vol. 8, no. 1, 2008, pp. 17–34 (p. 18).

26 See Tyler, 'Classificatory Struggles', p. 500.

27 Lisa McKenzie, *Getting By: Estates, Class and Culture in Austerity Britain* (Bristol: Policy Press, 2015), p. 112.

28 McKenzie, p. 112; Tyler, 'Classificatory Struggles', p. 501.

29 Rhian E. Jones, p. 96.

30 Skeggs, *Class, Self, Culture*, p. 2.

31 Compellingly, radge can been used as a noun to describe a 'lascivious woman', according to the *OED*. This definition chimes with the mobilisation of the chav figure to describe a young woman who, as already discussed, is viewed as unable to correctly 'perform' femininity. Importantly, however, Anais reclaims this description (lascivious as in lewd and lustful) in order to reaffirm control over her own identity and that of her female friends on island El Radgio. See 'radge, *adj.* and *n.2*', *OED Online*, Oxford University Press, www.oed.com/view/Entry/266773.

32 Eve Kosofsky Sedgwick, *Between Men: English Literature and Male Homosocial Desire* (New York, NY: Columbia University Press, 1985), pp. 1–2.

33 On Loch Lomond sits Inchcailloch (or Inch-Cailleach) which means Island of the Cowled Woman, Old Woman, or Nuns. Briefly mentioned in *Rob Roy* (1817) by Walter Scott (who calls it the 'Isle of Women' in a note to his novel), it is thought to be an ancient site of female sanctuary. Loch Lomond is 80 miles from Edinburgh, the same distance away as the loch in Fagan's text. See Fagan, p. 190; and see Walter Scott, *Rob Roy* (Cambridge, MA: The Riverside Press, 1956), p. 219, and Edward Francis Finden and William Finden, *Landscape Illustrations of the Waverley Novels with Descriptions of the Views*, vol. 1 (London: Charles Tilt, 1832), p. 18.

34 Tyler, *Revolting Subjects*, p. 186.

35 Ibid., p. 221 (notes).

36 Skeggs, *Class, Self, Culture*, p. 86.

37 Welshman, *Underclass*, p. xi.

38 Skeggs, *Class, Self, Culture*, p. 87.

39 Tyler, *Revolting Subjects*, p. 186.

40 Fiona McCulloch, '"Daughter of an Outcast Queen" – Defying State Expectations in Jenni Fagan's', *The Panopticon*', *Scottish Literary Review*, vol. 7, no. 1, 2015, pp. 113–131, (p. 114, p. 115). Elsewhere, McCulloch has described 'cosmopolitical autonomy' thus: 'The infinite cosmos, uncharted and without territorial borders, serves as an ideal trope for cosmopolitanism's capacity to dismantle divisions and mobilize itself as an endless and renewable energy'. See Fiona McCulloch, *Cosmopolitanism in Contemporary British Fiction: Imagined Identities* (Basingstoke: Palgrave Macmillan, 2012), p. 2.

41 McCulloch, *Scottish Literary Review*, p. 123.

42 Ibid., p. 130.

43 Kelly, *Irvine Welsh*, p. 64.

44 Ibid., p. 64.

45 Chris Bambery, *A People's History of Scotland* (London: Verso, 2014), p. 316.

46 Scott, *The Demotic Voice*, pp. 96–97.

47 The suggestion is not that Fagan is simply a 'female Irvine Welsh' but that the connected approaches of both writers to working-class Edinburgh illuminate important engagements with the wider dynamics of class. Alan Bissett convincingly warns against reductive readings which label new working-class writers as the 'Scouse Irvine Welsh' or the 'black Irvine Welsh'. He has complained of an obsession with comparing all new writing in either non-Standard English or about working-class life to Welsh and therefore reducing such work to a standardised mode of working-class experience.

This, in turn, reveals a middle-class metropolitan class bias, argues Bissett. See Alan Bissett, 'We Can't All Be Irvine Welsh', *The Guardian*, 16 November 2006, www.guardian.co.uk/books/booksblog/2006/nov/16/negativedialect.
48 Sinfield, p. xxii.
49 Ibid., p. xvii.
50 Foucault, *The Birth of Biopolitics*, p. 67.
51 Bett, 'Poetry in Image', *The Skinny*. In the same interview, Fagan adds:

> There's something like 289 languages spoken in British schools today. [...] We're all used to hearing every accent, every voice [...] it's a wee bit old fashioned to think that English literature is English literature and there is one way to do things. The world novel means to make new, so to reject anything that's doing something in a new way is just crazy.

52 McCulloch, *Scottish Literary Review*, p. 130, p. 115.
53 Kelly, *Irvine Welsh*, p. 26.
54 Ibid., p. 28.
55 Foucault argues that such emerging forms of control were central to both the formation of capitalism and the capitalist mode of production. He has observed that 'the development and generalization of disciplinary mechanisms constituted the [...] dark side' of a 'formally egalitarian juridical framework' which gave rise to the bourgeoisie as the 'politically dominant class'. Foucault, *Discipline and Punish*, p. 222.
56 Welsh quoted in Kelly, *Irvine Welsh*, p. 28. Another Edinburgh writer, Ian Rankin, has described the place as a 'schizophrenic city', according to Horton, who herself describes it as 'a civic body repressing and abjecting its darker, more troublesome elements'. See Horton, p. 222.
57 Skeggs, *Class, Self, Culture*, p. 56.
58 Janet Semple, *Bentham's Prison: A Study of the Panopticon Penitentiary* (Oxford: Oxford University Press, 1993), p. 2, p. 17. Original emphasis.
59 Bentham, 'Panopticon; or, the Inspection-House', p. 46.
60 Foucault, *Discipline and Punish*, p. 203.
61 McCulloch, *Scottish Literary Review*, p. 114.
62 Ibid., p. 117.
63 Foucault, *Discipline and Punish*, p. 206.
64 Ibid., p. 214.
65 Ibid., p. 214.
66 Tyler, *Revolting Subjects*, p. 12.
67 See Fagan, *The Panopticon*, p. 289.
68 McCulloch, *Scottish Literary Review*, p. 130.

6 Sunjeev Sahota and the Racialised Worker

Class, Race, Violence

There is a passage in Sunjeev Sahota's 2011 novel *Ours are the Streets* when Imtiaz Raina is recalling how his father Rizwan would explain working long hours as a taxi driver in Sheffield. 'But we are doing it all for you', he remembers being told. 'It will all be worth it in the end'.[1] For Imtiaz, as a second-generation British Pakistani and first-person narrator of the novel, this 'guilt trip', as he describes it, speaks to another type of journey; it explains a distinctive experience of immigration and reveals the motivations of people like his father who moved to Britain. Rizwan's inclusive use of 'we' puts focus on the collective, on postwar migrants and British subjects from Pakistan speaking to the wider diaspora community in what is now the former colonial centre. 'You will understand when you have children of your own', he assures Imtiaz. But, with the death of his Abba on the streets of South Yorkshire and the abrupt ending of this cross-generational journey, the son sees only failure and rejection. 'Maybe I understand too much', Imtiaz says in anger:

> We were meant to become part of these streets. They were meant to be ours as much as anyone's. That's what you said you worked for, came for. Were it worth it, Abba? Because I sure as hell don't know. I used to just slam the door and stand with my back to it wondering, What end? Whose end? When is this fucking end? Because what's the point, man? What's the point in dragging your life across entire continents if by the time it's worth it you're already at the end? Ameen.[2]

It is the passage from which the novel's title is indirectly drawn, here with a stress on uncertainty and doubt ('they were meant to be', 'were it worth it') whereas 'ours are the streets' is declarative and affirming. This latter sense of ownership and belonging is thrown into ironic relief by Imtiaz's questioning of his late father. What does the supposed 'end' represent? What is life like for this young, working-class British Asian in the twenty-first century? For Imtiaz, it is an experience felt and understood as exclusion, both from the streets (for him, they are not 'ours') and from the racialised national identity of the country of his birth. The processes of what are, following on from the last chapter, another form of abjection will be the central focus of this sixth and final chapter. My primary reading is of Sahota's debut novel but I also provide an analysis of work and migrant labour in its follow-up, *The Year of the Runaways* from 2015, towards the end of the chapter. Both novels, I argue, work at the intersections of race and class to examine the figure of the working-class 'other' as a critique of the racialised logics of capital.

The street as a social and political site has a significant position in the British imaginary when thinking about identities linked to class, region, and nation. It has been a dominant feature of twentieth-century working-class history and cultural representation in particular. I discussed in Chapter Three, for example, how Pat Barker's novel, her debut like Sahota's, takes a title which puts together two dominant features of class history to play with their meanings. In *Union Street*, it is indicative of a union of women, not a trade union but equally as political, living in the same location and leading connected but subtly different lives. It is a site of plurality and multiplicity in Barker's text then, one which draws together connecting struggles. In the title used by Sahota, it is potentially a site of collective belonging: this place is 'ours'; it is not simply 'mine'. So, there is a suggestion of solidarity and collective ownership. But, it can also be a space of exclusion, setting up distinctions between 'ours' and 'theirs'. Sahota's novel probes such class-inflected connotations by drawing out an experience of the streets as a racialised space and, importantly, as a highly contested one. It has been a key site in the expression of and fight against racism: from violence directed towards people of colour and the fascistic claiming of the street as a white space to, and often in response, the location for direct anti-fascist action and practice. The National Front in the mid-1970s, for example, attempted 'to mark out and reclaim territory that they believed had been conceded to racialised minorities by strategically deploying graffiti, random violence and increasingly, marches in ethnically diverse areas'.[3] The street is also a site of confrontation then, often a political location which has been used in various ways for protest, agitation, violence, organisation, the dissemination of knowledge, and the staging of ideological debate. In Sahota's novel, many of these ways of thinking about the street as political and social are mobilised to examine questions of nationhood and belonging. Edward Said describes the 'universal practice of designating in one's mind a familiar space which is "ours" and an unfamiliar space beyond "ours" which is "theirs"'. This, Said argues, is 'a way of making geographical distinctions that *can* be entirely arbitrary'.[4] Such distinctions in Sahota's novel connect to the 'imagined community' of Benedict Anderson's powerful formulation; it is the imagined national community of Britain that Imtiaz and his family expect to be able to call 'ours' but it always remains, for Imtiaz in particular, unattainable. He feels, or is made to feel, outside of Britain, these streets are 'theirs'; he is excluded from and by the 'formal universality of nationality as a socio-cultural concept'.[5]

The possessive pronouns, 'ours' and 'theirs', come up frequently in *Ours are the Streets*. It is a novel which tells the story of the radicalisation of Imtiaz as a young, working-class Muslim from Sheffield who is plotting to bomb Meadowhall, the large shopping complex on the edges of the city. The narrative alternates between Britain and Pakistan and a life lived in both; the crossing of these geographical and imaginative borders is what Imtiaz is partly trying to work through. To his uncle, Tauji, he describes a profound sensation of being stuck: 'We don't really know what we're about. I guess. Who we are, what we're here for'.[6] The emphasis is on the plural again, like his father's use of 'we', with a wider, generational sense of what is initially identified as a structure of feeling specific to children of immigrants. However, Imtiaz then adds, as means of clarification:

> But that weren't nothing like what I wanted to say. Even to me it just sounded like the usual crap I'd been hearing for years. I wanted to talk about why I felt fine rooting for Liverpool, in a quiet way, but not England. I wanted to talk about why I found myself defending Muslims against whites and whites against Muslims. About why I loved Abba but had still wished him dead. But I couldn't think of how to say any of what I wanted. "I mean, we're the ones stuck in the middle of everything. Like we're not sure whose side we're meant to be on, you know?".[7]

This is a familiar experience of struggling to explain and understand an 'in-between' position, of being no longer at the point of departure or at the place of arrival. It is often both an indefinite journey marked by class (consider Raymond Williams's 1960 novel *Border Country* with the protagonist Matthew Price repeatedly 'crossing' the borders between his Welsh working-class childhood and his middle-class adult life in England) and by race and ethnicity (in his 1986 essay 'The Rainbow Sign', for instance, Hanif Kureishi describes feeling rejected by his birthplace, England, and his father's, Pakistan) which can often lead to a crisis of identity. John McLeod has called this 'perilous intermediate position' expressed by Kureishi as 'living "in-between" different nations, feeling neither here nor there, unable to indulge in sentiments of belonging to either place'.[8] But he also notes how such a position has been reconsidered and renegotiated 'as a site of excitement, new possibilities, and even privilege'.[9] In other contemporary work by authors writing specifically about British Asian experience, Sara Upstone argues that there has been a more assured sense of what 'being British' means. In referencing the work of Kureishi, Hari Kunzru, and Monica Ali, she suggests: '[T]he confidence of many British-born protagonists suggests they are not as confused as their classic representation of "caught between two cultures" implies. [...] [T]he British-born/raised generation announces its agency so that, against alienation, there is also a more defiant British-born sensibility'.[10] So, where does Imtiaz in *Ours are the Streets* fit in here? He can neither access exciting new ways of forming an affirmative concept of British identity nor does he feel that the 'stuck between' experience adequately speaks to his own fractured, often contradictory sense of belonging. What he begins to formulate is a response which emerges out of specific historical and political contexts as well as the material conditions of being young, working class, British, Muslim, and a child of a migrant Pakistani couple.

Sahota himself is a son of immigration, his father having moved to England from India in 1966, his mother in 1978, three years before he was born. Similarly, his paternal grandparents were migrants, having to flee newly-created Pakistan in 1947. Originally from Derbyshire, Sahota now lives in Sheffield. He was named as one of *Granta's* top twenty British writers under forty in 2013 and *The Year of the Runaways* was shortlisted for the Booker Prize in 2015. Sahota has said in interview that the novel, as a form, has been of particular importance to how he thinks about his own identity: 'their language was a way of making sense of myself and my role: who I was as a child of immigrants, who I was as a Briton, as an Englishman, and as a global citizen. The novel was part of that wider conversation I was having about myself'.[11] What novels he has read, and crucially when, have been a source of seeming fascination for critics and interviewers. Much of the press coverage around Sahota mentions or often leads with his 'revelation' that he first read a novel at the age of eighteen.[12] This speaks to both the commercial need for a 'hook' on a news story about a contemporary novelist but also of the kinds of cultural capital it is presumed an author must have, particularly if the novel is held (problematically) as an exclusively 'high literary form'. What is of more interest to my reading, however, is the narrative focus of the first book Sahota read in his late teens: Salman Rushdie's *Midnight's Children* (1981). It is a story concerned with the shifting borders of identities and nations and the ways in which these are historically, politically, and imaginatively imposed and transcended. In both *Ours are the Streets* and *The Year of the Runaways*, the central characters begin to draw on and out similar memories of struggle from Britain's history, notably its (neo)colonial past and present, and beyond its twenty-first-century borders: in India, Pakistan, Kashmir, and Afghanistan. These are the longer histories of violence and struggle that Imogen Tyler argues must be part of a contemporary analysis of the racialising forms of social abjection.

As I discussed in the previous chapter, abjection works to bracket, draw, and construct boundaries and part of that construction is the crafting of the 'other'; it is that which is both deemed disgusting and must be expelled but which also defines that society or specific ideology performing the act of expulsion. Crucially, it is a spacialising theory, one of bordering; it works to generate a space between. Further, McLeod has described borders as 'important thresholds, full of contradiction and ambivalence'. He adds: 'They both separate and join different places. They are intermediate locations where one contemplates moving beyond a barrier'.[13] There are a number of compelling configurations and constructions here then, when thinking about class, work, labour, race, and immigration: for instance, borders, space, policing, contamination, fear, anxiety, threat, and the imagined foreign body. Tyler reads abjection through subject and state formation, noting how the 'borders of the subject and the state are continually being made and unmade'.[14] A focus on citizenship, social class, and migrant illegality draws out the 'longer histories of violence and struggle that converge within the bordering practices of the political present'.[15] Ulla Rahbek has noted the significance of borders in *Ours are the Streets* but places emphasis on how and why they are transgressed by those 'fenced-in' by 'invisible cultural and religious borders'; 'And this lack of belonging leads [Imtiaz] to plan the ultimate border crossing', concludes Rahbek, 'as a suicide bomber'.[16] What is significant in Sahota's writing, however, is the way he examines the political imposition and policing of borders. These include physical and geographical borders as well cultural and social ones. They are marked out by notions of nationhood and belonging which are shaped by the intersections of race and class. It is not simply that Imtiaz is 'fenced-in' but that he is kept out. According to Tyler, there are various forms of social abjection crafted and mobilised by neoliberal governmentality to justify and legitimise 'the reproduction and entrenchment of inequalities and injustices'.[17] Borders work, then, through the fabrication of difference and the imposition of alterity as a means of justifying control, inequality, and violence. This can be seen in the construction of racial difference as a means of 'justifying' colonialism and in the demonisation of the working class to fabricate explanations for the inequalities of capitalism. How and where do these two socially constructed, political practices intersect?

As was noted in the Introduction, Paul Gilroy describes how racial meanings are malleable, they can alter and be struggled over: 'If it is conceived as a continuous and contingent process in the same sense as class formation, race formation can also relate the release of political forces which define themselves and organize around notions of "race" to the meaning and extent of class relationships'.[18] So, perceptions of racial difference change and are constructed socially for political purposes. 'Race', as a political category, is the result of this social and historical process. Gilroy adds: '"Race" has to be socially constructed and politically constructed and elaborate ideological work is done to secure and maintain the different forms of "racialisation" which have characterised capitalist development'.[19] David Roediger's assertion that the 'production' of racial differences 'is itself part of the logic of capital' offers a useful way of 'keeping race and class simultaneously in view'.[20]

And it is this sense of both as 'mutually entangled', as Gilroy suggests, that draws attention to both the similarities and differences between these two political formations.[21] There are contrasting ways in which race and class work but the focus on process is significant. Crucially, they are contingent and continuous whilst being irreducible to one another. Racialisation is a historical and social process working in ways comparable (but not identical) to the various social dynamics of class formation which E. P. Thompson skilfully and powerfully identifies in *The Making of the English Working Class*. However, Roediger has warned that the 'class first' position of some labour and socialist historians reduces, and therefore, marginalises race-based inequality and significantly hinders the potential for broad, productive solidarities to emerge across various, interlocking sites of struggle against the logic of capital.[22] As Stuart Hall describes in his memoir, Thompson was scathing of *Policing the Crisis* (the 1978 book Hall edited with Chas Critcher, Tony Jefferson, John Clarke, and Brian Roberts and which was so influential on Gilroy's *There Ain't No Black in the Union Jack*) because of the 'analytical weight [it] gave to race'.[23] So, there is a historical failure here, one traceable in some work from the left on class in Britain. This chapter critiques Sahota's elucidation of what is a complex interplay between race, class, and capital in the twenty-first century, one connected to the history of empire.

The way Imtiaz in *Ours are the Streets*, for instance, attempts to make sense of such complicated historical processes is a useful way of thinking about the language and the form of the novel. It is written as a diary or extended letter to his wife Rebekah, daughter Noor, and his wider family. Crucially, it is a fragmentary form – a way of sketching down his thoughts – and the interlocking scraps represent lives broken up and scattered. In part, this is explained by the displacement of a long history of immigration, of that sense of being 'in-between' as discussed above. Imtiaz's visit to his family's home village in Pakistan gives expression, at a formal level, to what has been an abiding feature of diaspora writing, one in which 'home' is imagined 'in fragments and fissures, full of gaps and breaches'.[24] This fragmentation works productively in *Ours are the Streets* by allowing the narrative to move quickly between various sites: the British Asian, working-class home of Imtiaz's childhood; the white, working-class home of his wife Rebekah's family; the streets of Sheffield; the village in Pakistan. And the connections between place are further drawn out in Sahota's fiction through geography and language. Meersbrook, where Rebekah lives, is called a 'hill station' by Imtiaz, echoing the ways in which the landscape of Pakistan is described.[25] And the similarities between Sheffield, which features in both novels, and the Punjab, where a number of characters in *The Years of the Runaways* come from, seem more than mere coincidence: five rivers converge at different points in the Yorkshire city (Sheaf, Don, Porter, Rivelin, and Loxley) while Punjab broadly translates as the 'land of five rivers' (Beas, Sutlej, Ravi, Chenab, and Jhelum). Punjabi is used throughout the second novel by the Indian migrant workers ('Sat sri akal' as a greeting, for example) but it stands separate from English; in contrast, the language used by Imtiaz as a British Pakistani in the first book merges Urdu and South Yorkshire dialect. The use of 'sempt' in place of 'seem' and 'were' instead of 'was' represents the voice of working-class Sheffield; it is accompanied by expressions such as 'Inshallah' meaning 'God willing' and 'Ammi' for mother. These are terms all used on the opening page of the novel which set-up and convey the specific vernacular of a British Pakistani northern working class. Sahota has described the novel as a 'capacious form', suggesting that 'you can throw almost anything at it and it remains robust. It's the access to interiority that distinguishes it'.[26] The complexity and flexibility such a form offers, therefore, provide a way of sketching out various critiques of how race and class intersect in the life of Imtiaz.

I have described *Ours are the Streets* as a diary and a long letter but it is also an extended prayer, a confession, an act undertaken to stall death, and it works as a correction to the assumptions projected onto Imtiaz as well as to what narrative will form after his planned terrorist attack.[27] Here, we see a different form of process, not only process as a social relation but as a working through, of writing and attempting to make sense of the experience of being 'made abject'. The dynamics of race play a significant part in initially blocking this productive act; Imtiaz has previously been excluded from such forms of writing. The social construction of racial difference has denied him access to an understanding of the very processes which are one of the causes of his abjection. He reveals:

> I really did enjoy English and Art and stuff like that. And wondered about growing up and writing plays or something [...]. Knew it'd never happen, like. For all the usual boring brown reasons. But I'm loving writing this. It's really helping. It's like normally I'm walking round and I'm just confused about how I'm feeling or what I'm thinking. But when I'm writing it's like I'm rummaging about inside myself, and I can just keep on rummaging until I find something that's not far off what it really is I want to say. Ameen.[28]

Imtiaz constructs a clichéd image of a writer: 'I ought to have been wearing glasses, or maybe one of those one-eyed jobs',[29] he jokes. But it is the dynamics of race which more directly explain his exclusion; he wrongly assumes that people of colour do not write and there is an accompanying cultural pressure on him not to do so. The latter not only comes from the British Pakistani community it seems but also emanates from the ways in which British Muslims are systematically denied access to freedom of speech and the forming of political opinions. Such repressions are what can lead to the taking up of extreme positions, Arun Kundnani has suggested. Spaces need to be created which allow for young Muslims to 'think critically and learn how to express their views in effective ways', he says.[30] The act of writing for Imtiaz is one such safe space but it is too late, he has already turned to forms of political violence. According to Said, what has politicised and troubled conceptions of Muslims in the 'West' is 'the almost total absence of any cultural position making it possible either to identify with or dispassionately to discuss [...] Islam'.[31] Sahota's novel is correcting this absence, allowing for a cultural position to be taken by Imtiaz, but this, in turn, serves to draw attention to how such a position was needed much earlier.

Ours are the Streets, therefore, explores the complex reasons why Imtiaz is drawn to extremism; it questions those decisions and provides a space to do so which connects race, class, and abjection. He experiences a shifting sense of home, relinquishing his foreigner or Englishman label ('valetiya'), to become 'rooted to my earth' in his family's Pakistani village.[32] Further, Pakistan is eventually identified as 'home home'.[33] This is a reversal of the journey his father originally undertook: from Pakistan to a new home in Britain. Imtiaz is moving from Sheffield, his birthplace, to the identification of a new sense of belonging through the complex social and mental processes of return. Crucially, the reasons for this reversal, what instigates it, are significant when thinking through the class dynamics of the text.

Rizwan Raina dies of a heart attack while at work, chasing a fare-dodging customer. The funeral is held in Pakistan, the service being the reason why Imtiaz visits the country of his father's birth. This fatal incident follows a number of racially-motivated attacks: 'Yesterday they took a leak in your taxi, last month they put a brick through your window. Maybe next time they'll just burn the thing',[34] Imtiaz says to Rizwan. There is a sense that this life of service, a kind of servitude which results in violence and oppression, is a failure; it is a disappointment which is understood in class terms: '[T]he worst time were always in that moment when he realised he were being pitied – because he only drove a taxi, because he had never managed to move away from this estate – and the shame would wash down over him'.[35] Imtiaz's father is a taxi driver throughout his life in Yorkshire, despite ambitions to move beyond such work after a successful college education in Pakistan. This trajectory is contrasted to his fellow Pakistani immigrants who enjoy what he sees as successful careers in Britain. The family live in an 'old-style terrace' and Imtiaz writes of his father being 'very proud that he'd paid the mortgage off and owned it fully'.[36] But the previous extract describes the shame Rizwan feels within the British Asian community. This is partly understood as a class failure and represents an awareness of class through struggle; here is class as a social relation. It is part of a racialised experience of class, one which has resulted historically in generations of Caribbeans, Indians, and Pakistanis undergoing a 'profound process of proletarianization on their arrival in Britain', according to Virdee.[37] Post-war migrant labour became, following the intensification of the racialisation of British nationalism, 'the unwanted reminders of an empire lost' and there was a 'restaging of the colonial encounter' within Britain.[38] Part of this process meant that British Asians came to 'occupy a distinctive position in class relations – as a racialized fraction of the working class'.[39] As McLeod states, the country 'was changed forever by its colonial encounters'.[40] Crucially, race, class, and immigration overlap here: 'the performative necessity of nationalist representations enables all those placed on the margins of its norms and limits – such as women, migrants, the working class, the peasantry, those of a different "race" or ethnicity – to *intervene* in the signifying process and *challenge* the dominant representations with narratives of their own'.[41] Imtiaz's writing in *Ours are the Streets* can be seen to be part of that challenge but it is one shaped by (and in turn which leads to) violence. Gilroy's explanation for such historical brutality enacted upon those situated on the margins is crucial here: Britain has failed 'to meet the historic challenge represented by the underlying difficulties of social and political transition with which the presence of post-colonial [...] people has been unwittingly bound up'. Gilroy adds:

> [T]hese chronic difficulties which periodically produce acute bouts of racial and national anxiety arise from melancholic responses to the loss of imperial pre-eminence and the painful demand to adjust the life of the national collective to a severely reduced sense of itself as a global power.[42]

What is significant, with regard to Sahota's writing and the social and political trajectory this study of working-class literature is tracking, is what Virdee describes as a 'postcolonial racism', one which can be traced from the primal scene of the New Right, the infamous Enoch Powell 'Rivers of Blood' speech of 1968, to the emergence of Thatcherism a decade later. '[T]he confident racism that had accompanied the high imperial moment mutated into a defensive racism', says Virdee, 'a racism of the vanquished who no longer wanted to dominate but to physically expel the racialized other from the shared space they occupied, and thereby erase them and the Empire from its collective memory'.[43] Part of this move was, adds Virdee, to 'manage the coming crisis of British capitalism by manipulating a racializing nationalism' and, crucially, 'maintain its class rule'.[44]

Such a racialised experience of class in a Britain after empire helps explain the life of Rizwan Raina and how it comes to be understood by his son. The racialisation of Britain and British as white, notably through successive Immigration Acts which eventually culminated in the Windrush Scandal of 2018, results in the forms of alienation felt by Imtiaz. As Gilroy and Virdee explain, these processes are ones which must be understood in relation to British capitalism and the forms it takes prior to, during, and after Thatcherism, from the New Right to the twenty-first century. So what does *Ours are the Streets* offer in way of a critique of capital and neoliberalism? In an insightful reading of 'Jihadi fiction', Jago Morrison suggests, albeit tentatively, that Sahota, unlike John Updike's novel *Terrorist* (2006), is more interested in exploring the 'psychology of a would-be terrorist' than examining a 'contemptuous view of the West' and critiquing the 'temples of consumerism'.[45] However, such a mode of critique is represented by Imtiaz whose target, after all, is one such 'temple': Meadowhall.

On his return to Sheffield, following his father's funeral, Imtiaz describes what he sees as he waits for his luggage at the airport: 'the shiny tiles, the flashing signs, the sparkling windows, just the wasteful meaningless brightness of everything. None of it felt real'.[46] This sense of artificiality continues on his arrival home: 'I stepped out of the fake car and went up the fake path and buzzed the fake doorbell'.[47] The powerful, accumulative effect of the repeated use of 'fake' is directly contrasted with how he feels in Pakistan: 'It were like for the first time I had an actual real past, with real people who'd lived real lives'.[48] There is an explicit parallel being drawn here, the use of 'real' on three occasions and in quick succession accentuates the sense of Britain as 'fake' (also deployed three times). These passages could be explained by the disorientating experience of cross-continental travel or put down to Imtiaz's paranoia, an exaggerated and simplified view of 'reality' by someone whose mental health appears to be deteriorating. But an awareness of the artificial being used as a mode of distraction, particularly for political purposes, is what Imtiaz hopes his daughter Noor will gain from his writing. 'Remember these material goods are just the things they try to dazzle you with so you won't notice what's really going on', he says.[49] The 'fake' is the promise of consumer capitalism, of an escapism which insidiously works to divert critical attention away from the actions of Western governments, both domestically and internationally. There is a critique of consumerism here then, contrary to Morrison's reading, but the alternatives to such political realities are tragically ill-conceived by Imtiaz.

'Terrorism is not the product of radical politics but a symptom of political impotence', according to Kundnani.[50] In *Keywords for Today* (edited by Colin MacCabe and Holly Yanacek), Islamic terrorism is described as seeking to claim 'its authority not from a political but from divine authority'.[51] However, as Tony Crowley has noted, '[t]here are few terms more politically significant than terrorism in its variable contemporary usage'.[52] Its dominant use is 'obfuscatory', suggests Crowley, and we must ask difficult and probing questions about its 'use of violence for political aims';[53] as Kundnani argues, 'terrorism is a mode of political action'.[54] The figure of Imtiaz Raina returns us to one of the early uses of the word, as *Keywords for Today* identifies: 'In Early Modern English, terror comes to stand for a state of fear provoked on the very edge of the social'.[55] This notion of peripheral existence and placement, both socially and politically, is a key factor in the violence perpetrated by and enacted upon Imtiaz. As Tyler has noted, colonial history as well as the 'neoliberal inequalities of the social and political present' must be considered here, as a way of both understanding and finding a solution to the cycles of violence which engulf the racialised working class. 'However difficult the task, we must', she urges, 'do the critical work of understanding the roots of contemporary forms of marginality as symptomatic of ongoing forms of colonial dehumanization'.[56] It is a difficult task because there are a number of dangers; namely, that acts of mass killing will be seen to be justified by what are nevertheless important methods of historical and political contextualisation or that the forms of political dissent which are traceable in narratives such as Imtiaz's are 'collapsed', as Kundnani puts it, into terrorism so that 'the only Muslim voice is the terrorist voice'.[57] Morrison identifies another problem, one which he describes as a 'significant lack' in Sahota's novel: 'Martyrdom itself remains fearfully unknowable', he says.[58] This may be so for the character of Imtiaz as the novel ends before the planned (and most probably aborted) attack on Meadowhall takes place. But Imtiaz is one of a 'cell' of four potential suicide bombers, all with different motivations, all groomed and coerced by a radical mentor, Abu Bhai. Two of the four (Faisal and Aaqil) do go ahead with their acts of 'martyrdom': Faisal attacks and murders American soldiers in Afghanistan; Aaqil bombs the British High Commission in Islamabad, killing six Britons. There are multiple criticisms of these bombings, particularly from Imtiaz's father and from Charag (the fourth member of Imtiaz's group who has no intention of becoming a suicide bomber). So, not only is there a complex picture drawn of the motivations and willingness to commit such brutal acts of 'martyrdom' but there are also several contrasting positions taken to these forms of violence. This is part of the novel's attempt to complicate an understanding of what is figured as a cycle of violence and to resist easy resolutions which contain and restrict critical discussion. Sahota is writing against the kind of simplistic and limiting media narratives Hanif Kureishi also touches upon in his fiction; in *The Black Album* (1995), after a bomb at Victoria Station in London, the central character Shahid Hasan 'wanted to be in the midst of chaos, not watching the event on television, where it would already have a form and explanation, robbing viewers of involvement'.[59] The difficulties of resisting such easy forms of understanding have increased and been complicated by the ways in which terrorism and its global socio-political contexts are understood after 11th September 2001. My reading of *Ours are the Streets* places it within a longer history, clearly situated within but not only as a product of, or singular response to, the post-9/11 period (or post-7/7 in Britain and the 2005 Islamic terrorist attacks on London's transportation system). This is not a novel about a singular theme: the violent Muslim male. It is a novel about various forms of historical and structural violence enacted upon the racialised other and the role of class in that process. The novel places Imtiaz's exclusion within the longer, historical processes, specific to Britain, of race, class, and colonialism.

Sahota has described his own frustrations at the 'rise' of the 9/11 novel, noting that authors have been 'falling over themselves to write the terrorist novel'.[60] He adds:

> The debates around terrorism, or illegal immigrants, or migration, are just so base and crude, and give no concession to nuances. The media and government want a simple narrative that comes with easy hooks, and gets easy catchwords and slogans out there, which will make people think that they're on top of the situation.[61]

What is required is what Kundnani describes as a focus on 'specific material circumstances', with added emphasis on 'the specific social and political histories' pertaining to race, class, immigration, empire, and capitalism.[62] It is in Sahota's second novel that these themes are explored more expansively through the notions of illegality, nationhood, and citizenship.

The Year of the Runaways tracks the lives of three Indian immigrants (Randeep, Avtar, and Tochi) in twenty-first-century Britain, living and working 'illegally' on building sites, in fast food takeaways, and in underground sewers removing toxic waste. The novel opens in Sheffield but quickly moves to several geographical and imaginative spaces familiar from both Sahota's debut and from the work of the other writers looked at in this book. In the final part of the novel titled 'Autumn',[63] Randeep, for example, who is married to a fourth central character in the narrative, a British woman Narinder, is living under a railway bridge in Derby, 'on the river, by the new flats'. Sahota writes:

> He found no bridge in that direction, only waterside bars and restaurants, and so he turned around and retraced his steps and carried on past the station and the flats, out towards the gasworks and factories. There weren't any joggers around here, just the odd fisherman thickly hidden. He walked on, convinced he'd gone too far, or that it had been a ruse to get him out of the gurdwara. Then he saw it: a wide, bottle-green bridge, beautiful in its way. Underneath it, three figures, all in shadow. Their chatter echoed coarsely. They were slumped against the wall in their sleeping bags and blankets.[64]

Here, once again then, is a deindustrial landscape, similar to that which is found in the work of Burn, Cartwright, and Raisin. Randeep is thrust to the edges of the city, a political and historical space marked by the dynamics of capital: gentrification, homelessness, the architectural fabric of industrialisation. However, there is a comparable yet slightly different conception of what the street represents here, compared to the contested political space discussed at the start of this chapter, and it is one which aligns Randeep with the social abjection experienced by Mick Little in Ross Raisin's *Waterline*. Elsewhere, for example, Avtar complains about being 'left [...] to die on the streets'.[65] So, the forms of exclusion which the street represents in *Ours are the Streets* are replicated in *The Year of the Runaways* as direct violence; there is an explicit fear of death which is part of a structural violence built on and produced by the inequalities of race and class.

Sahota has spoken of how his writing connects to a structure of feeling emanating from a distinct political understanding of historical and social change as a process of deindustrialisation. 'When I think of the places I grew up, which were vibrant working-class communities', he says, 'and then the decimation of the manufacturing industry and the mining industry that Thatcher caused in the 1980s, a sense of betrayal from that time still hangs in the air today in many communities in the North of England'.[66] It is the violence of capital being tracked here and, for Sahota, this must be read within a postcolonial context, one which engages with the history of immigration into working-class areas. Expanding on what he identifies as the impact of deindustrialisation, he adds:

> What that does to a community, how the blame for that is fixed on a government, and the sense of displacement caused by new communities coming in, is fascinating. The children of those new groups create a new dynamic and a unique nexus of conditions that is quite specific to the North.[67]

Compellingly, the experience of abjection suffered by what are identified as 'new communities' cuts across potential racial, ethnic, and religious solidarities in *The Year of the Runaways* because it is predicated on class inequalities. Randeep is homeless after a police raid on the house he shares with several other immigrants in Sheffield. After moving to the East Midlands, where he struggles to find work or accommodation, he looks for help from the local gurdwara mentioned above but is advised to join the homeless men under the railway bridge; he identifies this as 'a ruse to get him out of the gurdwara'. When asked later about visiting, Randeep responds: 'We all did. But the people, they complain. They say we're unclean. That we smell. Which we do. So let us come and use the shower once a day, right?'.[68] It is presumed that the gurdwara will act as a place of refuge and support but the response Randeep receives in Derby, as an Indian Sikh and homeless migrant, shows how abjection works across ethnicity and faith as well as upon racialised inequalities.

The Kristevan notion of contamination has a social effect: the formation of a supposed 'underclass'. The designation of the 'foreign body' as 'unclean' and as carrying an unpleasant odour ('we smell') marks it out for expulsion, even from those communities in which it might be expected solace and support could be found.

Crucially, however, Randeep is homeless because of the way the neoliberal state has mobilised its forces in order to define notions of illegality. Social abjection works through the construction of social norms imposed by the state, in this instance represented by the police and the raid on Randeep's Sheffield home. As Imogen Tyler argues 'British citizenship is a legal, political and social field of intelligibility that abjectifies some people outside of the realms of citizenship altogether, constituting them as illegal but also, paradoxically, fixing, capturing, and paralysing them within the borders of the state'.[69] Randeep finds himself in the 'position of being outside the legal protections of citizenship, but nevertheless subject to the full force of state power'.[70] This is akin to what Giorgio Agamben describes as a state of exception, 'an anomic space in which what is at stake is a force of law without law'; it is a form of state power which is figured as being deployed out of 'necessity', one constructed as objective when it is, in fact, a 'subjective judgement'.[71] According to Agamben, '[t]he question of borders becomes all the more urgent' here and 'exceptional measures' imposed to both 'protect' but also construct borders 'find themselves in the paradoxical position of being juridical measures that cannot be understood in legal terms, and the state of exception appears as the legal form of what cannot have legal form'.[72] This state of emergency at times of national crisis, which found new expressions during the Bush-Blair 'war on terror', has often meant indefinite detentions and deportations or extraditions without fair hearing; in the USA in particular it has resulted in the introduction of orders which 'radically erases any legal status of the individual, thus producing a legally unnameable and unclassifiable being'.[73] What Randeep's outside/inside position in the UK represents is one of the many contradictions of neoliberal capitalism: the need for migrant labour at the same time as the crafting of a myth concerning the illegal immigrant. Such notions of illegality are linked to what I looked at in Chapter Four during the discussion of Ross Raisin's *Waterline* and what Tyler has identified as a 'liberal paradox': 'deepening democracy through citizenship, and the abjection of "illegal" populations from the rights and protections of citizenship through the enforcement of often brutal and inhumane immigration controls'.[74] So, it is a notion of democracy defined and secured by including 'citizens' yet excluding often racialised 'others' through violent means. The figure of the national abject is constructed in order to create fear and anxiety and therefore justify state action. The experience of migrant workers like Randeep and his friend Avtar is one of living on what Anne McClintock has described as the 'impossible edges of modernity', these are abject zones, according to McClintock they draw 'attention again to the spatial dimensions of abjection'.[75]

Randeep becomes separated from Avtar who finds what he thinks is paid work in the West Midlands. He is in fact held as a slave in a shed in the back garden of his 'boss' and works during the day removing a huge globe of fat, a fatberg, from an underground sewer. Sahota writes:

> Avtar threw Romy their torch – the defunct lamps on their helmets had never been replaced – and they wound tape around the tops of their boots so too much of the thicker shit wouldn't find its way in. [...] [T]he dark water came to his knees. Things bobbed on the surface – ribbons of tissue, air-filled condoms that looked like silver fish floating dumbly towards the light. A furry layer of moss waved back and forth across the curve of the brickwork. Everything seemed bathed in a gelatinous gleam.[76]

As well as evoking mining imagery which takes us back to Chapter One – miners helmets which no longer work properly, descending underground to work, taking a pick axe to hack at the fatberg – there are compelling connotations of the Kristevan notion of abjection here: fluids, scum, and disgust. It is an extreme form of precarity which carries echoes of the industrial society of the previous century and what Virdee identifies above as the historical proletarianisation of, in particular, migrant workers from India. And what works as a literal example of social abjection is identified as playing a key role within the dynamics of capitalist society: the imagery of 'things' bobbing to the surface, of being expelled but refusing to be suppressed by the violence of the present. It is a society addicted to waste, one which blocks the system designed to process it, and the very people abjected by this society are the ones tasked, or more aptly forced with dealing with what is described by Sahota as a 'writhing ten-foot maggot stuck to the side of the tunnel'.[77] Those constructed and defined as human waste within the national imaginary are having to remove the real waste, the 'gelatinous gleam' which seems to infect everything. It is a disgusting process – morally and physically – but it is also an act of displacement, one performed in order to maintain both the physical and political structures of British society. The figurations of work and racialised labour in Sahota's novel, therefore, reveal the concealments and contradictions of capital.

By focusing on the formation of social abjection in such processes, it is possible, across Sahota's writing, to hold together race and class; there is the potential of keeping them simultaneously in view, as Roediger suggests, through a critique of capitalism which illustrates the dynamics of both as social and political formations. It is this focus on the intersection of race and class which simultaneously draws out one of the key relationships between deindustrialisation and demonisation based on the mutually entangled forms of racial and class inequalities. These are the social and historical processes which form the structural conditions for twenty-first-century capitalism; they are also the sites from which solidarities need to be forged in order to overcome the violence of neoliberalism.

Notes

1 Sunjeev Sahota, *Ours are the Streets* (London: Picador, 2011), p. 70.
2 Ibid., p. 70.
3 Virdee, p. 130. The British National Party moved away from the National Front policy of direct street action (as discussed in Chapter Three) but this has since been a central plank of the English Defence League's strategy under the leadership of Tommy Robinson.
4 Edward Said, *Orientalism* (London: Penguin, 2003), p. 54. Original emphasis.
5 Anderson, p. 5.
6 Sahota, *Streets*, p. 137.
7 Ibid., pp. 137–138.
8 John McLeod, *Beginning Postcolonialism* (Manchester: Manchester University Press, 2000), p. 214.
9 Ibid., p, 214.
10 Sara Upstone, *British Asian Fiction: Twenty-First-Century Voices* (Manchester: Manchester University Press, 2010), p. 7.
11 Katy Shaw, 'Living by the Pen: In Conversation with Sunjeev Sahota', *English*, vol. 66, no. 254 (pp. 263–271), p. 265. In the same interview, Sahota comments on the necessity of the novel form to develop and change in order, he says, 'to address the newer concerns of the world we live in' and suggests that 'language in novels has to change to reflect more effectively the world out there' (p. 267).
12 See Yvette Huddleston, 'He Hadn't Read a Novel Until He Was 18. Now Sunjeev Sahota Is Vying for the Man Booker', *Yorkshire Post*, 9th September 2015; Andrew McMillan, 'Sunjeev Sahota Interview: Rise and Rise of the Man Booker Shortlisted Author', *Independent*, 25th September 2015.
13 McLeod, p. 217.
14 Tyler, *Revolting Subjects*, p. 46.
15 Ibid., p. 46.
16 Ulla Rahbek, '"Repping Your Ends": Imagined Borders in Recent British Multicultural Fiction', *Literature & Theology*, vol. 27, no. 4, December 2013 (pp. 426–438), p. 430, p. 432.
17 Tyler, *Revolting Subjects*, p. 8.
18 Gilroy, p. 36.
19 Ibid., p. 35.
20 David Roediger, *Class, Race, and Marxism* (London: Verso, 2017), p. 7.
21 Gilroy, p. 38.
22 Roediger, p. 6.
23 Stuart Hall (with Bill Schwarz), *Familiar Stranger: A Life Between Two Islands* (London: Penguin: 2018), p. 265. See also Gilroy's critique of Thompson in *There Ain't No Black in the Union Jack*, p. 55.
24 McLeod, p. 211.
25 Sahota, *Streets*, p. 106.
26 Shaw, 'In Conversation', p. 265.

27 It is left uncertain whether or not Imtiaz goes ahead with the planned bombing of Meadowhall; it is very unlikely that it does. The attack is delayed at first (see *Ours are the Streets*, p. 288) and the novel ends as Imtiaz speaks to his dead father, asking him to sit with him as he goes to sleep, immediately after he has informed Rebekah of his plans on the evening before the second attempt.

28 Sahota, *Streets*, p. 26.

29 Ibid., p. 151.

30 Arun Kundnani, *The Muslims are Coming! Islamophobia, Extremism, and the Domestic War on Terror* (London: Verso, 2015), p. 182.

31 Said, *Orientalism*, pp. 26–27.

32 Sahota, *Streets*, p. 98.

33 Ibid., p. 259. It is another character, Fahim, who describes Pakistan as 'home home' but Imtiaz agrees, writing: 'I said that were the most sensible thing he'd said in years' (p. 259).

34 Sahota, *Streets*, p. 72.

35 Ibid., p. 73.

36 Ibid., p. 30.

37 Virdee, p. 111. Virdee's book carefully tracks the different experiences of migrant workers in Britain from the late-eighteenth century and explains how these forms of proletarianization, although they differ at various moments throughout the twentieth century in particular (see Virdee, p. 161), are racialised.

38 Virdee, p. 107.

39 Ibid., p. 112.

40 McLeod, p. 205.

41 Ibid., p. 119. Original emphasis.

42 Gilroy, p. xxxvii.

43 Virdee, p. 114.

44 Ibid., p. 117.

45 Jago Morrison, 'Jihadi Fiction: Radicalisation Narratives in the Contemporary Novel', *Textual Practice*, vol. 31, no. 3 (pp. 567–584), p. 577. Morrison offers an illuminating reading of novels by Mohsin Hamid and J.M. Coetzee (as well as Updike and Sahota) suggesting that 'we are invited to question what we think we know about radicalisation, jihadis and the counterterrorist response to them' (p, 570).

46 Sahota, *Streets*, p. 278.

47 Ibid., p. 279.

48 Ibid., p. 115.

49 Ibid., p. 75.

50 Kundnani, p. 289.

51 Colin MacCabe and Holly Yanacek, eds., *Keywords for Today: A 21st Century Vocabulary* (Oxford: Oxford University Press, 2018), p. 349.

52 Tony Crowley, 'Keywords: Terrorism', *Key Words: A Journal of Cultural Materialism*, vol. 14, 2016 (pp. 116–118), p. 116.

53 Ibid., p. 117.

54 Kundnani, p. 103.

55 McCabe and Yanacek, p. 348. By tracking the use of the word, *Keywords for Today* identifies an important development from this early understanding: 'a word initially used to describe emotional states experienced at the very margins of the social is now limited entirely to describing emotional states experienced at the very heart of social and political life' (p. 350).

56 Tyler, *Revolting Subjects*, p. 41.

57 Kundnani, p. 267.
58 Morrison, p. 576.
59 Hanif Kureishi, *The Black Album* (London: Faber and Faber, 2010), p. 103.
60 Shaw, 'In Conversation', p. 269.
61 Ibid., p. 266.
62 Kundnani, p. 69, p. 61.
63 The novel is structured by four parts relating to the seasons ('Winter', 'Spring', 'Summer', 'Autumn') and ends with a short epilogue.
64 Sunjeev Sahota, *The Year of the Runaways* (London: Picador, 2015), pp. 379–380.
65 Ibid., p. 351.
66 Shaw, 'In Conversation', p. 267.
67 Ibid., p. 267.
68 Sahota, *Runaways*, p. 381.
69 Tyler, *Revolting Subjects*, p. 14.
70 Ibid., p. 62.
71 Giorgio Agamben, *State of Exception* (Chicago, IL: The University of Chicago Press, 2005), p. 39, p. 30.
72 Ibid., p. 1.
73 Ibid., p, 3. Agamben's writings on the figure of the *homo sacer* are also relevant here: individuals stripped of legal rights but kept alive in a basic, highly restricted state. See Giorgio Agamben, *Homo Sacer: Sovereign Power and Bare Life* (Stanford, CA: Stanford University Press, 1998).
74 Tyler, *Revolting Subjects*, p. 93.
75 McClintock quoted in Tyler, *Revolting Subjects*, pp. 35–36.
76 Sahota, *Runaways*, p. 382.
77 Ibid., p. 383.

Conclusion
Class Matters

This book has been an attempt to analyse a small selection of novels as sites through which to read the complex processes of capital, using them to examine and explore the workings of class in twenty-first-century Britain. It has traced articulations of class experience from deindustrialisation, using the Miners' Strike of 1984/1985 as a strategic starting point, through to social abjection and demonisation. A historicisation of class in Britain has been a defining focus and the mapping of what is a complex trajectory through deindustrialisation has been undertaken in order to draw attention to the lasting impact of class, how it works, and how it is used in emerging new ways. *The Working Class and Twenty-First-Century British Fiction: Deindustrialisation, Demonisation, Resistance* is not a definitive account or survey of contemporary working-class fiction, however. A definitive account, if at all possible, would need to cover more texts and provide an extensive analysis of what is, encouragingly, an upsurge in writing that could loosely be described as working class. Categorising authors and novels comes with an array of problems and the categories themselves are not pre-determined but defined by the processes of selection. The six writers who form the central focus here have been selected because their respective texts articulate something specific and distinctive about class, work, and neoliberalism; they figure the latter as a project with a particular political intention designed as an attack on the working class. That is why my focus has been on how the dynamics of contemporary neoliberal capital have been felt, experienced, and understood through deindustrialisation, class struggle, inequality, trauma, social abjection, and racism. These texts all challenge conceptions of homogeneity and static forms of social class. Therefore, to end this book it will be useful to remember where it started: with E. P. Thompson's notion of class as a process, as an active formation rather than simply a descriptive term, 'something which in fact happens (and can be shown to have happened) in human relationships'.[1] The notion of class naming and the struggle to define what class and inequality are and what they represent, as well as on the heterogeneity rather than a perceived homogeneity of the working class, are vital to understand what class means, why it matters, and how it continues as an active formation.

This book has engaged with several approaches to the novel and has been concerned with how contemporary writers have worked with and through the registers and literary techniques of a variety of formal modes. Bertolt Brecht argued that we need different methods to reveal truth, that it 'must be expressed in many ways'. 'New problems appear and demand new methods', he wrote. 'Reality changes; in order to represent it, modes of representation must also change'.[2] The profound changes brought about by the twenty-first century demand the same. Neoliberalism continues to remodel and reconstitute itself and society. There have been radical changes to class, particularly since 1979, which require continued theorisation if contemporary examples of writing about class are to be identified and analysed. There has also been a deliberate attempt to figure class as anachronistic and redundant, symbolised by New Labour's uncoupling of class from inequality but also traceable through the broad embrace of the neoliberal project by mainstream British politics. More encouragingly, and in response, a critical discourse around contemporary formations of class has emerged which presents an opportunity to instigate new ways of thinking about fiction. This book is presented as a contribution to such a renewal. One of the exciting (but equally often anxiety-inducing) aspects of working on twenty-first-century material is that the field and terms of reference are continually being adjusted and altered. New work on working-class writing, both in theory and practice, is now being developed at a time when there is an opportunity, once more, to begin to shift the focus onto the inequalities of class and cultural production. Kit de Waal has been an important figure here and alongside *Know Your Place: Essays on the Working Class by the Working Class*, edited by Nathan Connolly and published in 2017, there is now *Common People: An Anthology of Working-Class Writers* (edited by de Waal and released in 2019) as well as a range of new novels on working-class life which have emerged and are emerging in the second and third decades of the twenty-first century. What are identified in my book are several productive sites of resistance from which debates engaged with contemporary capitalism, work, and class are possible; there are many more. New ways of articulating and mapping class are needed. These must acknowledge the dramatic changes brought about by contemporary capitalism and, in the case of literary fiction, use the flexibility of the novel as a form to illuminate the complex, complicated, and shifting formations of class. I have specifically selected fiction that engages with these concepts of change and process; here are texts which foreground class as a fundamental experience, one which is not static, stable, or pre-determined but is shaped by and around social discourse and the dynamics of neoliberalism. They are authors who imagine and capture capital through the pressures placed on class experience, namely the processes of political struggle, inequality, deindustrialisation, nostalgia, trauma, social abjection, and racialised violence. And, as noted, they represent an emerging corpus but are not as far as the boundaries of the critical field on working-class writing should be drawn.

As de Waal has persuasively argued, there are a number of potential stumbling blocks when thinking about and supporting working-class writing, none more so than the persistent problem of 'social mobility'. The author of *My Name is Leon* (2016) explains thus:

> I've always had a problem with the idea of cherry-picking the most able or the most driven rather than lifting whole communities out of poverty, providing better standards of education and better living conditions for all. Worse than that, the notion of social mobility has always smacked of: "How can we help you to be more like us?" It seems to say that to be working class is to be a failure.[3]

Social mobility as it is figured within stories about the working class is often part of a discourse of meritocracy. As David Alderson has noted, the narrative of escape has 'a long tradition in working-class writing: that of the exceptional individual who leaves [their] class behind'.[4] When it comes to novels of this type, the assumed reader is a member of a generic middle class and the move out of the working class represents an escape into the culture of the former, one which is never explored or interrogated but simply accepted as superior to that of the latter. There is no critique of middle-class culture or dominant class logic. What is really important here though is that social mobility, in this form, is accommodated by the logic of neoliberal discourse. For Raymond Williams, the ladder metaphor often deployed to laud meritocracy reveals how social mobility and capitalism are compatible; '[I]t is a device that can only be used individually; you go up the ladder alone', notes Williams, who adds that it is an 'alternative to solidarity'.[5] In *Against Meritocracy: Culture, Power and Myths of Mobility*, Jo Littler argues that the metaphor of mobility 'promises opportunity whilst producing social division'.[6] She adds: '[I]t endorses a competitive, linear, hierarchical system in which by definition certain people must be left behind. The top cannot exist without the bottom. Not everyone can "rise"'.[7] So, the figuration of an individual (rather than a collective) escape carries with it powerful and damaging implications. Only one person at a time can go up the metaphorical ladder and they often use what is being 'escaped' from as a means of supporting that escape: writing about the working class to escape the working class, for example. Such methods of mobility do not question or radically change class structures sustained by inequality and division; rather, they help to perpetuate the idea that the people who have already arrived at the escapee's destination are there on merit, they have got there by hard work, this is a valuable and worthwhile place to be. And there is a further problem here: narratives of escape, despite the upward mobility of a central 'exceptional' individual, draw class formations as stable and static. The working class are in danger of being presented as backward or culturally bankrupt, often with moments of nostalgic or romanticised reverence. Such stories risk demonising the society from which the protagonist, figured as the moral centre of the novel, flees. The class from which the individual escapes, therefore, is described as if it must be escaped. Such a move risks placing the blame on the working class rather than probing the workings of wider societal structures; it also crafts a myth of agency and raises a pertinent question: how is only one person among a multitude able to resist and 'rise'? Think of what Alan Sinfield asks about Winston Smith in George Orwell's *1984* (1949): 'Why should not the proles resist? Why should only Winston see through it all?'.[8] Again, it is the focus on the individual rather than on collective solidarity that is the problem here. And it raises a further question: for who are such narratives of escape being written? Kit de Waal has spoken of how the publishing industry only selects and allows through specific narratives, particularly when it is seeking to create what she describes as 'just another product for middle-class consumption'.[9] One damaging trend has been, particularly since the Brexit vote, the anthropological journalistic studies of 'left behind' areas, as noted in the Introduction, often deciding what they will find in working-class communities before they have arrived. Here is another form of filtering. It is a move which can construct and project, depending on who the writer is or who they chose to speak to and for, an idea of the 'authentic' working-class individual: the one who has escaped and returns, or who has escaped and now can offer an insight into the reality of the place they have escaped from. It is a pitfall which can be avoided, and it is a problem of cultural production rather than the fault of any individual writers, but it always risks perpetuating conceptions of class which serve inequality. In my, albeit narrow, selection of texts, I have attempted to avoid such problems of perpetuation. The specific focus of *The Working Class and Twenty-First-Century British Fiction* has been on work, on deindustrialisation, and on the ways class naming is deployed and can be resisted, something which connects all the six main chapters. What both the continuities and the shifts, from David Peace to Sunjeev Sahota, represent are a mapping of neoliberalism. The novels studied across this book name and resist the processes which have labelled the working class as the 'enemy within'; they provide sites of resistance to the damaging logics and inequalities of capital. And they represent not an escape from class but an affirmation that class matters.

Notes

1 Thompson, p. 8.
2 Brecht, 'Popularity and Realism', p. 83, p. 82.
3 Kit de Waal, 'Make Room for Working-Class Writers', *The Guardian*, 10th February 2018, www.theguardian.com/books/2018/feb/10/kit-de-waal-where-are-all-the-working-class-writers-.

4 David Alderson, 'Making Electricity: Narrating Gender, Sexuality, and the Neoliberal Transition in *Billy Elliot*', *Camera Obscura 75*, vol. 25, no. 3, 2011 (pp. 1–27), p. 11.

5 Raymond Williams quoted in Jo Littler, *Against Meritocracy: Culture, Power and Myths of Mobility* (Abingdon: Routledge, 2018), p. 3.

6 Jo Littler, *Against Meritocracy: Culture, Power and Myths of Mobility* (Abingdon: Routledge, 2018), p. 3.

7 Ibid., p. 3.

8 Sinfield, p. 115.

9 de Waal, *The Guardian*, 10th February 2018.

Bibliography

Adorno, Theodor W., 'Reading Balzac', in Rolf Tiedemann, ed., *Notes to Literature: Volume One* (New York, NY: Columbia University Press, 1991), pp. 121–136.

Adorno, Theodor, Walter Benjamin, Ernst Bloch, Bertolt Brecht, and Georg Lukács, *Aesthetics and Politics* (London: Verso, 2007).

Agamben, Giorgio, *Homo Sacer: Sovereign Power and Bare Life* (Stanford, CA: Stanford University Press, 1998).

—— *State of Exception* (Chicago, IL: The University of Chicago Press, 2005).

Alderson, David, 'Making Electricity: Narrating Gender, Sexuality, and the Neoliberal Transition in *Billy Elliot*', *Camera Obscura* 75, vol. 25, no. 3, 2011, pp. 1–27.

Anderson, Benedict, *Imagined Communities* (London: Verso, 2006).

Antonucci, Lorenza, Laszlo Horvath, and André Krouwel, 'Brexit Was Not the Voice of the Working Class nor of the Uneducated – It Was the Squeezed Middle', The London School of Economics and Political Science, 13 October 2017, http://blogs.lse.ac.uk/politicsandpolicy/brexit-and-the-squeezed-middle/

Arnot, Hugo, *The History of Edinburgh, from the Earliest Accounts, to the Year 1780 [...]: With an Appendix* (Edinburgh: Thomas Turnbull, 1816).

Bambery, Chris, *A People's History of Scotland* (London: Verso, 2014).

Barker, Pat, *Union Street* (London: Virago, 1982).

Barr, Damian, *Maggie & Me* (London: Bloomsbury, 2013).

Baudrillard, Jean, 'The Evil Demon of Images and The Precession of Simulacra', in Thomas Docherty, ed., *Postmodernism: A Reader* (Hertfordshire: Harvester Wheatsheaf, 1993), pp. 194–199.

Beckett, Andy, 'Political Gothic', *London Review of Books*, 23 September 2004, www.lrb.co.uk/v26/n18/andy-beckett/political-gothic

Belsey, Catherine, *Critical Practice* (London: Routledge, 1991).

Benjamin, Walter, 'Left-Wing Melancholy', in Walter Benjamin, *Selected Writings Volume 2, 1927–1934* (Cambridge, MA: Harvard University Press, 1999).

—— *Selected Writings Volume 2, 1927–1934* (Cambridge, MA: Harvard University Press, 1999).

—— *Illuminations: Essays and Reflections* (New York, NY: Schocken Books, 2007).

—— 'Theses on the Philosophy of History', in Walter Benjamin, *Illuminations: Essays and Reflections* (New York, NY: Schocken Books, 2007), pp. 253–264.

—— 'What Is Epic Theater?', in Walter Benjamin, *Illuminations: Essays and Reflections* (New York, NY: Schocken Books, 2007), pp. 147–154.

Benson, Richard, *The Valley: A Hundred Years in the Life of a Family* (London: Bloomsbury, 2014).

Bentham, Jeremy, 'Panopticon; or, the Inspection-House', in John Bowring, ed., *The Works of Jeremy Bentham* (Edinburgh: William Tait, 1838–1843).

Bentley, Nick, *Radical Fictions: The English Novel in the 1950s* (Oxford: Peter Lang, 2007).

Berlant, Lauren, *Cruel Optimism* (Durham, NC: Duke University Press, 2011).

Bett, Alan, 'Poetry in Image: Jenni Fagan on Taking *The Panopticon* to the Screen', *The Skinny*, 13 January 2015, www.theskinny.co.uk/books/features/poetry-in-image-jenni-fagan-on-taking-the-panopticon-to-the-screen

Betteridge, David, 'Introduction', in David Betteridge, ed., *A Rose Loupt Oot: Poetry and Song Celebrating the UCS Work-in* (Middlesbrough: Smokestack Books, 2011), pp. 21–31.

Betteridge, David, ed., *A Rose Loupt Oot: Poetry and Song Celebrating the UCS Work-in* (Middlesbrough: Smokestack Books, 2011).

Beynon, Huw, ed., *Digging Deeper: Issues in the Miners' Strike* (London: Verso, 1985).

Bissett, Alan, 'We can't all be Irvine Welsh', *The Guardian*, 16 November 2006, www.guardian.co.uk/books/booksblog/2006/nov/16/negativedialect

Bloomfield, Barbara, 'Women's Support Group at Maerdy', in Raphael Samuel, Barbara Bloomfield, and Guy Boanas, eds., *The Enemy Within: Pit Villages and the Miners' Strike of 1984–5* (London: Routledge & Kegan Paul, 1986), pp. 154–165.

Bourdieu, Pierre, et al., *The Weight of the World* (Stanford, CA: Stanford University Press, 1999).

Boym, Svetlana, *The Future of Nostalgia* (New York, NY: Basic Books, 2001).

Brecht, Bertolt, 'Popularity and Realism', in Theodor Adorno, et al., *Aesthetics and Politics* (London: Verso, 2007), pp. 79–85.

Breman, Jan, 'A Bogus Concept', *New Left Review*, vol. 84, November/December 2013, pp. 130–138.

Brooker, Joseph, 'Orgreave Revisited: David Peace's *GB84* and the Return to the 1980s', *Radical Philosophy*, vol. 133, September/October 2005, pp. 39–51.

Brown, Wendy, 'Resisting Left Melancholy', *boundary 2*, vol. 26, no. 3, 1999, pp. 19–27.

Burn, Gordon, 'Wired Up and Whacked Out', *The Sunday Times*, 25 August 1991, pp. 36–37.

—— 'Books: Books of the Year', *The Independent*, 29 November 1997, www.independent.co.uk/life-style/books-books-of-the-year-1296850.html

—— 'After the Flood', *The Guardian*, 15 November 2003, www.theguardian.com/books/2003/nov/15/featuresreviews.guardianreview10

—— *Alma Cogan* (London: Faber and Faber, 2004).

—— 'The "English disease"', *The Guardian*, 7 May 2004, www.theguardian.com/music/2004/may/07/1

—— *The North of England Home Service* (London: Faber and Faber, 2004).

—— 'Living memories', *The Guardian*, 11 June 2005, www.theguardian.com/books/2005/jun/11/featuresreviews.guardianreview33

—— *Best and Edwards: Football, Fame and Oblivion* (London: Faber and Faber, 2006).

——— *Born Yesterday: The News as a Novel* (London: Faber and Faber, 2008).

Campbell, Beatrix, *Wigan Pier Revisited: Poverty and Politics in the 80s* (London: Virago, 1984).

Cartwright, Anthony, *The Afterglow* (Birmingham: Tindal Street Press, 2004).

——— *Heartland* (Birmingham: Tindal Street Press, 2010).

——— *How I Killed Margaret Thatcher* (Birmingham: Tindal Street Press, 2012).

Chaplin, Sid, *The Day of the Sardine* (Leeds: The Amethyst Press, 1983).

Collini, Stefan, 'Blahspeak', *London Review of Books*, vol. 32, no. 7, 8 April 2010, pp. 29–34.

Colls, Robert, 'Born-again Geordies', in Robert Colls and Bill Lancaster, eds., *Geordies: Roots of Regionalism* (Edinburgh: Edinburgh University Press, 1992), pp. 1–34.

Colls, Robert and Bill Lancaster, eds., *Geordies: Roots of Regionalism* (Edinburgh: Edinburgh University Press, 1992).

Common, Jack, *Kiddar's Luck* (Newcastle: Bloodaxe Books, 1990).

Connolly, Nathan, ed., *Know Your Place: Essays on the Working Class by the Working Class* (Liverpool: Dead Ink, 2017).

Craig, Carol, *The Tears that Made the Clyde: Well-being in Glasgow* (Argyll: Argyll Publishing, 2010).

Crowley, Tony, *Standard English and the Politics of Language* (Basingstoke: Palgrave Macmillan, 2003).

——— 'Keywords: Terrorism', *Key Words: A Journal of Cultural Materialism*, vol. 14, 2016, pp. 116–118.

Cunningham, David, 'The Contingency of Cheese: On Fredric Jameson's *The Antinomies of Realism*', *Radical Philosophy*, vol. 187, September/October 2014, pp. 25–35.

Cunningham, Valentine, '"In the Darg": Fiction Nails the Midlands Metalworker', in H. Gustav Klaus and Stephen Knight, eds., *British Industrial Fictions* (Cardiff: University of Wales Press, 2000), pp. 36–53.

Davies, Dan, 'David Peace: In The Light', *Esquire*, 30 August 2013, www.esquire.co.uk/culture/article/4717/in-the-light-by-david-peace/

Davies, Tony, 'Unfinished Business: Realism and Working-Class Writing', in Jeremy Hawthorn, ed., *The British Working-Class Novel in the Twentieth Century* (London: Edward Arnold, 1984), pp. 125–136.

de Waal, Kit, 'Make Room for Working Class Writers', *The Guardian*, 10 February 2018, www.theguardian.com/books/2018/feb/10/kit-de-waal-where-are-all-the-working-class-writers-

Dean, Jodi, *The Communist Horizon* (London: Verso, 2012).

Debord, Guy, *Society of the Spectacle* (Detroit, MI: Black & Red, 1970).

DeLillo, Don, *Underworld* (London: Picador, 1997).

Denning, Michael, *Mechanic Accents: Dime Novels and Working-Class Culture in America* (London: Verso, 1987).

Docherty, Thomas, ed., *Postmodernism: A Reader* (Hertfordshire: Harvester Wheatsheaf, 1993).

Doctorow, E.L., *Ragtime* (London: Penguin, 2006).

Dorril, Stephen and Robin Ramsay, *Smear! Wilson and the Secret State* (London: Grafton, 1992).

Duvall, John N., ed., *The Cambridge Companion to Don DeLillo* (Cambridge: Cambridge University Press, 2008).

Duvall, John N., 'Introduction', in John N. Duvall, ed., *The Cambridge Companion to Don DeLillo* (Cambridge: Cambridge University Press, 2008), pp. 1–12.

Eagleton, Terry, 'At the Coal Face', *The Guardian*, 6 March 2004, www.theguardian.com/books/2004/mar/06/featuresreviews.guardianreview20

Eddo-Lodge, Renni, *Why I'm No Longer Talking to White People About Race* (London: Bloomsbury, 2018).

Fagan, Jenni, *The Panopticon* (London: Windmill Books, 2013).

———— 'I Went From Growing Up In Care To Being A Best Selling Granta Author – By Jenni Fagan', *Marie Claire*, 30 August 2013, www.marieclaire.co.uk/blogs/544200/

Fairclough, Norman, *New Labour, New Language?* (London: Routledge, 2000).

Fielding, Steven, *A State of Play: British Politics on Screen, Stage and Page, from Anthony Trollope to The Thick of it* (London: Bloomsbury, 2014).

Finden, Edward Francis, and William Finden, *Landscape Illustrations of the Waverley Novels: with Descriptions of the Views*, vol. 1 (London: Charles Tilt, 1832).

Fisher, Mark, *Capitalist Realism: Is There No Alternative?* (Winchester: Zero Books, 2009).

———— *Ghosts Of My Life* (Winchester: Zero Books, 2013).

Foster, John and Charles Woolfson, *The Politics of the UCS Work-In* (London: Lawrence and Wishart, 1986).

Foucault, Michel, *Discipline and Punish: The Birth of the Prison* (London: Penguin, 1991).

———— *The Birth of Biopolitics: Lectures at the College de France* (Basingstoke: Palgrave Macmillan, 2010).

Fox, Genevieve, '"I Wanted to Be Truthful and Authentic': Book Club Interview with Ross Raisin', *The Telegraph*, 2 December 2011, www.telegraph.co.uk/culture/books/bookclub/8930921/I-wanted-to-be-truthful-and-authentic-Book-Club-Interview-with-Ross-Raisin.html

Fraser, Frankie, *Mad Frank's Underworld History of Britain* (London: Random House, 2012).

Freeman, John, ed., *Granta 123: Best of Young British Novelists 4* (London: Granta Publications, Spring 2013).

Freud, Sigmund, 'Mourning and Melancholia', in Adam Phillips, ed., *The Penguin Freud Reader* (London: Penguin, 2006), pp. 310–326.

Gąsiorek, Andrzej, *Post-War British Fiction: Realism and After* (London: Edward Arnold, 1995).

Gibbon, Peter and David Steyne, eds., *Thurcroft: A Village and the Miners' Strike. An Oral History by the People of Thurcroft* (Nottingham: Spokesman, 1986).

Gilroy, Paul, *There Ain't No Black in the Union Jack* (Abingdon: Routledge, 2002).

Grundy, Lynne, Christian Kay, and Jane Roberts, *A Thesaurus of Old English* (Glasgow: University of Glasgow, 2015) http://oldenglishthesaurus.arts.gla.ac.uk/

Hadley, Louisa and Elizabeth Ho, '"The Lady's Not for Turning": New Cultural Perspectives on Thatcher and Thatcherism', in Louisa Hadley and Elizabeth

Ho, eds., *Thatcher & After: Margaret Thatcher and Her Afterlife in Contemporary Culture* (Basingstoke: Palgrave Macmillan, 2010), pp. 1–26.

Hadley, Louisa and Elizabeth Ho, eds., *Thatcher & After: Margaret Thatcher and Her Afterlife in Contemporary Culture* (Basingstoke: Palgrave Macmillan, 2010).

Hall, Stuart, 'The Toad in the Garden: Thatcherism Amongst the Theorists' in Cary Nelson and Lawrence Grossberg, eds., *Marxism and the Interpretation of Culture* (London: Macmillan Education, 1988), pp. 35–73.

—— 'The Great Moving Right Show', in Stuart Hall, *The Hard Road to Renewal: Thatcherism and the Crisis of the Left* (London: Verso, p. 1990), pp. 39–56.

—— *The Hard Road to Renewal: Thatcherism and the Crisis of the Left* (London: Verso, 1990).

Hall, Stuart with Bill Schwarz, *Familiar Stranger: A Life Between Two Islands* (London: Penguin: 2018).

Hanley, Lynsey, *Estates: An Intimate History* (London: Granta Books, 2008).

Harris, John, 'Britain Is in the Midst of a Working Class Revolt', *The Guardian*, 17 June 2016, www.theguardian.com/commentisfree/2016/jun/17/britain-working-class-revolt-eu-referendum

Hart, Matthew, 'An Interview with David Peace', *Contemporary Literature*, vol. 47, no. 4, Winter 2006, pp. 547–569.

—— 'The Third English Civil War: David Peace's "Occult History of Thatcherism', *Contemporary Literature*, vol. 49, no. 4, Winter 2008, pp. 573–596.

Harvey, David, *The Condition of Postmodernity: An Enquiry into the Origins of Cultural Change* (Oxford: Blackwell, 1990).

—— *A Brief History of Neoliberalism* (Oxford: Oxford University Press, 2007).

—— *The Enigma of Capital and the Crises of Capitalism* (London: Profile Books, 2011).

Hawthorn, Jeremy, ed., *The British Working-Class Novel in the Twentieth Century* (London: Edward Arnold, 1984).

Hayward, Anthony, *Which Side Are You On? Ken Loach and His Films* (London: Bloomsbury, 2004).

Haywood, Ian, *Working-Class Fiction from Chartism to Trainspotting* (Plymouth: Northcote House, 1997).

Head, Dominic, 'H. E. Bates, Regionalism and Late Modernism', in David James, ed., *The Legacies of Modernism* (Cambridge: Cambridge University Press, 2011), pp. 40–52.

Heffernan, Nick, *Capital, Class & Technology in Contemporary American Culture: Projecting Post-Fordism* (London: Pluto Press, 2000).

Hewison, Robert, *The Heritage Industry: Britain in a Climate of Decline* (London: Methuen, 1987).

Hilliard, Christopher, *To Exercise Our Talents: The Democratization of Writing in Britain* (Cambridge, MA: Harvard University Press, 2006).

Hobsbawm, Eric, 'The Forward March of Labour Halted?', in Eric Hobsbawm, *Politics for a Rational Left: Political Writing 1977–1988* (London: Verso, 1989), pp. 9–22.

—— *Politics for a Rational Left: Political Writing 1977–1988* (London: Verso, 1989).

Hoggart, Richard, *The Uses of Literacy: Aspects of Working-Class Life* (London: Penguin, 2009).

Hollowell, John, *Fact & Fiction: The New Journalism and the Nonfiction Novel* (Chapel Hill, NC: The University of North Carolina Press, 1977).

Horton, Patricia, '*Trainspotting*: A Topography of the Masculine Abject', *English*, vol. 50, Autumn 2001, pp. 219–234.

Hutcheon, Linda, *Poetics of Postmodernism: History, Theory, Fiction* (London: Routledge, 1988).

Ipsos MORI, 'State of the Nation 2013 – Ipsos MORI Poll for British Futures', Ipsos MORI, 14 January 2013, www.ipsos-mori.com/researchpublications/researcharchive/3111/State-of-the-Nation-2013.aspx

James, David, 'Relocating Mimesis: New Horizons for the British Regional Novel', *JNT: Journal of Narrative Theory*, vol. 36, no. 3, 2006, pp. 420–445.

—— 'Introduction: Mapping Modernist Continuities', in David James, *The Legacies of Modernism* (Cambridge: Cambridge University Press, 2011), pp. 1–20.

—— *The Legacies of Modernism* (Cambridge: Cambridge University Press, 2011).

Jameson, Fredric, *Postmodernism, or, the Cultural Logic of Late Capitalism* (London: Verso, 1992).

—— *The Cultural Turn: Selected Writings on the Postmodern, 1983–1998* (London: Verso, 1998).

—— 'Marxism and Postmodernism', in Fredric Jameson, *The Cultural Turn: Selected Writings on the Postmodern, 1983–1998* (London: Verso, 1998), pp. 33–49.

—— *The Antinomies of Realism* (London: Verso, 2013).

Jefferson, Douglas and Graham Martin, eds., *The Uses of Fiction: Essays on the Modern Novel in Honour of Arnold Kettle* (Milton Keynes: The Open University Press, 1982).

Jones, Owen, *Chavs: The Demonization of the Working Class* (London: Verso, 2011).

Jones, Rhian. E., *Clampdown: Pop-Cultural Wars on Class and Gender* (Winchester: Zero Books, 2013).

—— 'On Peterloo, Poetry, and the Politics of Protest History', *New Socialist*, 5 November 2018, https://newsocialist.org.uk/peterloo-poetry-and-politics-protest-history

Kaplan, Cora, 'The Death of the Working-Class Hero', *New Formations*, vol. 52, 2004, pp. 94–110.

Kelly, Aaron, *Irvine Welsh* (Manchester: Manchester University Press, 2005).

Kelly, Richard T., 'North East State of Mind', *New Writing North Review*, November 2009, pp. 24–31.

Kelman, James, 'A Note on the War Being Waged by the State Against the Victims of Asbestos', in James Kelman, *Some Recent Attacks: Essays Cultural & Political* (Stirling: AK Press, 1992), pp. 59–63.

—— *Some Recent Attacks: Essays Cultural & Political* (Stirling: AK Press, 1992).

—— '*And the Judges Said...*' *Essays* (London: Secker & Warburg, 2002).

—— *Kieron Smith, Boy* (London: Penguin, 2009).

Kennedy, Joe, *Authentocrats: Culture, Politics and the New Seriousness* (London: Repeater Books, 2018).

Kirk, John, *The British Working Class in the Twentieth Century: Film, Literature and Television* (Cardiff: University of Wales Press, 2009).

Klaus, H. Gustav, *James Kelman* (Plymouth: Northcote House, 2004).

Klaus, H. Gustav and Stephen Knight, eds., *British Industrial Fictions* (Cardiff: University of Wales Press, 2000).

Klein, Naomi, *The Shock Doctrine: The Rise of Disaster Capitalism* (London: Penguin, 2007).

Kosofsky Sedgwick, Eve, *Between Men: English Literature and Male Homosocial Desire* (New York, NY: Columbia University Press, 1985).

Kundnani, Arun, *The Muslims Are Coming! Islamophobia, Extremism, and the Domestic War on Terror* (London: Verso, 2015).

Kureishi, Hanif, *The Black Album* (London: Faber and Faber, 2010).

Kristeva, Julia, *Powers of Horror: An Essay on Abjection* (New York, NY: Columbia University Press, 1982).

Lacey, Stephen, *Tony Garnett* (Manchester: Manchester University Press, 2007).

Lancaster, Bill, 'Newcastle – Capital of What?', in Robert Colls and Bill Lancaster, eds., *Geordies: Roots of Regionalism* (Edinburgh: Edinburgh University Press, 1992), pp. 53–70.

——— 'Gordon Burn, 1948–2009', *North East Labour History Journal*, vol. 41, April 2010, pp. 172–177.

Laybourn, Keith, *A Century of Labour: A History of the Labour Party* (Stroud: Sutton Publishing, 2001).

Lea, Daniel, 'Trauma, Celebrity, and Killing in the "Contemporary Murder Leisure Industry"', *Textual Practice*, vol. 28, no. 5, 2014, pp. 763–781.

Littler, Jo, *Against Meritocracy: Culture, Power and Myths of Mobility* (Abingdon: Routledge, 2018).

Loach, Loretta, 'We'll be Here Right to the End... And After: Women in the Miners' Strike', in Huw Beynon, ed., *Digging Deeper: Issues in the Miners' Strike* (London: Verso, 1985), pp. 169–179.

Lott, Tim, 'The Loneliness of the Working-Class Writer', *The Guardian*, 7 February 2015, www.theguardian.com/commentisfree/2015/feb/07/loneliness-working-class-writer-english-novelists

Luckhurst, Roger, *The Trauma Question* (Abingdon: Routledge, 2008).

Lukács, Georg, *The Historical Novel* (Harmondsworth: Penguin, 1969).

MacCabe, Colin, and Holly Yanacek, eds., *Keywords for Today: A 21st Century Vocabulary* (Oxford: Oxford University Press, 2018).

MacInnes, Colin, *Absolute Beginners* (London: Allison & Busby, 2011).

Mantel, Hilary, *The Assassination of Margaret Thatcher: Stories* (London: 4th Estate, 2014).

———, 'The Assassination of Margaret Thatcher', *The Assassination of Margaret Thatcher: Stories* (London: 4th Estate, 2014), pp. 203–242.

Marqusee, Mike, 'No Redemption', *Red Pepper*, March 2009, www.redpepper.org.uk/No-redemption/

Marx, Karl, 'Critique of the Gotha Programme', in Karl Marx and Friedrich Engels, *Selected Works* (London: Lawrence and Wishart, 1968), pp. 319–335.

Marx, Karl and Friedrich Engels, *Selected Works* (London: Lawrence and Wishart, 1968).

McCulloch, Fiona, *Cosmopolitanism in Contemporary British Fiction: Imagined Identities* (Basingstoke: Palgrave Macmillan, 2012).

—— '"Daughter of an Outcast Queen" – Defying State Expectations in Jenni Fagan's *The Panopticon*', *Scottish Literary Review*, vol. 7, no. 1, 2015, pp. 113–131.

McDonald, Paul, *Fiction from the Furnace: A Hundred Years of Black Country Writing* (Sheffield: Sheffield Hallam University Press, 2002).

McKenzie, Lisa, *Getting By: Estates, class and culture in austerity Britain* (Bristol: Policy Press, 2015).

McLeod, John, *Beginning Postcolonialism* (Manchester: Manchester University Press, 2000).

McNamee, Eoin, 'Hand-Held Narrative', *The Guardian*, 30 April 2004, www.theguardian.com/books/2004/apr/30/news.comment

McNeill, Dougal, *Forecasts of the Past: Globalisation, History, Realism, Utopia* (Oxford: Peter Lang, 2012).

Milne, Seumas, *The Enemy Within: The Secret War Against the Miners* (London: Verso, 2004).

Milner, Andrew, *Class* (London: SAGE Publications, 1999).

Mirowski, Philip, *Never Let a Serious Crisis Go to Waste: How Neoliberalism Survived the Financial Meltdown* (London: Verso, 2014).

Morrison, Jago, 'Jihadi Fiction: Radicalisation Narratives in the Contemporary Novel', *Textual Practice*, vol. 31, no. 3, pp. 567–584.

Mulhern, Francis, '*Culture and Society*, Then and Now', *New Left Review*, vol. 55, 2009, pp. 31–45.

Nel, Philip, 'DeLillo and Modernism', in John N. Duvall, ed., *The Cambridge Companion to Don DeLillo* (Cambridge: Cambridge University Press, 2008), pp. 13–26.

Nelson, Cary and Lawrence Grossberg, eds., *Marxism and the Interpretation of Culture* (London: Macmillan Education, 1988).

O'Brien, Phil, 'An Interview with Anthony Cartwright', *Contemporary Literature*, vol. 56, no. 3, Autumn 2015, pp. 397–420.

—— 'The Deindustrial Novel: Twenty-First Century British Fiction and the Working Class', in Ben Clarke and Nick Hubble eds., *Working-Class Writing: Theory and Practice* (London: Palgrave Macmillan, 2018), pp. 229–246.

Orwell, George, *The Road to Wigan Pier* (London: Penguin, 2001).

Peace, David, *Occupied City* (London: Faber and Faber, 2009).

—— *GB84* (London: Faber and Faber, 2010).

Phillips, Adam, ed., *The Penguin Freud Reader* (London: Penguin, 2006).

Pickering, Michael, and Kevin Robins, 'A Revolutionary Materialist with a Leg Free', in Jeremy Hawthorn, ed., *The British Working-Class Novel in the Twentieth Century* (London: Edward Arnold, 1984), pp. 77–92.

Pizer, Donald, 'John Dos Passos in the 1920s: The Development of a Modernist Style', *Mosaic*, vol. 45, no. 4, December 2012, pp. 51–67.

Rahbek, Ulla, '"Repping Your Ends": Imagined Borders in Recent British Multicultural Fiction', *Literature & Theology*, vol. 27, no. 4, December 2013, pp. 426–438.

Raisin, Ross, *Waterline* (London: Penguin, 2011).

Ramdin, Ron, *The Making of the Black Working Class in Britain* (London: Verso, 2017).

Reid, Alistair J. and Henry Pilling, *A Short History of the Labour Party* (Basingstoke: Palgrave Macmillan, 2005).

Roediger, David, *Class, Race, and Marxism* (London: Verso, 2017).

Rowbotham, Sheila, *Woman's Consciousness, Man's World* (Harmondsworth: Penguin, 1973).

Rowland, Antony, *Poetry as Testimony: Witnessing and Memory in Twentieth-Century Poems* (Abingdon: Routledge, 2014).

Said, Edward, *Orientalism* (London: Penguin, 2003).

Samuel, Raphael, Barbara Bloomfield, and Guy Boanas, eds., *The Enemy Within: Pit Villages and the Miners' Strike of 1984–5* (London: Routledge & Kegan Paul, 1986).

Sahota, Sunjeev, *Ours are the Streets* (London: Picador, 2011).

────── *The Year of the Runaways* (London: Picador, 2015).

Savage, Mike and Fiona Devine, 'The Great British Class Survey – Results', *BBC*, 3 April 2013, www.bbc.co.uk/science/0/21970879

Seymour, Richard, *Corbyn: The Strange Rebirth of Radical Politics*, 2nd edition (London: Verso, 2017).

Scott, Jeremy, *The Demotic Voice in Contemporary British Fiction* (Basingstoke: Palgrave Macmillan, 2009).

Scott, Walter, *Rob Roy* (Cambridge, MA: The Riverside Press, 1956).

Semple, Janet, *Bentham's Prison: A Study of the Panopticon Penitentiary* (Oxford: Oxford University Press, 1993).

Shaw, Katy, *David Peace: Texts and Contexts* (Eastbourne: Sussex Academic Press, 2011).

────── 'Living by the Pen: In Conversation with Sunjeev Sahota', *English*, vol. 66, no. 254, 2017 pp. 263–271.

Sinclair, Upton, *The Jungle* (London: Penguin, 1986).

Sinfield, Alan, *Literature, Politics and Culture in Postwar Britain* (London: Continuum, 2004).

Skeggs, Beverley, *Formations of Class & Gender* (London: SAGE Publications, 1997).

────── *Class, Self, Culture* (London: Routledge, 2004).

Standing, Guy, *The Precariat: The New Dangerous Class* (London: Bloomsbury Academic, 2011).

Stevens, Geoff, 'Black Country Dialect Poets', *The Blackcountryman*, vol. 5, no. 2, 1972, pp. 43–44.

Storey, David, *This Sporting Life* (London: Penguin, 1986).

Strangleman, Tim, '"Smokestack Nostalgia," "Ruin Porn" or Working-Class Obituary: The Role and Meaning of Deindustrial Representation', *International Labor and Working-Class History*, vol. 84, 2013, pp. 23–37.

Swales, Kirby, 'Understanding the Leave Vote', NatCen Social Research, 7 December 2016, https://whatukthinks.org/eu/wp-content/uploads/2016/12/NatCen_Brexplanations-report-FINAL-WEB2.pdf

Tannock, Stuart, 'Nostalgia Critique', *Cultural Studies*, vol. 9, no. 3, 1995, pp. 453–464.

Taylor, D.J., 'La Divine Thatcher: How Novelists Responded to Maggie', *The Guardian*, 19 June 2015, www.theguardian.com/books/2015/jun/19/margaret-thatcher-1980s-how-novelists-responsed

Thompson, E.P., *The Making of the English Working Class* (London: Penguin, 1991).

Tiedemann, Rolf, ed., *Notes to Literature: Volume One* (New York, NY: Columbia University Press, 1991).

Todd, Selina, *The People: The Rise and Fall of the Working Class* (London: John Murray, 2015).

Trilling, Daniel, *Bloody Nasty People: The Rise of Britain's Far Right* (London: Verso, 2013).

Tyler, Imogen, 'Chav Mum Chav Scum', *Feminist Media Studies*, vol. 8, no. 1, 2008, pp. 17–34.

—— *Revolting Subjects: Social Abjection and Resistance in Neoliberal Britain* (London: Zed Books, 2013).

—— 'Classificatory Struggles: Class, Culture and Inequality in Neoliberal Times', *The Sociological Review*, vol. 63, 2015, pp. 493–511.

Tyler, Imogen, and Bruce Bennett, 'Against Aspiration', *What Is Aspiration? How Progressives Should Respond* by CLASS: Centre for Labour and Social Studies, August 2015, pp. 6–8 http://classonline.org.uk/pubs/item/what-is-aspiration

Umney, Charles, *Class Matters: Inequality and Exploitation in 21st Century Britain* (London: Pluto Press, 2018).

Upstone, Sara, *British Asian Fiction: Twenty-First-Century Voices* (Manchester: Manchester University Press, 2010).

Vall, Natasha, *Cultural Region: North east England, 1945–2000* (Manchester: Manchester University Press, 2011).

Vardy, Christopher, 'Historicising Neoliberal Freedom: *GB84* and the Politics of Historical Fiction', *Open Library of Humanities*, vol. 4, no. 2, 24 October 2018, pp. 1–32.

Voloshinov, V.N., *Marxism and the Philosophy of Language* (Cambridge, MA: Harvard University Press, 1986).

Virdee, Satnam, *Racism, Class and The Racialized Outsider* (London: Palgrave, 2014).

Warner, Alan, '*Waterline* by Ross Raisin – Review', *The Guardian*, 13 July 2011, www.guardian.co.uk/books/2011/jul/13/waterline-ross-raisin-review

Waugh, Patricia, *Metafiction: The Theory and Practice of Self-Conscious Writing* (London: Routledge, 2001).

Wayne, Mike, *England's Discontents: Political Cultures and National Identities* (London: Pluto, 2018).

Welsh, Irvine, *Trainspotting* (London: Vintage, 2004).

Welshman, John, *Underclass: A History of the Excluded, 1880–2000* (London: Hambledon Continuum, 2006).

White, Gregor, 'Book Review: *Waterline*, by Ross Raisin', *Daily Record*, 30 September 2011, www.dailyrecord.co.uk/news/local-news/book-review-waterline-ross-raisin-2735498

Williams, Raymond, *Culture and Society 1780–1950* (Harmondsworth: Penguin, 1963).

—— 'A Lecture on Realism', *Screen*, vol. 18, no. 1, Spring 1977, pp. 61–74.

—— *Marxism and Literature* (Oxford: Oxford University Press, 1977).

—— 'Region and Class in the Novel', in Douglas Jefferson and Graham Martin, eds., *The Uses of Fiction: Essays on the Modern Novel in Honour of Arnold Kettle* (Milton Keynes: Open University Press, 1982), pp. 59–68.

—— *Towards 2000* (Harmondsworth: Penguin, 1985).

—— *Keywords: A Vocabulary of Culture and Society* (London: Fontana Press, 1988).

—— 'Mining the Meaning: Key Words in the Miners' Strike', in Raymond Williams, *Resources of Hope: Culture, Democracy, Socialism* (London: Verso, 1989), pp. 120–127.

—— *Resources of Hope: Culture, Democracy, Socialism* (London: Verso, 1989).

—— *Culture and Materialism: Selected Essays* (London: Verso, 2005).

—— 'The Welsh Industrial Novel', in *Culture and Materialism: Selected Essays* (London: Verso, 2005), pp. 213–229.

Williamson, Bill, 'Living the Past Differently: Historical Memory in the North-East', in Robert Colls and Bill Lancaster, eds., *Geordies: Roots of Regionalism* (Edinburgh: Edinburgh University Press, 1992), pp. 148–167.

Index

Note: Page numbers followed by "n" denote endnotes.

Absolute Beginners (MacInnes) 55, 58
Adam, Robert 115
The Adelphi 50
Adorno, Theodor 1, 68
The Afterglow (Cartwright) 1, 18, 67, 68, 70, 71, 73, 75, 76, 81, 83, 85
Against Meritocracy: Culture, Power and Myths of Mobility (Littler) 153
Alderson, David 153
Alma Cogan (Burn) 18, 57
Anderson, Benedict 40, 134
aspiration 8–9
The Assassination of Margaret Thatcher (Mantel) 84
Authentocrats (Kennedy) 15, 84

Bambery, Chris 122
Barker, Pat 70, 134
Barr, Damian 84
Bataille, Georges 115
Baudrillard, Jean 56
Beckett, Andy 43n8
Benjamin, Walter 31, 103
Bennett, Bruce 8, 9
Bentham, Jeremy 115, 125
Bentley, Nick 58
Berlant, Lauren 73
The Black Album (Kureishi) 143
Blair, Tony 7, 75–76, 78–79, 146
Bloody Nasty People (Trilling) 79
Bourdieu, Pierre 73
Boym, Svetlana 53, 56, 61, 63
Brecht, Bertolt 31, 59, 152
Breman, Jan 105
Brexit 15, 16, 17, 84, 123, 154
British National Party (BNP) 77, 79–81
Brooker, Joseph 34, 43n8

Brown, Wendy 104
Burn, Gordon 1, 43; working-class nostalgia and 47–66
The Busconductor Hines (Kelman) 94

Callaghan, James 11
Cameron, David 16
Campbell, Beatrix 103
Capote, Truman 51
Cartwright, Anthony 1, 63, 102; deindustrial novel and 67–89
Chaplin, Sid 49, 50, 62
Cinderheath 79–81, 85
class inequality 8, 9, 11–12, 17, 52, 79, 82, 114, 118, 123, 130, 152, 153
Class Matters (Umney) 15
Clegg, Nick 16
Cogan, Alma 56, 57
cognitive mapping 18, 23n108
collective memory 56
Collini, Stefan 8
Colls, Robert 50, 53
colonial dehumanization 143
Common, Jack 50
Connolly, Nathan 4
consciousness, of class 3, 6, 18
Conservative-Liberal Democrat Coalition Government 16
Conservative Party 8, 16, 98
Corbyn, Jeremy 2, 3, 16
Crowley, Tony 71, 142
cultural capital 14, 85, 136
Cunningham, David 34
Cunningham, Valentine 68, 72, 87n38

Davies, Tony 68, 81
The Day of the Sardine (Chaplin) 49
Debord, Guy 48, 52, 57

deindustrialisation 2, 5, 47, 53, 60, 67,
  69, 73, 82–83, 85, 93, 97–98, 100,
  145, 151
DeLillo, Don 51, 52, 61, 62
demonisation 2, 5, 17, 114, 137,
  147, 151
Deng Xiaoping 9
Denning, Michael 109
de Waal, Kit 3, 152–154
disneyfication 63, 99
Doctorow, E.L. 51, 58
documentary realism 35
Dos Passos, John 34

Eagleton, Terry 33
economic liberalism 7, 16, 19n27, 76
Eddo-Lodge, Renni 4
'Elitism and English Literature,
  Speaking as a Writer' (Kelman) 94
*The Enemy Within: The Secret War
  Against the Miners* (Milne) 39
The Enigma of Capital (Harvey) 9
*England's Discontents: Political
  Cultures and National Identities*
  (Wayne) 7–8, 16, 19n27, 22n98, 69,
  70, 76, 86n15
Erikson, Kai 102
European Union (EU) Referendum 15

Fagan, Jenni 1, 110, 127; revolting
  class and 114–132
Fairclough, Norman 8–9
*Fiction from the Furnace: A Hundred
  Years of Black Country Writing*
  (McDonald) 68
Fielding, Steven 77, 78
Fisher, Mark 27, 48, 60
Foster, John 98
Foucault, Michel 39, 115, 125,
  132n55
Fowler, Ellen Thorneycroft 68
Freud, Sigmund 102
Friedman, Milton 10

Gąsiorek, Andrzej 62
GB84 (Peace) 1, 4, 18, 27–36,
  38–43, 43n8, 67, 84; occult
  history 43n8
gentrification 61, 100, 145
Gilroy, Paul 4, 77, 107, 137, 138,
  141, 142
Gordon Burn Prize 18
Great British Class Survey 14
Griffin, Nick 80

Hadley, Louisa 83
Hall, Stuart 11–13, 68, 78, 104, 138
Hanley, Lynsey 2, 3, 12
*Happy Like Murderers: The Story
  of Fred and Rosemary West*
  (Burn) 51
Hart, Matthew 28
Harvey, David 7, 9, 29, 38, 61, 79,
  99, 100
Hayek, Friedrich 10, 11
Heartland (Cartwright) 1, 67, 72, 73,
  76–81, 85
Heath, Edward 96
Hill, Archie 68, 72
Ho, Elizabeth 83
Hogan, Edward 69
Hoggart, Richard 54, 55
How I Killed Margaret Thatcher
  (Cartwright) 1, 67, 68, 72–74, 81,
  82, 85
Hutcheon, Linda 52

imagined community 40, 134
industrial capitalism 69, 95, 103
industrialism 68, 69
Iron Towns (Cartwright) 85

James, David 53, 70
Jameson, Fredric 1, 23n108, 29, 33,
  34, 51
Jones, Owen 6, 8, 21n76, 52, 79, 118
Jones, Rhian E. 3, 6, 52, 118–120
Joseph, Keith 11, 97
The Jungle (Sinclair) 51

Kaplan, Cora 7, 78, 79
Kelly, Aaron 11
Kelman, James 71, 93, 95, 103, 108
Kennedy, Joe 15, 16, 84
Keywords for Today 142, 143
Kiddar's Luck (Common) 50
Kieron Smith, Boy (Kelman) 94
Kirk, John 12, 53, 70, 107
Klaus, H. Gustav 94
Klein, Naomi 10
Know Your Place (ed. Connolly) 4
Kundnani, Arun 140, 142, 144
Kureishi, Hanif 135, 143

Lacey, Stephen 34
laissez-faire economics 125
Lancaster, Bill 48
liberal paradox 106
Liddle, Roger 7

linguistic otherness 72
Littler, Jo 153
Loach, Ken 36
Lott, Tim 2, 3
Luckhurst, Roger 101–102
Lukács, Georg 34, 81

MacInnes, Colin 55, 59
Macmillan, Harold 50, 56
Maggie & Me (Barr) 84
Mailer, Norman 51
Majorism 16
*The Making of the Black Working
    Class in Britain* (Ramdin) 40
*The Making of the English Working
    Class* (Thompson) 6, 138
Mandelson, Peter 7
Mantel, Hilary 84
Marx, Karl 10, 82, 107
Matanda, Abondance 4
May, Theresa 16
McClintock, Anne 146
McCulloch, Fiona 122, 124, 126, 129
McDonald, Paul 68
McGregor, Ian 37
McKenzie, Lisa 120
McLeod, John 136–137, 141
McNamee, Eoin 45n55
McNeill, Dougal 34
Midnight's Children (Rushdie) 136
Miners' Strike of 1984/1985 2,
    27–46 151
Mirowski, Philip 10, 14
Mont Pelerin Society 10
Morrison, Jago 142
Mosleyite thirties 58
Mulhern, Francis 79
Murray, David Christie 68
Murry, John Middleton 50
My Name is Leon (de Waal) 153

National Coal Board (NCB) 29
National Union of Mineworkers
    (NUM) 29
Nel, Philip 34
neoliberalism 2, 6–10, 12, 14,
    16–18, 28–30, 33, 39, 48, 76,
    78, 84, 98, 100, 114, 120, 152;
    ideologies 1
New Labour 7–9, 75–80, 119
New Labour, New Language?
    (Fairclough) 8
The North of England Home Service
    (Burn) 1, 43, 47–49, 51–53, 55–62

Occupied City (Peace) 35
O'Flynn, Catherine 69
Orwell, George 33, 50, 154
Osborne, George 16
Ours are the Streets (Sahota) 1, 133,
    135–143, 145
Oxford English Dictionary (OED)
    28, 29, 117

The Panopticon (Fagan) 1, 114, 117,
    122–124, 127, 130
Paton, Kirsteen 100
Peace, David 1, 4, 84; class war and
    31; Miners' Strike, occult history
    28; strike novel and 27–46
Pelling, Henry 75
Pizer, Donald 34
Policing the Crisis (Hall et al.) 138
populism 13
postcolonial racism 141
poverty 6, 8, 9, 33, 51, 107, 122, 153
Powell, Enoch 80
private finance initiatives (PFIs) 19n27

racialisation 107, 137, 138
racist riots of 1919 106
Ragtime (Doctorow) 51, 52, 58
Rahbek, Ulla 137
Raisin, Ross 1, 100, 101, 145; class
    mourning and 93–113
Ramdin, Ron 40
Reagan, Ronald 10
realism 34, 59, 81
Reid, Alistair 75
Reid, Jimmy 98
The Road to Wigan Pier (Orwell) 33
Roediger, David 137–138
*A Rose Loupt Oot: Poetry and Song
    Celebrating the UCS Work-In*
    (ed. Betteridge) 99
Rowbotham, Sheila 75
Rowland, Antony 72, 73
Rushdie, Salman 136

Sahota, Sunjeev 1, 4, 67, 105, 110;
    racialised worker and 133–150
Said, Edward 134, 140
Savage, Mike 14
Scott, Jeremy 72, 108, 122
Sedgewick, Eve Kosofsky 121
Semple, Janet 125
Seymour, Richard 16
Shaw, Katy 27, 31, 32, 43n8
Shelley, Percy Bysshe 3

Shostakovich, Dmitri 35
Sillitoe, Alan 62, 70
Sinfield, Alan 11, 59, 123, 127, 154
Skeggs, Beverley 7, 9, 41, 121, 125
Smear!: Wilson and the Secret State (Dorril) 45n55
Social Democratic Party (SDP) 13
social mobility 153
social realism 33, 34, 49, 51, 58, 62, 68, 70, 81
social trauma 48
Somebody's Husband, Somebody's Son: The Story of Peter Sutcliffe (Burn) 51
Steele, Tommy 54
Stevens, Geoff 72
Storey, David 57, 62
Strangleman, Tim 74

Tannock, Stuart 53
Taylor, D. J. 83
Terrorist (Updike) 142
Thatcher, Margaret 7, 9–10, 30, 31, 40, 97, 101, 104
Thatcherism 7, 10–13, 16, 39, 40, 67, 82, 97, 118
'Third Way' 7, 8
This Sporting Life (Storey) 57
Thompson, Bobby 49, 54, 55
Thompson, E. P. 6, 138, 151
Thomson, Bobby 53
Thurcroft: A Village and the Miners' Strike, An Oral History by the people of Thurcroft (ed. Gibbon and Steyne) 32, 35, 38, 41
'The Titan Crane' (Whittingham) 99
Todd, Selina 9, 11, 14, 56
Trainspotting (Welsh) 117, 123, 124
trauma 48–49, 61, 72–73, 81, 94, 102, 129
Trilling, Daniel 79, 80
Tyler, Imogen 6, 8–10, 14, 39, 106, 107, 114, 115, 118, 119, 122, 137, 143

Umney, Charles 15, 17
underclass 9, 107, 118, 120, 121, 124, 128, 146
Underworld (DeLillo) 52
Union Street (Barker) 70, 71, 134
Updike, John 142
Upper Clyde Shipbuilders (UCS) 95, 96, 101
Upstone, Sara 135

Vardy, Christopher 39, 42, 45n47
Virdee, Satnam 40, 76, 80, 106, 141, 142
Voloshinov, V.N. 71, 86n33

Warner, Alan 93
Waterline (Raisin) 1, 4, 93–96, 98, 101–103, 105, 108–110, 128, 145, 146
Waugh, Patricia 30
Wayne, Mike 7, 22n98, 68–70
welfare capitalism 11, 21n64, 33
Welsh, Irvine 117, 123–125
Welshman, John 107
Whittingham, Brian 99, 100
Wigan Pier Revisited: Poverty and Politics in the 80s (Campbell) 103
Williams, Raymond 2, 3, 13, 14, 27, 34, 58, 69–71, 153
Williamson, Bill 55
Windrush Scandal of 2018 142
Wolfe, Tom 51
Woolfson, Charles 98
working-class identity 48, 53, 69
working-class nostalgia 47–66
working-class writing 3, 70, 152–153

The Year of the Runaways (Sahota) 1, 134, 136, 138, 144, 145
Young, Francis Brett 68